FAIRS AND FESTIVALS OF INDIA

FAIRS AND FESTIVALS OF INDIA

Editor-in-Chief
Swami Chidatman Jee Maharaj

ANMOL PUBLICATIONS PVT. LTD.
NEW DELHI - 110 002 (INDIA)

ANMOL PUBLICATIONS PVT. LTD.
H.O.: 4374/4B, Ansari Road, Daryaganj,
New Delhi-110 002 (India)
Ph.: 23278000, 23261597
B.O.: No. 1015, Ist Main Road, BSK IIIrd Stage
IIIrd Phase, IIIrd Block,
Bangalore - 560 085 (India)
Visit us at: www.anmolpublications.com

Fairs and Festivals of India

First Published, 2009
ISBN 978-81-261-3607-0

PRINTED IN INDIA

Printed at Mehra Offset Press, Delhi.

Contents

Preface

India colourful and vibrant, a land as diverse as its people. A mosaic of faiths, cultures, customs and languages that blend harmoniously to form a composite whole. One of the world's oldest living civilizations—which gave to the world—the concept of zero, the primordial sound Aum..., Yoga and Buddhism.

She is old. She is young. The two diametrically opposite, different yet unique and dynamic faces of India coexist even at this turn of the millennium. With a history of heritage, learning and civilisation dating back to almost 5000 years or perhaps even more, the modern India presents itself as an ideal country. From snow clad mountains to breezy sparkling blue sea side. From arid deserts with shifting sand dunes to lush green country sides. From ancient relics and architectural ruins dating back into antiquity to modern cities, India has it all.

To the north it is bordered by the world's highest mountain chain, where foothill valleys cover the northernmost of the country's maximum states. Further south, plateaus, tropical rain forests and sandy deserts are bordered by palm fringed beaches. Its southernmost tip is the meeting point of three Oceans.

India is a land of staggering contrast with a mingling of the tradition and modernity that is an unique experience to be in India. One will forever remember the stay in this wonderful Homeland-a land truly of mystery and enchantment. Only India can offer such an astonishing variety of contrasts.

She has given birth to numerous spiritual leaders and founders of some of the popular religions of the present day world. India probably has the most religious diversity in any country. It's the birthplace of Hinduism, Buddhism, Sikhism and Jainism and is among the few places to have a resident

Zoroastrian population. India with her veritable treasure trove of culture, mysticism, philosophy, art, music and architecture to name a few. Much of India's classical music is devotional and the North Indian Hindustani and South Indian Carnatic streams are distinct and both have a complex 'raga' framework. The legacy of dance in India is tremendous. The classical dances of India are numerous such as Kathakali of Kerala, Bharatnatyam of Tamil Nadu, Kuchipudi of Andhra Pradesh, Manipuri and Odissi from Orissa are the prominent dance forms in this country that sways to an altogether novel beat. The Yakshagana, nautanki and puppetry are ancient folk forms that live on till date. The earliest specimens of Indian painting are the ones on the walls of the Ajanta Caves dating back to 2nd century BC. The Mughals had a huge impact on Indian art. The influence of Persian art brought placid garden scenes, illustrations from myths, legends and history into Indian art. Word craft, handicrafts, architecture and sculpture all contribute to this rich and varied domain. Indian literature, both in English and in the vernacular, is ever more popular around the world.

The book aims at presenting perspectives of different aspects of Indian culture. It has topics on Indian classical music and dance, painting, ayurveda and yoga which are traditional and indigenous system of physical and mental wellbeing, language, philosophy and excellence achievements by Indian in the different branches of science and social sciences. It also includes our ancient religious and classic literature.

It is hoped that this book will be welcomed by the general readers as also scholars who are interested in the Indian heritage.

—Editors

1

Great Fairs of India

Kumbha Mela

The pilgrimage occurs four times every twelve years, once at each of the four locations. Each twelve-year cycle includes the Maha (great) Kumbha Mela at Prayag, attended by millions of people, making it the largest pilgrimage gathering around the world. The observance of Kumbha Mela is based upon the following story : thousands of years ago, perhaps in the Vedic period, gods and demons made a temporary agreement to work together in obtaining *amrita* (the nectar of immortality) from the Milky Ocean, and to share this equally. However, when the Kumbha (pot) containing the amrita appeared, the demons ran away with the pot and were chased by the gods.

For twelve days and twelve nights (equivalent to twelve human years) the gods and demons fought in the sky for the possession of this pot of amrita. It is said that during the battle, drops of amrita fell on to four places : Prayag, Haridwar, Ujjain and Nasik. Thus, Kumbha mela is observed at these four locations where the nectar fell.Kumbha Mela is attended by millions of people on a single day. A ritual bath at a predetermined time and place is the major event of this festival.

Other activities include religious discussions, devotional singing, mass feeding of holy men/women and the poor, and religious assemblies where doctrines are debated and standardized. Kumbha Mela (especially the Maha Kumbha Mela) is the most sacred of all the Hindu pilgrimages. Thousands of holy men/women (monks, saints, sadhus) grace the occasion by their presence. The suspiciousness of Kumbha Mela is in part attributed to the gathering of thousands of holy men/ women at one place on earthAccording to astrologers, the 'Kumbh Fair' takes place when the planet Jupiter enters Aquarius and the Sun enters Aries.

On Mahavir Jayanti, much emphasis is also placed on self control. Thus, the controlling of the senses and emotions takes precedence. Evening meals are eaten before sunset and Jains are enjoined not to lose control of their emotions.

On this day, typically four kinds of donations are made. These donations are intended to instil a sense of generosity and compassion for the less fortunate. It is also intended to remind Jains to not be too attached to material possessions. The four kinds of donations recommended for every Jain include:

Gyan daan: sharing of knowledge

Abhay daan: protecting people from bad actions

Aushad daan: donating medicines

Ahaar daan: giving food

The *Maha Kumbh Mela* ("great festival of the pot of nectar of immortality") is held every three years in each of four different locations, returning to each of four places every twelve years. An Ardh (half) Mela (festival) takes place six years after the Maha Kumbh in each location. Kumbh Mela is a sacred Hindu pilgrimage and bathing festival that takes place at the following four locations of India:

1. *Prayag* (near the city of Allahabad, in the state of Uttar Pradesh) at the confluence of three rivers Ganga (Ganges), Yamuna and Saraswati
2. *Haridwar* (in the state of Uttaranchal) where the river Ganga enters the plains from Himalayas.
3. *Ujjain* (in Madhya Pradesh), on the banks of Ksipra river
4. *Nasik* (in Maharashtra) on the banks of Godavari river.

The observance of Kumbh Mela is based upon the following legend: Thousands of years ago, in the Vedic period, gods and demons made a temporary agreement to work together churning amrita (the nectar of immortality) from the Ksheera Sagara (primordial ocean of milk), and to share the nectar equally. However, when the *Kumbh* (urn) containing the amrita appeared, the demons ran away with it and were chased by the gods. For twelve days and twelve nights (equivalent to twelve human years) the gods and demons fought in the sky for possession of this pot of amrita. It is said that during the battle, drops of amrita fell at four places: Prayag, Haridwar, Ujjain and Nashik. Thus, the Kumbh Mela is observed at these four locations where the nectar fell.

Astrology and Kumbh Mela: The precise dates of the *Kumbh Mela* are astrologically determined, based upon the positions of the Sun, the Moon and Jupiter. At Prayag, the *Maha Kumbh Mela* is held in the month of Magha (January/ February in the Gregorian calendar). The highest spiritual merit is attached to bathing on the new moon day, when Jupiter is in Taurus and both the Sun and Moon are in Capricorn. At Haridwar, the Kumbh Mela is held in the months of Phalgun and Chaitra (February/March/April), when the Sun passes to Aries, the Moon is in Sagittarius and Jupiter is in Aquarius. In Ujjain, the festival is held in the month of Vaishakha (May), when other planets are in Libra, the Sun and Moon are in Aries and Jupiter is in Leo. At Nashik, the Kumbh Mela takes place in the month of Shravana (July), when the Sun and Moon are in Cancer and Jupiter is in Scorpio.

It is also said that the elixir of life is filled in a Kumbh (Pot) in Swarg (heaven) so with certain combination of Sun-Moon-Jupiter combination, the elixir falls from heaven to earth, and kumbh mela is held on that locations.

Rituals of Kumbh Mela: The Triveni Sangam, or the intersection of Yamuna River and Ganges River, where devotees perform rituals.

Kumbh Mela is attended by millions of people on a single day. The major event of this festival is a ritual bath at the banks of the rivers in each town. Other activities include religious discussions, devotional singing, mass feeding of holy men and women and the poor, and religious assemblies where doctrines are debated and standardized. Kumbh Mela (especially the Maha Kumbh Mela) is the most sacred of all the Hindu pilgrimages. Thousands of holy men and women (monks, saints and sadhus) attend, and the auspiciousness of the festival is in part attributable to this.

Once every 12 years, millions of the world's most zealous Hindu pilgrims gather at the confluence of the Ganges and Yamuna rivers near the city of Allahabad for the greatest of India's immersion rituals, the Maha Kumbh Mela. This year's Maha Kumbh Mela is particularly auspicious, being the first of the new millennium and coinciding with an astrological planetary alignment occurring only once every 144 years. By the time the 2001 Kumbh Mela ends on February 21st, approximately 70 million saints, sinners, Sadhus, faith healers, preachers, gurus, charlatans and devotees from across India and the world will have participated in perhaps the single most colossal gathering of humanity since the dawn of time.

In Hindu mythology, Gods and demons fought over the pot (Kumbh) of the divine nectar of immortality. The Gods ultimately obtained the pot of nectar, spilling some back on the earth, upon four cities in northeastern India: Allahabad, Ujjain, Nasik and Haridwar. The Kumbh Mela rotates between these sites every four years. Allahabad, (the modern name of the holy city Prayag, meaning "holiest of the holy") located at the confluence of the Ganga, and Yamuna rivers is considered the most sacred and important location for the Mela.

Hindus believe that during this year's Kumbh Mela a bath in the Sangam (the holy confluence of the Ganga and Yamuna rivers) will cleanse them of their sins, and grant an escape from the endless cycle of reincarnation.

The Maha Kumbh Mela is truly a microcosm of Indian society at its most spectacular. The six-week spectacle is a passion filled festival, which transcends creed, caste and religion. For the throngs of Hindu devotees who will travel here it is a chance at salvation.

Of the 70 million or so attendees at the Kumbh, most are rural villagers and commoners who have traveled for days, weeks or even months by any means possible on a personal search for the divine. Carrying bundles of provisions on their heads, unprepared for the low temperatures, they will sleep on the open ground; eat whatever is available and brave conditions that most westerners would find unimaginable. They have come for the opportunity of a lifetime, the opportunity for a miraculous dip into the cleansingly frigid waters of the Ganges on this sacred occasion.

I had arrived in New Delhi on January 19th, 2001 meeting my friend from past trips, Satkamal Singh, a Sikh cab driver. We would leave the next morning for the fifteen-hour road trip to Allahabad. Acting as my translator, guide, negotiator, photographic assistant and personal security officer, Satkamal would be an integral part of my plan to chronicle the biggest Kumbh in history.

A key component of this trip was my desire to photograph Sadhus, India's religious holy men, many of whom have decided to forgo normal life, renounce all belongings, and live nomadic or reclusive lives sustained by herbs, handouts and hashish. Protected by the armor of nakedness, the most militant of the Sadhus, the Nagas, were top on my priority list. Nagas, whose ascetic traditions date back more than 2000 years, have on occasion defended Hinduism against the fervor of a younger religion, Islam. The Nagas are considered the most Holy and revered among the Sadhu sects. The term "holy" however, can sometimes be a misnomer since India's Sadhus are not all seekers of God. The unmistakable dress (or lack there of) does impart respect among the faithful, but it is a known fact that some Sadhus are criminals wanted by police for murders, rapes, swindling or trade in contraband and narcotics.

During my days in the Sadhu camps, I met fascinatingly bizarre characters, many of whom have taken on various penances as signs of ultimate devotion.

I spent time with Amar Bharti Baba, a man who's now petrified arm has been held aloft for the past 27 years. I met Radhey Puri Naga Baba, a man standing on one leg for nearly a decade, his feet swollen to twice their normal size. I visited the midget Sadhu, Bawan Giri Baba, a 62 year old who stands barely two feet tall. Countless others who make up the 180,000 or so Sadhus who attend the Kumbh, bury themselves in the sand, sleep on piles of thorn bushes or remain silent for years. Some are regarded as prophets, saints and gurus-others as outcasts or criminals. In my days with the Sadhus I was questioned, blessed, dismissed, and hustled. I was offered spiritual advice, tea, marijuana and hashish more times than I can count.

Apart from the Sadhu ashrams, the entire Mela grounds were a riot of sights, sounds, smells, colours and movement. Among the crowd were some 5000 barbers, on site to service the millions who elected to have their heads shaved before bathing in the Sangam. A shaved head costs around 10 Rupees (25 cents)-a small price to pay for a spiritual advantage (Hindu's believe that each strand of hair is the equivalent of buying a cow for the God of your fancy). Shaving one's head therefore speeds up one's journey to heaven.

Intermingled with the barbers were legions of beggars who offered yet another way to create good Karma for one's self. I witnessed even the poorest of pilgrims filling a beggar's extended hand with anything from a rupee to a cup of rice. Beggars in India provide a unique type of symbiotic relationship with those who are more fortunate. Begging allows those who are able to give, the opportunity to do a good deed. Beggars come in all types, but none were more heart wrenching than the hundreds of lepers at the Kumbh. Many were wheeled in on makeshift wooden carts or carried on the backs of family members.

Almost all the lepers were covered with wool blankets, their effected limbs bandaged with hopelessly soiled rags. Partial limbs protruded from beneath blankets for all to see, many lacked fingers, toes, or entire hands and feet. The most unfortunate lepers, with advanced disease, quivered and shook uncontrollably, as if shivering, despite the stifling mid day heat. Meanwhile, just steps away, processions of gilded coaches draped in silk, announced the arrival of important religious leaders. Competing for attention in this already deafening cacophony, were the chants of passing processions, intermingled with loudspeakers that blasted anything from religious mantras, to announcements in Hindi about cattle insurance and cigarettes. The decibel level seemed to deafen all but the most calloused Indian ears.

At one point I decided to call my wife back in California, using one of the many STD phone booths set up in small shacks on the Mela grounds. STD phones, ubiquitous in India, resemble taxi-meters; an L.E.D. read-out displays the cost in Rupees as the call progresses. Once my connection was made I shouted into the receiver and struggled to hear my wife's responses. Conversation was nearly impossible so finally; I held the phone in the air to let her experience the incredible din. As my phone bill neared two hundred Rupees, I noticed the phone booth operator grinning from ear to ear...I'm sure this was the most expensive call of the day.

Amravati in Indralok and presented Indra, the ruler of the celestial regions, with a garland of eternal flowers. Indra, casually passed the garland to the divine elephant, Airawat, under whose feet it got crushed. Durvasa, known for his wrath, cursed Indra that he would be deprived of his powers and his position. The demon king Bali attacked and overcame Indra. The gods pleaded with Vishnu, who recommended the divine nectar, Amrita, which bestows immortality.

To extract this, the oceans were churned at once by the gods and the asuras. The pot of ambrosia was handed to Brihaspati, (Jupiter) Surya, (Sun) Chandrama (Moon) and Shani (Saturn). In the process of the ensuing tussle to get it, which lasted 12 god-days, equal to 12 human years, a few drops spilled from the kumbh or pitcher in which the Amrita was being carried. This nectar fell at Allahabad, Haridwar, Nasik and Ujjain, sanctifying these places.

The Kumbha Mela is held at these four sacred places-on the banks of the holy Ganga at Haridwar where it descends from the mighty Himalayas to the plains of India, at the confluence of the Ganga, Yamuna and the mythical Saraswati called the Triveni Sangam at Prayag or Allahabad, beside the river Kshipra at Ujjain and on the banks of the Godavari at Nasik. At each of the four places the Kumbh festival is celebrated once every twelve years, coinciding with one round of Jupiter through the zodiac. Since the three cosmic powers played their role, the Kumbha is celebrated when Jupiter, the Sun and Moon are in particular astrological positions in the almanac. When the Sun enters Mesh Rashi and Jupiter enters Kumbha Rashi in the month of Vaishakhi (April-May), it is held at Haridwar, where it was last celebrated in 1998.

In the month of Magh (Jan-Feb) when the sun enters Makar Rashi and Jupiter enters Mesh Rashi and Vrishabh Rashi, it is celebrated at Prayag, Allahabad, where the last Kumbha Mela in 2001 was a particularly auspicious festival which occurs once every 144 years. The Kumbha Mela at Ujjain and Nasik are known as Simhastha because various planets transit in Simha Rashi (Zodiac Leo). When the Sun enters Mesh Rashi (Aries) and Jupiter enters Simha Rashi, the Kumbha is celebrated at Nasik, where it was celebrated in August 2003.

It is celebrated at Ujjain when Jupiter enters Leo and there is a combination of 10 Punyaprad Yog or various specified factors. It was last celebrated in Ujjain in 1992 and the forthcoming Kumbha will be held in Vaishakh (April-May) 2004. A Kumbha procession defies description-it must be experienced to be known. It is heralded by the conjunction of planets at an auspicious time and place, and it is the convergence of a spiritual energy that has it's own compelling power.

The colour and style of the traditional dresses of every region of India inter-mingle here against the backdrop of shades of saffron everywhere. Sadhus and sannyasins of every kind are represented here in the many colours and images: saffron and pure white, red and black, matted locks, shaved heads; ashes and sandalwood, vermillion and orange pastes; kopins, robes, digamber; beads, stones, glass and metal in necklaces, amulets, bracelets, rings; large kundals through pierced ears; trishuls, machetes, swords and weapons of a different age; the kamadhenu or mendicants bowl, khappar or coconut shell receptacle; flower-bedecked; flags, chattris and palanquins-ceremonial processions and age-old rituals... The sounds of the war-like cries of ash-smeared Naga sadhus intermingle with the many sounds in the congregation of elephants, camels and horses as though time has stood still for centuries. The beating drums, the ringing bells, the blowing conch shells and the chants are a strange call of the stirring soul.

And in this relentless march is a vibrancy and an energy impossible to define. In recent years, the Kumbha Melas have attracted high media attention, international participation and celebrity status as an event. For the devout, it remains an occasion to be cleansed and purified. For the tourist, it has colour, flavour, exotica. For the spiritually inclined it is a power-house of spiritual energy, the greatest meeting-ground of saints and mahatmas, where there always exists the possibility of darshana of the enlightened and the crossing of milestones on the path.

Kumbh Mela (the Urn Festival) is a Hindu pilgrimage that occurs four times every twelve years and rotates between four locations: Prayag, Haridwar, Ujjain and Nashik. Each twelve-year cycle includes one *Maha Kumbh Mela* (*Great* Kumbh Mela) at Prayag, which is attended by millions of people, making it the largest gathering anywhere in the world.

According to Hindu creation myths, the gods once fought a great battle over the *kumbh* (pitcher) containing the nectar of immortality. In the scuffle, four drops of the nectar spilled onto the earth, splashing on the ground of Allahabad, Nasik, Ujjain and Haridwar.

A huge *mela* (fair) is held at each of the cities, attracting vast numbers of Hindu holy men, especially the naked *saddhus* and *nagas*, or militant Hindu monks. For India's 670 million plus Hindus, the four cities involved in the Kumbh Mela cycle are among the seven most sacred cities on the pilgrimage circuit.

The triennial pilgrimage attracts millions from all over the country. In Haridwar ('Gateway to the Gods') in 1998, more than 10 million Hindus came and washed in the Ganges in the sacred area where the river leaves the mountains and enters the plains.

The Allahabad Kumbh Mela is the largest and holiest of all melas. Two of Hinduism's most important rivers, the Ganges and the Yamuna (as well as the mythical River of Enlightenment), converge here and Hindus consider that the confluence, known as the *sangam*, has great soul-cleansing properties. All pious Hindus hope to bathe here at least once in their lives. In 2001 around 70,000,000 people visited Allahabad during the Mela, with more than 15,000,000 pilgrims bathing on one day alone!

The once-in-a-144-years mega event, the Maha Kumbha Mela, is here. We dig out some legends associated with the Kumbha Mela and its esoteric meaning The Mahakumbha. This is your chance to attain *moksha*. It's now or never, because only once in 144 years do you get to see this unique combination of the spiritual energies.

The much awaited and hyped *Mahakumbha mela* will be held at the holy land of Allahabad, India, through January till Mahashivratri in February. According to astrologers, the Kumbha mela takes place when the planet Jupiter enters the sign of Aquarius and the Sun enters into Aries.A ritual bath at Sangam, where the three rivers—Ganga, Yamuna and Saraswati—meet, at a predetermined time and place is the major part of this mela. Other activities include religious discussions, *yajnas* or sacrificial fire ceremony, devotional singing, mass feeding of holy men and women and the poor, and religious assemblies where doctrines are debated.

The *Kumbha mela* is periodically celebrated every 12 years at one of the four holy places of Hardwar, Nasik, Ujjain and Allahabad. But a culmination of 12 times 12 will be in this year and as it coincides with a step into the new millennium, it is expected to increase spiritual vibrations globally. In 1989, over 15 million people attended the Kumbha mela at Allahabad and the *Gunnies Book of World Records* noted it as the greatest number of people assembling for a common purpose.

Many foreign visitors aim to make it to the mela including New Agers Richard Bach, Billy Graham and Paulo Coelho. Writes Pandit Rajmani Tigunait, spiritual head of the Himalayan Institute in their website: "Many visitors will be traveling from the United States; others will be joining from 20 other countries." For this special occasion, many saints and sages, totally engrossed in their sadhana in the Himalayas will emerge for a bath at Sangam.The political parties also have an ace up their sleeves.

The Week reports that the Vishwa Hindu Parishad (VHP) plans to unveil a model of the Ram Temple, to be built at Ayodhya, which is nearly complete, at a secret location in Jaipur. Designed by Gujarat-based architect Chandrakant Sompura, it is crafted by Chandresh Pandey from Jaipur. Kumbha literally means a pitcher. Astrological representation of Aquarius denotes a man holding a pitcher. The reference is to the pot filled with the nectar of immortality that emerged after the gods and demons churned the milky ocean. However, the symbolism inherent when we speak of Kumbha far transcends the literal translation.

Our scriptures tell us that the trinity of gods—Brahma (creator), Vishnu (whose name literally means the divine light that pervades everything, protector) and Shiva (destroyer), and all goddesses, including Mother Earth with her seven islands, and all knowledge in the form of the four Vedas—Rig, Yajur, Sama, Atharva—are present in the Kumbha. So Kumbha is symbolic of all that is and all that exists. In essence, the Kumbha mela is a celebration of all knowledge and all life. Though *kumbha* refers to an overflowing pot, it also refers to a body filled with knowledge.

The nectar, or divine knowledge, lies within this kumbha, which is nothing but our body and we simply have to churn it to bring this knowledge out. If we look into the origins of the Kumbha mela, we find that this pitcher symbolises sharing and not hoarding. In *Vishnu Purana* a beautiful story is told of the war between the *rakshasas* (demons) and the *devatas* (gods). According to this, the demons were always fighting with their peace-loving brothers, the *devatas*. One day, the gods went to Brahma and asked for help: "If we continuously lose our brothers and sisters in the never-ending war with the demons, we will all perish." Brahma advised them to ask Vishnu for help. Vishnu responded: "If you churn the great milky ocean, you will find a golden pot of nectar. And a drop of nectar will make you immortal. Since you are not strong enough to churn the ocean yourselves, you must take the demons' help." Now, the gods were more distressed. They voiced their fear: "If the demons know that the reward is immortality, they will forcibly take the nectar and create more trouble. And if we don't tell them the reason, they will not agree to the churning."

But Vishnu assuaged them and the perplexed gods convinced the demons to help them. It was no mean task to churn the vast milky ocean. Serpent Vasuki, Vishnu's seat, offered to be the rope and Vishnu incarnated as a turtle on whose back rested the mountain Meru. And so began the fantastic churning. After much hard work, a vicious smoke emerged, which filled the skies. This was not nectar, but deadly poison! With people choking to death, this poison could not be ignored. Who would save them? Then the lord of the netherworld, Shiva, came forward and drank the poison. Today, after this sacrifice, Shiva is worshipped as the savior from death.

The churning resumed and shortly came out the golden pot of nectar. As soon as the pot came out, Indra, the lord of heavens, signaled Dhanwantari, the primordial physician, who leapt forward, grabbed the pot of nectar and ran away. The demons, quicker than him, pursued him relentlessly. Indra sought aid from Jupiter (the *dev* guru), Surya (the sun), Moon and Saturn to protect Dhanwantari and preserve the Kumbha. This long chase lasted 12 days, which was the equivalent of 12 years on earth. During this chase, which traversed all realms of the universe, Dhanwantari rested only four times, placing the Kumbha on the ground. And each time a few drops of the holy nectar spilled onto the earth in that place.

These four places—Nasik, Ujjain, Hardwar and Allahabad in India—are today the centers of the Kumbha mela. In another legend, a demon named Shankhasura (*shankha*: conch, *asura*: demon) sent forth legions of creatures from the bottom of the sea to capture the sacred Vedas. And as the dark waters swallowed the knowledge of the mantras in the Vedas, the higher values of life also sank into the depths. Slowly, acts of charity and other forms of selfless service vanished. Fear, hunger, sleep and sex became the motivating forces for all human activities. Striving to appease their insatiable desires, humans plundered all. Scared, the gods sought refuge in the caves of Mount Kailash. Now, the conch demon demolished natural law and ushered in his reign with calamities—earthquakes, volcanoes, droughts. Chaos stalked the earth, and with the gods in hiding, the sages intervened.

They meditated on Vishnu, the protector and nourisher, asking him for aid. In response to their plight, Vishnu advised them: "With a singular aim and disciplined mind, join forces to gather the knowledge of the Vedas once again. While you fulfill this task I will bring the benevolent forces of nature from their hiding place and dwell with them at Prayaga Raja (now Allahabad, India)."

After the sages' departure, Vishnu assumed the form of an enormous fish, and vanquished Shankhasura. He then summoned the gods from their hiding place and brought them to Prayaga Raja, where they were joined by the other two of the trinity, Brahma and Shiva. Meanwhile the sages, through dhyana, discovered where the Vedas were hidden, fished them out of the mud, and joined the assembly at Prayaga Raja. There they asked Vishnu's permission to bring the knowledge of the Vedas into practice for the benefit of all creation. Granting their request, Vishnu said: "The secret of success lies in sacrifice, and the Vedas tell us how to walk this path. In every aspect of creation there is a continuous ceremony of sacrifice. Leaves decompose and nourish other organisms. Nothing in creation is meant for itself.

The greatest among all sacrifices is the *ashwamedha* (the horse sacrifice) performed for the larger welfare. They train and tame their "horses", the mind and senses, and finally they share this harnessed energy with all living beings. This form of sacrifice nourishes humankind and every other form of life." So all present performed the *ashwamedha yajna*.

The ritual lasted 12 years, and when it was completed the ecosystem was back into balance. Even the creatures from the netherworld were transformed. And with the natural world once again bursting with vitality, peace and prosperity reigned. The sages and gods requested Vishnu to bless the sacred Prayaga Raja: "May the energy emitting from Prayaga Raja guide humanity through all eternity." Hence, today this place is known as *brahma kshetra* (the field of pure consciousness) and *tirtha raja* (the lord of all holy places). According to the *Padma Purana* these events took place when the Himalayas were still in their infancy and the area around Badrinath, now well above the timberline, was covered by a lush forest.

From that time on Prayaga Raja has been regarded as a spiritual center. Great sages—Markandeya, Chyavana, Pulastya, Bharadvaja—guided their students through prolonged, intense practices here. Noble kings—Pururava and Bharata—whose dedication to spiritual practices and acts of charity earned them the status of *raja rishi* (royal seers), instituted a series of group practices here that went on, uninterrupted, for decades.

These stories remind us that a materially successful society eventually ends up with a Shankhasura, a demon who systematically drowns the higher values of life. "Whether myth or fiction, for centuries these legends have inspired people to find the sacred in the mundane," writes Tigunait. "Most religions teach us that the spiritual and the worldly cannot coexist. What solace! These stories imply that there is no mediator between the aspirant and God, no rigid rules or laws.

Simply listen to the voice of your heart, they say, and surrender the fruits of your deeds to the Almighty, who dwells in this sacred land." In this one national event the nectar of love, satsang, knowledge and grace is distributed to all without any discrimination. Even Mahatma Gandhi, in his autobiography, wrote: "...and then the Kumbha mela arrived. It was a great moment for me. I have never tried to seek holiness or divinity as a pilgrim, but 1.7 million people cannot be hypocrites."

During the Hindu festival, Kumbh Mela, millions of people congregate to bathe in the waters of certain rivers on auspicious days to cleanse their souls. Depending on the year of the 12-year cycle, sages, yogis, and devotees gather in temporary cities for a month of music, dancing, prayers, and ceremonies. Based on the ancient doings of gods who consecrated four sites along the banks of rivers with the honey of immortality, Kumbh Mela is the Hindu equivalent of a holy pilgrimage.

As the story goes, there was a pot, the kumbh, full of the elixir or nectar of immortality. Yet the gods fought over who got to carry the pot, and in the process, four drops fell at four different places. These came to be known as Prayag, Hardiwar, Ujjain, and Nasik, and they correspond to the four Kumbh Melas that take place every three years. On astrologically propitious days, determined by the paths of planets, the nectar is said to return to these rivers so that bathing in them will bring peace and purification.

Prayag occurs at the point where the Ganges and Yamuna Rivers meet the fabled Saraswati River. Haridwar brings people to the Ganges, where it flows from the Himalaya Mountains onto the wide valley. Ujjain occurs at the Ksipra River, while the Godavari River is the site of the Kumbh Mela called Nasik. The exact dates of each pilgrimage vary from year to year, depending on when the Sun enters Aries and Jupiter enters Aquarius.

The Kumbh Mela in 2001 attracted as many as 20 million people on a single day. That's perhaps the largest convergence of people in the history of Earth. Both the holy men, including ascetics, sages, sadhus, yogis, and the devout believer, the devotee, meet for weeks of meditations, ritual bathing, and exchanges of wisdom. They occupy a giant, tented city, broken up into marketplaces, ashrams or temples for meditation, and living quarters.

Some days are more holy for bathing than others, according to the stars, and on these days non-Hindus are asked to respectfully stay out of the water. Otherwise, the banks are crowded with throngs of tourists and Hindus alike, praying, playing music on drums, burning incense, saying prayers, and reciting mantras. It is a remarkable ceremony that blends mythology, culture, and deep, spiritual beliefs.

Periodical or annual fairs-Melas as they are known-on river banks, lake-shores, beaches and sacred places are held by Hindus to commemorate important events or in honour of

Gods or Goddesses. These melas find a mention in our epics and Puranas and therefore, are a prominent feature of Hinduism from time immemorial. The most important of these melas is the KUMBH MELA.

The origin of this mela is still obscure. May be it originated as a meeting place for the main religious heads in the country who could lay down canons for the whole community as Hinduism has no supreme hierarchial head. A large number of religious heads, ascetics, high priests, philosophers and wandering mendicants form the major part of pilgrims who visit the Kumbh Mela. It is the prospect of their "Darshan" that draws the crowds. It is said about this mela that the earth was made sacred at four places by contact with the "KUMBH"-jar-filled with "amrit"-nectar.

It is believed that the gods became emaciated as a result of the curse by a saint and wanted to regain their old strength and vigour by drinking the nectar. But they knew that they would not be able to churn the ocean by themselves and bring up the Kumbh, filled with the nectar-the Elixir of Immortality that was lying on the bed of the ocean. So they approached the Asuras-the demons who were their inveterate enemies, to join hands with them in churning the ocean. For that help, the gods promised the Asuras that they would be given a portion of the nectar when the pot of nectar is brought up from the depths of the ocean.

The Asuras readily agreed. Then the gods and the demons started churning the ocean with Mandar mountain as the rod for churning and Vasuki, the great Cobra serpent for the thick string. As the vigorous churning progressed the ocean began to yield its treasures one by one. In all thirteen precious things came out from the sea. Lastly the Sage Dhanwantri appeared with the coveted jar of nectar in his hands. The Asuras who were physically stronger than the gods seized the Kumbh. At that moment Lord Indra's son Jayant, assumed the form of a gregarious rook-a ferocious bird-whisked away the jar from the hands of the demons and flew high up in the sky. The bird on its way to heaven rested at Nasik, Ujjain, Prayag and Haradwar. He took twelve days to reach paradise from the ocean. As each divine day is reckoned to be equivalent to an earth year, the KUMBH MELA is celebrated once in twelve years at each of these four places.

Another version of this story says that when the Gods and Asuras struggled for the possession of the kumbh nectar spilled from the jar and fell at these four places. The Mela is not held at all the four places on the same date but in turn and hence we have a Kumbh Mela every three years. But at Prayag-Allahabad-where the three holy rivers Ganga, Yamuna and the hidden Saraswati meet-the Sangam of these rivers-and the river-bed is extensive, the Kumbh Mela attracts a large multitude of people.

The sight is truly spectacular ! Next to this Mela at Prayag, the Kumbh Mela at Haradwar is gorgeous too. It is a stupendous pageant as millions upon millions of inspired people step into the ice-cold water at dawn. Disregarding the heavy expenses and the long tiring journey people come from all parts of the country and band together to form the world's and most colourful religious concourse-the KUMBH-MELA which comes after twelve long years of waiting. Hindus regard that a dip in the holy Ganga specially at Haradwar which is believed to be the gangadwar of ancient mythology.

As in ages gone by, the powerful call of Kumbh Mela still draws millions of people from all over India. It is indeed fantastic to behold the ancient past blending so naturally with the reality of the present world. The large gatherings of millions are seen once every six years in Ardha-Kumbh Mela and once in twelve years in the Kumbh melas. In these Kumbh Melas there are hermits and sages from the higher reaches of the Himalayas, Pilgrims, Swamis and missionaries from South of India and from far away lands like America. The faces of unlead ash-smeared sadhus, known as "Digambers", add to the mystic atmosphere. Bringing all of these together to the same place and at the same time certainly speaks of the overpowering strength of religious traditions in India and also of their staunch faith in their own religious precepts.

As the auspicious Kumbh Mela at Haradwar draws near thousands of emergency shelters spring up-modern tents, old style bamboo cottages like those used long ago by ancient sages. Atop of these flutter thousands of coloured flags of various religious sects. A common feature of this mela is fakirs sitting with their twisted limbs on their sharp spikes and ascetics standing on their heads.

As the auspicious hour for the dip draws near some 100,000 Sadhu take out a procession, which is led by a Sadhu, riding an unsadled horse, followed by caprisoned elephant behind which the holy men march in long files. The whole corsage proceeds in regal splendour down to the water's edge with some of the Sadhus reclining under gorgeous parasols in decorated palanquins. The route of the procession is lined with crowds of pilgrims. A ripple runs through the crowd as the first sect of Sadhus steps into the water to be followed by wave after wave of Sadhus dip in the holy river.

Then excited people enter the water to have their holy bath. In the ancient literary works the importance of Haradwar as one of the seven holy cities of the Hindus is highly emphasised. It is at Haradwar, rightly known as the "gateway to reach the gods" that the great holy Ganga enters the plain after a journey of two hundred miles through the rugged mountains.

Thus beauty and sanctity are seen together at Haradwar. Wooded hills, cradle the youthful Ganga not yet defiled by city wastes, as she emerges from the protective girdle of the majestic Himalayas, holding forth a promise of a million years in heaven no deities need to be propitiated, no temple bells are required to be rung! Just a bath in the magic waters of the Sacred Ganga at Haradwar and you reach nearer to heaven.

As evening falls at Haradwar and hundreds of lighted floats go bobbing down in the waters of Ganga, pilgrims sitting around the fire narrate the mythical episode of the churning of the sea by the gods and the demons for a continuous thousand years to finally bring out from the sea the KUMBH containing the elixir of immortality. The crowds listen to the legend of the fight between the gods and the demons to take possession of that Kumbh and also to the many stories that have sprung from that one episode. Apart from the Hindu devotees, there are a great many who came with truly pious sentiments. It is to such people that the Kumbh and Ardh-Kumbh melas owe their tremendous impact and popularity. Joyous and free, calm and tranquil the faithful ones leave the Melas at complete peace with themselves. The holy river and the All-powerful god in whom their faith becomes more implicit, convince them that they are a step ahead in their quest for achieving "MOKSHA"-freedom from mortality.

Ganga Sagar Fair

Gangasagar Mela is the largest fair celebrated in West Bengal. This fair is held where the Ganga and the Bay of Bengal form a nexus. Hence the name Gangasagar Mela.

The river Ganga which originates in the Gangotri glacier in the snow clad Himalayas, descends down the mountains, reaches the plains at Haridwar, flows through ancient pilgrimage sites such as Benares and Prayag, and drains into the Bay of Bengal. Sagar Island, at the mouth of the river Hooghly in Bengal (accessed from Diamond Harbour), where the Ganga breaks up into hundreds of streams, and drains into the sea, is honored as a pilgrimage site.

A dip in the ocean, where the Ganga drains into the sea is considered to be of great religious significance particularly on the Makara Sankranti day when the sun makes a transition to Capricorn from Sagittarius and this town becomes home to vast fairs, drawing visitors and recluses from all over the state. There is a common belief among the locals that the girls who take the holy dip get handsome grooms and the boys get beautiful brides. When they are done with the ritual obligations, they head towards the Kapilmuni Temple situated nearby, to worship the deity as a mark of respect.

A Dip for Moksha: The village priest leading his horde of devotees chants *sab teerth baar baar, Ganga Sagar ek bar*. You can go to all the holy places, but a pilgrimage to Ganga Sagar equals them all. A dip means redemption for all wrong done. This place is Sagar Island, on the confluence of the Ganga with the Bay of Bengal. The day "Makar Sankranti" or the last day of the month of *Paus* (December).

Legend has it that, before joining the sea, the Ganga watered the mortal remains of King Sagar's 60000 sons liberating their souls once and forever. It was standing on the Sagar Island that the mythical Kapil Muni condoned the sins of the sons of King Sagar who had dared to stop the horse blessed at Lord Indra's Aswamedha Yagna and tied it to a post near his temple. It is this legend that attracts people to this little island in a remote southern corner of West Bengal.

The Ganga Sagar *mela* (fair) is the largest annual assemblage of devotees in India. The greatness of the mela can be assessed from the fact that over a million pilgrims come from far-flung corners of India and beyond, speaking different languages and belonging to diverse castes and creeds, for a sacred dip at this holy confluence. For this, no invitation is given. No propaganda is carried out and overall no authority exists for carrying out the mela.

It is indeed a tough journey. A few days in packed buses and trains bring the pilgrims to Calcutta. From there, again a long bus journey to ferry *ghats* or jetty in Sunderbans area, followed by crossing the tidal river stretching for miles across. The last leg involves either walking or traveling by a local bus upto 30 kilometres depending on the location of embarkation point.

The journey can be tiring but religious fervour of the pilgrims overcomes all hardships. *Kapil Muni ki jai, Kapil Muni ki jai*, (Hail Kapil Muni), the din rises above the grinding motors of the launches ferrying the pilgrims across the Ganga and the countless buses plying between Calcutta and Namkhana. The problem of traveling doesn't deter even the weak and vulnerable. Old people in their eighties, and village women carrying babies and little children in tow are a common sight.

The never ending stream of pilgrims keeps pouring in throughout the day and night before the auspicious day and occupies any available space on the sandy beach. They move about the place in groups, many displaying saffron and red flags, identifying the religious *Akhara* (group) they belong to as well as acting as beacon to the members who stray out of the group.

People walks to the sound of the bells, blowing conch shells and chanting prayers. Strains of devotional songs can be heard from far and near. And, the ceaseless din of loudspeakers. An array of shops, stacked with heaps of vermilion, rudraksha, colourful beads, conch shells line the pathways. Many a visitor stands wide-eyed before the shops selling everything from food stuff, household utensils to remote controlled toys.

People crowd around the *naga sadhus* (naked ascetics) without whom the Ganga Sagar mela is incomplete. Sitting naked in little huts near the temple and enjoying a *chillum of ganja*, (cannabis) they are also the target of tourists' camera. While devotees jostle in front of numerous temporary shrines of Hindu deities to pay homage, Kapil Muni's temple remains the chief attraction. The temple of Kapil Muni, as we see it today, is by no means the spot where the sage meditated. It went under the sea millennium ago followed by the many others built in its place, which subsequently was also swallowed, by the advancing sea.

The present one was built only a few decades ago, quite a bit away from the sea. The tall dome of the temple is visible from a distance. In the temple, three images engraved in stone are displayed, the one in the middle is that of Kapil Muni. The sage is seen in a *jogasana*; his eyes wide open, looking towards the sea with millions of devotees before him. The idols of Ganga and King Sagar flank Kapil Muni and the horse of the sacrificial yagna stands at a distance.

The typical Ganga Sagar pilgrim is a country rustic, generally elderly, hardy, remarkably disciplined and fervent in his devotion. His dhoti seldom going below his knees, a cloth bound packet, containing everything needed for survival, on his head. And, of course, his women – heavily tattooed and clad in colourful saris.

As the night, pregnant with the auspicious moment, descends, all wait for the precise hour to take the dip. The sandy track to the water's edge is crowded with people who sit around fires before proceeding for the bath, chanting devotional songs and prayers. The seaside presents a spectacle in the darkness before dawn with the large bonfire lit by the bathers to keep off the cold. At midnight, the high tide drives the pilgrims back. The biting cold wind of mid – January from across the sea lashes the bare body. But there is a confidence on their faces and a kind of fire in their eyes. The confidence in God and the fire of earnest faith makes them brave the chill.

The stars in the sky have quite a long time to fade when the moment of truth comes. As soon as the priest announces, the auspicious pre-dawn hour, the crowds surge forward to meet the tide with a loud chorus *Kapil Muni ki jai* and plunge into the sea. Suddenly the place is charged with the extraordinary power of the believers.

After taking their holy dips, the shivering devotees trudge the one kilometre expanse leading to the brightly lit temple of Kapil Muni, where prayers were performed. Coconuts, flowers, vermilion, sweets, and money are offered to the image of the ancient sage.

The bustle of activity continues for quite sometime in the morning as the pilgrims perform a series of rituals including the symbolic *godan* to Brahmins. A calf is symbolically handed over to the Brahmin priest by the devotee. Many perform the symbolic crossing of the river of blood, *baitarani* to attain moksha or transcendation. It is interesting to observe the people, clutching the tail of a cow and wading through a puddle a few paces. Many people shave their heads and perform the last rites of departed relatives.

A number of marriages are solemnized on the beach during the day. Also, many local girls get married to the sea. This will ensure that theoretically they never become widows, even if their menfolk, braving the rough sea and tiger infested jungle for a living, die.

It is no wonder that for many tourists from abroad, like though French couple I met, Sagar mela is something more than a mammoth religious congregation. They have visited the mela twice and found "something which has disappeared from France and Europe at least half a century ago".

But the majority of the pilgrims take it easy. After the rituals are complete, they dry their clothes and hair, cook their food on open fires, eat and rest. Happy, contented and smiling, having made the pilgrimage.

The Ganga Sagar mela continues to throb with life, with the energy of millions of pilgrims. The pilgrimage may be extremely tough, but the pilgrims know that the visit will purify their souls. The visit fulfils their lifelong desire and often one can see tears of joy rolling down their cheeks. That is the magic of religion.

The arrival of the English New Year in the eastern part of India coincides with Gangasagar pilgrimage and fair, the second largest congregation of mankind known to the religious and domestic tourism history of the country after the holy Kumbha Mela. That Kumbha is observed once in four years at alternate location in north, central and central-west parts of the country makes Gangasagar all the more unique. Because, Gangasagar fair and pilgrimage is held annually on the Sagar Island's southern tip in the Ganges delta atop the Bay of Bengal, attracting flocks of the faithful from all parts of India and even from neighbouring countries, like Nepal, Bhutan and Bangladesh. Pilgrims from all walks of life have been visiting this holy place—famous for the mythical shrine of Sage Kapil—to offer prayers at his temple, after taking once-in-a-life-time dip in the confluence of River Ganges and the Sea.

Transition of the Sun from Sagittarius to Capricorn, during the winter solstice in the northern hemisphere is known as Makar Sankranti. From this day begins the six-month long Uttarayana, considered very auspicious for attaining higher worlds hereafter. Hence, Makar Sankranti—call it Lohri, Pongal or Sankranti; the festival conveys the bond of brotherhood and the spirit of oneness despite all odds—is celebrated throughout India as the festival of new harvest. It has been a traditional way of giving thanks to Mother Nature for her bounty. This is the period when the winter starts receding, paving way for the summer and the time when farmers bring home their harvest. In the coastal regions of south, it is a festival dedicated to Indra. In North India, a ritual bath in the river is important on this day. Khichri is eaten and given away as charity, and people also distribute rice and lentils to the poor and needy.

In Maharashtra and north India, a special dish called tilgul/ tilua, or laddoos made of jaggery and sesame seed, the chief crop of the season, is popular. In Gujarat and Rajasthan it is celebrated as the Kite flying day.

Traditionally, this period is considered the most auspicious time of the Hindu calendar. As per Mahabharata, the dying Bhishma waited—for this Solar transition—on a bed of arrows for his last breath, after felling to the arrows of Arjuna. According to other religious scriptures the Sun on this day visits the house of his son Shani, who is said to be the lord of Makar Rashi. Ordinarily, the father-son duo does not get along nicely but for this day when Sun makes it a point to visit his son. From Uttarayana starts the time of the Gods, while Dakshinayana is said to be their 'night', giving upper hand to the evil.

The auspicious things are done during this time. It was on this day when Lord Vishnu ended the rein of terror of the demon Asuras by finishing them off and burying them under the Mandar Mountain. It is also believed that Bhagirath—mythically credited with bringing down the purest of all river, mother Ganges to this planet—finally led Ganga near the Kapil Muni Ashram, at the present day Ganga Sagar, and performed 'tarpan' with her holy waters for the salvation of his unfortunate ancestors (60,000 descendants of King Sagar of Lord Rama's clan). He thus liberated their souls from the old curse of Sage Kapil, the presiding deity at the Gangasagar temple. Mythical belief goes that those who die in this period have no rebirth.

The beginning of January has therefore been the most favoured time of annual domestis tourism since time immemorial attracting thousands of worshippers—against all odds invloved in reaching the far flung remote island of Sagar in the bygone era—from down south, west and north alike. Times now have changed to the maximum positive levels with direct ferry services, all motorised and well-monitored against the overloading mishaps. Special bus and train services are available from Kolkata during January 12 to 15 to mark the Makar Sankranti Mela on the Sagar Island. Large vessels of Kolkata Port Trust and other public organisations are available from

Kolkata and about 110 KMs downstream, besides the Ganges at Kashinagar Point (Lot 08) and Namkhana, to ferry the pilgrims across the river to the island for an onward 45 minute bus journey to the fair grounds. Direct buses are posted to pick up and drop mela bound or returning pilgrims at Howrah and Kolkata Bus Stands, which run between these points and Namkhana and back.

The traditional fair still serves as the most attractive cause for domestic travel of the rural tourists to the east as it did in the ancient past. The myth that the Kapil Muni Temple only emerges out of water on the Makar Sankranti day to receive prayers of the devout, remains the catch-point to bring herds of natives from interiors of Gujarat, Kerala, Tamil Nadu, Maharashtra, Andhra and Karnataka. So has been the case with the dedicated masses from Haryana, Rajasthan, MP, UP, Bihar or Himachal, Punjab and Jammu. Nobody knows how and when the notion spread across the span of India! The Gangasagar fair on its peak day on January 14th attracts no less than a mini India in all its hues and traditions, serving as the time-tested bond of oneness of the nation enriched with unique range of cultural and linguistic variety.

The devastating Tsunami, last year, proved in arrival of almost no visitor from the southern states, specially Tamil Nadu and Andhra. And the heavy rains that played havoc in the same regions and Maharashtra in the past and recent months have again diminished the chances of the east-ward journey of the southern pilgrim. Yet, the fair administration is pepped up to welcome no less than five lac visitors that will again turn this tiny island of Bengal into a mini India, for some days at least. So hurry up and gear for the annual call of wander-lust—"Eastward Ho..!"

The Ganga Sagar fair attracts almost half a million people every year who take a holy dip at the confluence of the Ganges-some in the hope of washing away their sins, others expecting to win spouses of their dreams.

The fair is held on Sagar island, 156 km south of here, for several days, but Wednesday was the most auspicious occasion when the holy bath takes place.

The day marks the Hindu auspicious day of Makar Sankranti that falls on the last day of the Bengali month of Poush. It also marks the winter solstice.

Legend has it that on Makar Sankranti, when the sun begins its northward journey, the doors of heaven are kept open. A bath at the auspicious hour promises deliverance.

A special prayer is performed for the sun god as a thanksgiving for a good harvest. During evening prayers, worshippers set leaf baskets filled with flowers and lighted earthen lamps filled with camphor adrift in the Ganges.

There is a common belief among locals that girls who take the holy dip get handsome grooms and the boys get beautiful brides.

Preparations for the stay of hundreds of thousands of pilgrims on Sagar island have been made. Temporary sheds of bamboo have been erected. Police pickets have been set up. "Tight security arrangements have been made. Police have installed metal doors. Sniffer dogs are being pressed into service," fair official Ashis Thakur said.

Scores of food stalls and curio shops have come up. But Hindu ascetics with their long dreadlocks, some in just a loin cloth, others smeared in ash are attracting the most attention.

Groups of pilgrims huddled in front of the sages as they deliver their discourses on spirituality on the sandy beaches of the island are a common sight.

Many of the sadhus are seen wearing costly goggles, yet others can be spotted with mobile phones-all objects they describe as gifts from disciples.

Hundreds of such interesting mendicants and sages are passing through Kolkata on their way to Sagar island. Several NGOs have set up resting camps and are even serving sumptuous vegetarian meals for free for them.

Makar Sankranti also entails preparing traditional rice-sweets called pithey in Bengali households.

The Eastern Railway has this year completed its remaining construction of broadguage tracks on the Diamond Harbour section from Laxmikantapur to Namkhana and the officials are trying their best to provide direct access to incoming trains from upland to this nearest railhead on way to Sagar. Beyond this point travellers to Sagar have to cross the Ganges—from two points—on vessels. Fair Administration the Namkhana—Chemaguri water route has traditionally been less secure for boat journeys due to silting of the river.

The Fair administration prefers Lot Number Eight—Kachuberia route for allowing round-the-clock plying of passenger vessels during the annual fair. The pilgrims, therefore, are advised to reach for the second route to avoid unavoidable delays during low tides and the resultant rush of waiting passengers, most of whom are taken to the fair and back by tour arrangers of hinterland states who usually are themselves unfamiliar to this problem. The next caution is to avoid package tours by vessel from Kolkata (Babughat) to Sagar.

The island shore near the Kapil Muni Temple and the sprawling fair ground has no jetty for berthing the boats and large vessels, booked by the package trip runners, stop well within the muddy waters to compel the pilgrims to trudge in thigh-deep water to get off and on. Plying of country boats and ferrying of pilgrims by fishing travellers is completely banned during the fair period to prevent mishap. Facilities besides the Railways and the Kolkata Port Trust, other Central agencies such as the Departments of Post and Communication make massive arrangements providing ISD, STD and Internet services to the visitors and the media 24 hours a day during the five-day fair.

The Coast Guard and the Navy, with their dorniers and howercrafts and divers, join-in the local administration to keep a strict vigil to prevent any accident or untoward incident. Volunteers of HAM brigade-posted with readily available alternate communication facility through their handsets-also aid the security agencies at all the sensitive points of the fair. Their association helped in preventing the lifting of children for trafficking. Besides, these volunteers are a boon in the wake of any unforeseen natural calamity. The traditional fair still serves as the most attractive cause for domestic travel of the rural tourists to the east as it did in the ancient past. The myth that the Kapil Muni Temple only emerge out of water on the Makar Sankranti day to receive prayers of the devout, remains the catch-point to bring herds of natives from interiors of Gujarat, Kerala, Tamil Nadu, Maharashtra, Andhra and Karnataka.

So has been the case with the dedicated masses from Haryana, Rajasthan, MP, UP, Bihar or Himachal. Nobody knows how and when the notion spread across the span of India! The Gangasagar fair on its peak day on January 14th attracts no less than a mini India in all its hues and traditions, serving as the time-tested bond of oneness of the nation, enriched with unique range of cultural and linguistic varieties.

Baneshwar Fair

Celebrated in : Dungarpur, 13 Kms from Udaipur, Rajasthan

Deity : Shivalinga

Temple : Mahadev Temple

Time of the Festivity : Month of February

The name 'Baneshwar' is derived from the revered Shivlinga, which is kept in the Mahadev Temple in Dungarpur. "Baneshwar means the 'Master of the Delta' in the local Vagdi language and this name was given to the Shivlinga. The Baneshwar fair is held at a small delta formed by the river Som and Mahi, from Magh Shukla Ekadashi to Magh Shukla Purnima.

Baneshwar fair in its present form is actually one of two fairs: one which used to be held in of Baneshwar Mahadev (Lord Shiva) and another fair, which started after the construction of the Vishnu Temple by Jankunwari, daughter-in-law of Mavji, á highly revered saint considered to be an incarnation of Lord Vishnu.

Two disciples of Mavji named Aje and Vaje built the Lakshmi Narain Temple near the confluence of rivers Som and Mahi. The 'pran-pratishtha' ceremony of the idols was performed on Magh Shukla Ekadashi and since then, the fair is held on this day. The large congregation that gathers here at the time of the fair pays homage to all the deities with equal reverence. On Magh Shukla Ekadashi, the priest-called the Mathadhish, arrives at the fair site from Sabla, in a huge procession. A 16 cms silver image of Mavji on horseback is also brought here. The river water supposedly becomes holier when the Mathadhish takes a bath. Hence, people bathe along with him in the river. The Bhils consign the ashes of their dead at the confluence of the rivers.

The Baneshwar fair is predominantly a tribal fair with more than half of the congregation consisting of Bhils. They revere Baneshwar Mahadev as well as Mavji. The majority of the gathering is from the Districts of Dungarpur, Udaipur and Banswara.

Worship and Offerings: The temple of Baneshwar Mahadev remains open from 5.00 a.m. to 11.00 p.m. during the fair. In the morning, saffron is applied to the Shivlinga after it is bathed and an 'aarti' of burning incense is waved before it. In the evening, 'bhabhut' (ash) is applied to the Linga and an 'aarti' with a fine-wick lamp is waved. Devotees offer wheat flour, pulses, rice, jaggery, ghee, salt, chillies, coconut and cash.

Prayers are offered five times a day in the temples of Lakshmi-Narayan and Brahma. Brass gongs are struck at the time of 'aarti'. During the fair, 'aarti' of Mathadhish is also performed and Raslila takes place at night in the Lakshmi Narayan Temple. Offerings, similar to those at the Baneshwar Temple, are made at these shrines too.

Cultural Programmes:The Bhils attending Baneshwar Fair sing traditional folk songs in high pitched voices sitting around a bonfire every night. Cultural shows are arranged by youngsters of the clan. Groups of villagers are also invited to participate in the programme.

The fair resounds with the gaiety of songs, folk dances, magic shows, animal shows and acrobatic feats. Adding to the excitement are the joy rides on merry-go-rounds and swings. The large number of shops in the fair provides an opportunity for buying and selling of essential goods and fancy articles.

Sonepur Cattle Fair

Location: Sonepur, Bihar

Time of the Year: Kartik Purnima/November every year

Duration: Fifteen days (approximately)

Cycle: Yearly

A visual extravaganza awaits all at the Sonepur Fair, where multitudes congregate on Kartik Purnima to offer obeisance to Harihar Nath and participate inwhat is the biggest cattle fair in Asia. Festivities stretch over a fortnight, giving visitors a feel of the pulse of Bihar.

According to the Indian Almanacalmanac, the full moon day of Kartik Purnima,or Purnima of the month of Kartik, which usually falls in November, is one of the most auspiciousof days. A number of big fairs are held at important paces of pilgrimage. The Harihar Chhetra Mela near Sonepur is one of the biggest fairs held in India and is also the biggest cattle fair pilgrimage and the Harihar Kshetra Mela, as the Sonepur Fair is also known, is one of the biggest.

Sonepur is located in the Saran district in the northern part of Bihar. This district shaped like a triangle is demarcated by three mighty rivers-the Ganga, Gandak, and Ghagra, demarcate this district, which is shaped like a triangle. Sonepur stands on the confluence of the Ganga and Gandak.

The Sonepur Fair is of great antiquity and in olden times would attract importance and in the olden times, it attracted traders from as far as Central Asia. Like the origin of the Harihar Nath Temple, the reason for the inception of the Sonepur Fair is lost in the labyrinth of time.

The site of the present fair was originally at Hajipur whileHajipur, and only the pujas used to be offered atin the temple at Sonepur. During the reign of the Mughal emperor Aurangzeb, the fair was shifted to Sonepur. During the period of British rule,In the pre-independence era, the European indigo planters used it as an occasion for social and sports gathering. The fair continues for about fourteen days but the few days before, during and after the Kartik Purnima draws the maximum crowds. The sleepy mango grove of the fair ground turns into a wonderland, sure to overwhelm the sophisticated urban visitor as well as the simple rural folk.

The temple of Harihar Nath is naturally the main objective of the visitors to the fair after they have taken their ritual bath in the swirling waters of the Gandak. The original temple is believed to have been built by Lord Rama on his way to the court of King Janak to win Sita. The age and origin of the present temple has puzzled scholars but it is supposed to be believed that Raja Man Singh had it repaired. The builder of the present temple was Raja Ram Narain, a prominent figure during the late Mughal period. The Birlas recently conducted repairs and extension work in the temple.

Special Attractions: Visiting the temple of Harihar Nath is naturally the main objective of the visitors to the fair after they have taken their ritual bath in the swirling waters of the Gandak. As in many other famous places of worship, a number of smaller temples of other deities surround the temple of Harihar Nath Mahadeo.

Once the puja sand the ablutions are over, the visitors abandon themselves to the various attractions offered in and around the sprawling mela ground. The village folk, particularly the women,as well as the others, are attracted to the array of shops selling all sorts of garments, weapons and furniture, toys, utensils, agricultural implements, jewelry and various handicrafts. The fair becomes merchandise virtual explosion of colours, music, dances, magic shows, cattle, merchants and handicrafts.

The area that attracts all, however, is the one wherethe elephants are lined up for sale. The Sonepur Fair is the only one where such a large number of elephants are sold. These are mainly purchased by different forest departments and people involved with logging operations. Apart from elephants, a large number of cattle, a wide variety of animals and horses are also brought to the fair for sale. Legends are also bought and sold in the fair.

The fair continues for about fourteen days but the few days before and after the auspicious day of Kartik Purnima draw the maximum crowds. The sleepy mango grove, where the fair is organized, turns into a wonderland, sure to overwhelm the sophisticated urban visitor as well as the simple rural folk.

Like so many places of pilgrimage in India, Sonepur also has its legend. It involves two kings both of who were turned into animals, a crocodile and an elephant, by the curse of sages who were offended by them. Those days, this area was supposed to have been girdled by hills with three towering peaks and a lake in the center.

Once, while bathing in the lake with a party of women, a Gandharva chief named Huhu made fun of Dewala Muni by playfully pulling his leg. The ire of the sage took the form of a curse that turned Huhu into a crocodile. The other accused person was Indradyumna, a king of the Pandyas, who was of a very pious nature but had offended the powerful sage, Agastya. The king had failed to notice the sage as he was in meditation when the sage visited him. The curse of the enraged Agastya turned Indradyumna into an elephant that took refuge in the woods surrounding the lake.

One day while the elephant came with a herd to the lake to bathe, the gandharva-turned-crocodile caught his leg in its powerful jaws. Not to be taken lightly, the king of elephants tried to pull the crocodile up on the bank in an effort to crush him under his feet. A mighty battle ensued, which was joined by other crocodiles and elephants. The contest went on for thousands of years without any one being able to overpower the other. But ultimately, the King Elephant weakened and prayed to the supreme god Vishnu (Hari) to save him. His prayer was answered and Vishnu cut down the crocodile with his chakra (disc).

The touch of the chakra, however, released Huhu from the curse and he went to heaven. Vishnu also released Indradyumna from his curse by touching his forehead and took the king to His abode, Vaikuntha. Sonepur is well connected by road from the nearest main to the nearby towns and cities. Moreover, Sonepur is 25 km. from Patna, which is well connected by air, rail and road to the other parts of the country.

The famed cattle fair is held at Sonepur, in Northern Bihar on the banks of the River Ganga.. It is one Of the Asia's largest cattle fair. The full moon day of the month of Kartik (November) is regarded as one of the most auspicious days for the Hindus. Sonepur situated on the confluence of the holy rivers Ganga and Gandak, has the reverence of a blessed ground and lasts for a fortnight. In ancient times the Royal Rajahs and Nawabs used to camp here. The Sonepur Fair has unique and historical importance.

A bath at the confluence and a visit to the Hariharnath temple here is the aim for thousands of devotees on the Kartika Purnima day. The sprawling mela ground here with the pulsating market has the widest possible range of cattle and commodities. The array of shops sells all sorts of merchandise. Sonepur Fair is the only one of its kind where a large number of elephants are sold. These are purchased mainly by forest departments and people involved with logging operations. Apart from elephants, a large number of cattle and horses are also brought to the fair for sale. Various folk shows, games and jugglers can be seen in the fair.

According to the Indian Almanac the full moon day of Kartik Purnima which usually falls in November is one of the most auspicious of days. A number of big fairs are held at important paces of pilgrimage. The Harihar Chhetra Mela near Sonepur is one of the biggest fairs held in India and is also the biggest cattle fair in Asia.

Sonepur is located in there Saran district in the northern part of Bihar. This district shaped like a triangle is demarcated by three mighty rivers–the Ganga, Gandak and Ghagra. Sonepur stands on the confluence of the Ganga and Gandak.

When the pujas and the ablutions are over, the visitors abandon themselves to the various attractions offered in and around the sprawling mela ground. The village folk, particularly the women, are attracted to the array of shops selling all sorts of merchandise. The area that attracts all, however, is the one where the elephants are lined up for sale. Sonepur Fair is the only one where such a large number of elephants are sold.

These are mainly purchased by different forest departments and people involved with logging operations. Apart from elephants, a large number of cattle and horses are also brought to the fair for sale.

What is billed as Asia's largest cattle fair, the Harihar Kshetra Mela, is all about the royalty this year. Elephants are being "gifted away" and horses have come to acquire a "caste lineage".

"Gift" is a euphemism for a semi-underhand deal to get around the law. The government did not know whether to allow elephants at the fair this time. But it is impossible to think of the Sonepur fair without the jumbos at the confluence of the Gandak and the Ganga.

Tradition has it that Vishnu rescued the pachyderm from the jaws of the crocodile. (In the south, the religious equivalent may be 'Gajendra Moksham'.) The 25-day fair, held in the month of Kartik, has gained a religious connotation. It starts each year with lakhs of people taking a dip at the confluence on Kartik Purnima.

The absence of elephants, in any case, would have robbed the fair, one of the prime tourist events outside the Buddhist circuit, of its main attraction for the foreign visitors. Most of them enjoy a jaunty, trundling ride atop the pachyderms.

There are quite a few elephants around and, if you go by claims, their owners have reversed the principles of modern economics. The owners of these giant animals, worth several lakhs of rupees, each have overnight turned magnanimous enough to give them away for free to total strangers.

The government officials seem to be comfortable about registering the transfer of ownership as donations. But as anybody else, they too know who sold which elephant to whom. After all, it is an age-old tradition. This is not to say that the owners of elephants are pleased with the Forest Department officials. "We have ownership certificates. Then why can't we sell them openly? What will happen to these creatures if our financial situation does not let us take care of them any longer," asked one of them.

As ever, the horses are a big draw. While they are put to gallop, the traders refer to their stock in caste terms. The distinction is made based on their build, colour and temperament. The 'Brahmin' ones are tall, attractive and white, with broad manes and a sober deportment. The 'Kshatriyas' are those that are tall, brown with a broad chest and big ears, aggressive yet obedient. The ones with thin legs and long necks are the 'Vaishyas'. The short, black ones, which consume more food but work less than others are the 'Sudras'.

There are oxen in large numbers, but apparently the demand for buffaloes and cows exceeds supply. The ban on transportation of cattle by trains has meant that the presence of good breeds from Punjab and Haryana has shrunk. Even the local varieties are not here in large enough numbers, though buyers have come from Assam and West Bengal. If the floods in northern Bihar are cited as one of the reasons, the success of the White Revolution in Bihar might well be another reason. People do not want to sell their cows; they want to retain them for their milk, which has a ready market. The milk cooperatives are active and the returns are handsome and certain.

On the other hand, there is great demand for the Rajasthan variety of goats among the peasants and the landless people who are now keen to rear the better species for more meat or milk. A fair, perhaps, reflects the changing face of the economy.

Tarnetar Fair

The Tarnetar Fair is one of the most important fairs of Gujarat. Various tribes like the *Kolis*, the *Rabaris*, the *Bharwards*, the *Khants*, the *Khanbis*, the *Charans* and the *Kathis*, get together to celebrate the famous legendary marriage of Draupadi with Arjuna, thereby retracing its origin to the times of the Mahabharata. Arjuna was the third of the five Pandavas of Hastinapur, who got married to Draupadi-the princess of this region, in the great Hindu epic, the Mahabharata.

Tarnetar Fair-(Trinetreshwer Mahadev Fair): This fair is held every year on the 4th, 5th and 6th day of the *Shukla Paksha* (Aug-Sept) in Tarnetar (a village near the industrial town of Thangadli) in Surendranagar district in the region of

Saurashtra. Also known as the Trinetreshwer Mahadev Fair, this three-day festival is held at the 14th century Temple of Shiva (Destroyer in the Hindu Holy Trinity of Creator-Preserver-Destroyer), or *Trinetreshwer* (Three-Eyed God) who is also popularly known as Tarnetar. Built in a traditional style on the banks of a rivulet, this impressive marble temple has a *kund* (reservoir) in which the temple is reflected.

'Historic Swayamvara': According to popular belief, this was the very place where Draupadi had her *swayamvara* (a ceremony where an Indian princess chooses a husband from amongst a number of eligible suitors invited to her father's court).

Arjuna was the great archer who performed the 'Matsyavedh' and won her hand. The matsyavedh required him to climb up on a pole erected in the centre of the kund, balance himself on the two scales, and pierce the eye of the rotating fish on the top of the pole with an arrow by looking at its reflection in the water.

The Tarnetar fair in Saurashtra represents a unique synthesis of folk music, folk art and colour. It highlights the true folk nature of the fair with folk dances like the Rasada (a Gujarati folk dance), performed by hundreds of women moving gracefully in a single circle to the accompaniment of four drums and jodja pava (double flutes). People are mesmerised by the number of bhajan mandalis (group of devotees singing songs in praise of the Lord) singing bhajans and kirtans (devotional songs) to the tune of folk instruments such as khartals, pakhawaj, dhol and tabla (a range of Indian percussion instruments).

Banganga Fair

The Banganga Fair is held annually on the full moon day of Vaishakh (April-May) near a rivulet 11 kms from the historical township of Bairath in Jaipur district. The stream is believed to have been created by Arjun, one of the Pandavas.

Visiting the Banganga Fair, taking a bath and paying homage to the holy sites in the vicinity at this time is therefore considered very auspicious by the pilgrims who come from Alwar, Behror, Jaipur, Bharatpur and many other places.

Devotees gather at the Shri Radha Krishnaji's temple in the morning, they take a bath at the ghats (a flight of steps leading to the water) of the Banganga river with the belief that it has powers to purify the soul. The people then proceed to the nearby shrines of Hanuman and Ganga Bihari and also visit the Shiva temple and the Math of Goswamiji.

Camel Festival

A lively and colourful event, the Camel Festival is organised by the Department of Tourism, Art & Culture, Rajasthan in Bikaner every year. January is just the right month for a desert spree, and Bikaner just the right place to see the Ships of the Desert. In the camel country Bikaner, these desert leviathans pull heavy cart loads, transport grain and even work at the wells.

The Camel Festival begins with a colourful procession of bedecked camels against the red sandstone backdrop of the Junagarh Fort, the festivity advances to the open sand-spreads of the grounds, followed by the best breed competition, the tug-of-war contest, camel dance and acrobatics, etc.

The camels display amazing footwork, dancing gracefully to the slightest direction of their trainers. Bridal, bridles, bejewelled necks, jingling anklets and long, lanky camel shadows on dusky sands cast a magical spell. Hundreds of tourists and thousands of locals and dignitaries revel in this man-and-animal affair organised especially for the tourists.

The evenings close with a different tenor and tempo altogether: a traditional rendezvous of renowned artists of Rajasthan and the local folk performers.

The jubilant skirt-swirling dancers, the awe inspiring fire dance, and the dazzling fireworks light up the fortified desert city of Bikaner.

Bikaner is connected by rail and road with all the major cities. The nearest airport is at Jodhpur (243 kms.)

Kaila Devi Fair

The annual fair of Kaila Devi, (Mahalakshmi or the goddess of wealth), is held at the village Kaila (24 kms to the south west) in Karauli district in the month of Chaitra (Mar-Apr), lasting for a fortnight. The temple of Kaila Devi is located on the banks of the Kalisil river in the hills of Trikut, 2 kms. to the north-west of Kaila village. Another attraction is the small temple dedicated to Bhairon, situated in the courtyard and facing the shrine of Kaila Devi is a temple of Hanuman locally called 'Languriya'.

Approximately 2 lakh devotees gather during the fair. The ritual of Kanak-Dandotis is observed by staunch devotees. They cover a distance of 15 to 20 kms to reach the temple, not on foot but by lying prostrate, making lines with their hands in that position, advancing up to the line drawn and repeating this procedure till they reach the temple.

While some eat food and take rest during the journey, others endure the rigours of the ritual without these.

Groups of Mina tribesmen arrive in a spirit of gaiety dancing, singing and creating a lively atmosphere. The spacious courtyard becomes the venue for dances and songs sung in praise of the guardian deity.

The nearest rail-head is Hindaun at a distance of about 48 Kms. Shri Mahavirji is another rail-head of the Western Railway near Kaila. The site is approachable by well maintained roads from Karauli, Hindaun and Mahavirji. During the fair, the State Transport as well as private operators provide bus services keeping in mind the huge inflow of pilgrims.

Shekhawati Fair

The Shekhawati Festival held on 10th and 11th February every year is organised jointly by the State Department of Tourism, District administrations of Sikar, Jhunjhunu and Churu.

Shekhawati, already famous for its frescoes, is fast becoming a rural tourism destination too. Travelling on horse back, the tourists get a closer view of the countryside and the people.

And they return with an indelible imprint of not only the friendliness of the people but also of the agricultural revolution sweeping the villages — the region now exports 80 percent of its crops whereas only a few years ago it could meet only 10 percent of its requirement through local production.

For a broad-based discovery of Shekhawati's culture, the festival is spread over a number of venues-Nawalgarh, Sikar, Jhunjhunu and Churu.

The programmes include a one day tour of the region, camel and jeep safaris, farm visits, rural games, cultural programmes, haveli competitions and fireworks.

Nawalgarh is the central venue of the festival and can be reached comfortably by train and road from Jaipur (140 kms by Road).

Nawalgarh also has some of the finest frescoes of Shekhawati. The Clock Tower is a famous landmark and the Roop Niwas Palace hotel occupies a place of pride in the town.

Rath Yatra (Car Festival)

Place: Puri, Orissa

Time: July

Significance: Chariot Festival

This spectacular chariot festival celebrated for 8 days, is held at the famous Jaganath Temple at Puri (Orissa). Thousands of devotees flock to Puri during the occasion as they believe that a glimpse of Lord Jagnnath in his chariot gives salvation. Images of Lord Jaganath-the Lord of the Universe, his sister Subhadra and brother Balbhadra are taken out in a procession in three immense chariots.

The main chariot is 14 meters high and 10 meters square with 16 wheels. The deities are brought out of the temple to the chariots by rhythmic movement called 'Pahandi' in a royal procession to the accompaniment of the beat of the 'cymbals' and drums and chanting of prayers by devotees. The pushing and shoving to seat Lord Jagannath on his chariot continues for hours. The god it seems is testing the perseverance of his devotees. The devotees in turn coax, cajole, they promise sweetmeats and other delicacies, when all this fails they call the Lord names and even give blows to the idol, all the while the surging crowd chants, sings and dances. It is believed that on these days Lord Jagannath will descend from his pedestal and mingle with his devotees with no barrier between them. After seating the idols, the traditional King of Puri sweeps the Chariots with a golden broom. Thousands of devotees pull these chariots to Gundicha Mandir, a temple 3 km away.

After a week, on 'Ashadha Sukla Dasami', the 10th day of the bright fortnight of Ashadha (June-July), return journey or 'Bahuda Yatra' of the deities commences in the same manner from Gundicha temple to the main temple like Rath Yatra. When two months of Ashadha fall in one year, Rath Yatra is observed as the festival of 'Nabakalebar' the old deities are buried within the temple premises ('Koilibaikuntha') and are replaced by new deities, carved out of Margosa trees for which there are set procedures. Double Ashadha occurs at intervals of 8 to 19 years. Construction of the chariots begin as early as April.

Orissa is a land of innumerable fairs and festivals celebrated round the year but the most spectacular of them is the Rath Yatra, hitherto known as the Car Festival to western world. This chariot procession on the main streets of Ahmedabad city features a lot of colourful chariots, trucks and other vehicles. The procession commemorates the journey of Lord Krishna to Mathura, leaving behind grieving Gopis. The massive procession begins at Jagdish temple in Jamalpur. The main chariots are dedicated to lord Krishna, his brother Balaram and sister Subadhra, followed by colourfully decorated elephants, trucks, motor vehicles, pilgrims on foot, acrobats and gymnasts.

The Period of Yatra: Every year in July, the sacred coastal town of Puri comes alive to celebrate the Rath Yatra of Lord Jagannath, one of the biggest festivals during the monsoon season. According to the Indian solar calendar, it falls two days after the new moon day of the month of Asadh.

The famous Car festival of Lord Jagannath falls on the second day of bright fortnight of the month of Ashada when the Lord with his brother and sister coming out from the 'Ratna Sinhasan' to the streets of Puri joins His devotees while visiting His birth place The Gundicha Ghar. After a stay of nine days the return journey starts for the temple.

According to legend Lord Jagannath said to have expressed His desire to visit His birthplace Gundicha Ghar once every year. According to others Subhadra wanted to visit Dwarka, her parents home therefore, her two brothers Jagannath and Balabhadra took her there on this day. According to Bhagavad Puran on this day. Krishna and Balaram went to Mathura on the invitation of Kansa to participate in the competition.

The entire Ratha Yatra is a symbolic humanisation of God. All rituals associated with the festival demonstrate an attempt to bring the God down from His pedestal of glory to a more human level. On the day of journey the three chariots the yellow coloured Nandighosa, blue coloured Taladwaja and Deviratha are lined up in front of the temple and then the deities are brought on to their respective Chariots. Once the king of Puri the living symbol of Lord Jagannath sweeps the chariots with scented water and golden broom, the pilgrims lined up with the rope pull the chariots on the Badadanda to Gundicha Ghar.

Regional Celebrations : Though this festival time is very special in India, the main Rath Yatra takes place in the holy town of Puri. At other places, those devotees of Lord Jagannath, who cannot make it to Puri, take out similar processions on a much smaller scale. Notable are the ones at Ramnagar (near Varanasi), Serampore (near Calcutta) and Jagannathpur (near Ranchi). Every year in mid-summer, Lord Jagannath, with his elder brother Balabhadra and sister Subhadra, goes on vacation, travelling on grand chariots, from his temple in Puri, to his garden palace in the countryside. This belief of the Hindus has given rise to one of the biggest religious festivals in India— the Rathyatra or the Chariot Festival. This is also the etymological origin of the English word 'Juggernaut'.

Jagannath, believed to be an avatar of Lord Vishnu, is the Lord of Puri—the coastal town of Orissa in eastern India. Rathyatra is of great significance to the Hindus, and especially to the people of Orissa. It is during this time that the three deities of Jagannath, Balabhadra and Subhadra are taken out in a grand procession in specially made gigantic temple-like chariots called raths, which are pulled by thousands of devotees.

Rathyatra of Ahmedabad: The Rathyatra of Ahmedabad stands next to the Puri festival in grandeur and crowd-pulling. Nowadays, there are not just the thousands of people who participate in the Ahmedabad event, there are also communication satellites which the police use under the global positioning system to chart the course of the chariots on a map on the computer screen to monitor them from a control room. This is because Ahmedabad Rathyatra has a bloody record. The last violent Rathyatra which the city saw was in 1992, when the city suddenly became surcharged with communal riots. And, as you know, is a very riot-prone state!

Rathyatra of Mahesh: The Rathyatra of Mahesh in the Hoogly district of West Bengal is also of historical repute. This is not only because it's the grandest and the oldest Rathyatras in Bengal, but because of huge congregation it manages to attract. The Mahesh Rathyatra of 1875 is of special historical significance: A young girl was lost in the fair and amongst many, the district magistrate Bankim Chandra Chattopadhya — the great Bengali poet and author of India's National song — himself went out to search for the girl. A couple of months later this incident inspired him to write the famous novel *Radharani*.

Rathyatra is a great festival because of its ability to unite people in its festivity. All people, rich and poor, brahmins or shudras equally enjoy the fairs and the joy they bring. You will be amazed to know that even Muslims participate in Rathyatras! Muslim residents of Narayanpur, a village of about a thousand families in the Subarnapur district of Orissa, regularly take part in the festival, from builiding the chariots to pulling the *rath*.

Ratha Yatra is one of the major Hindu festivals associated with Lord Jagannath held at Puri in Orissa state, India. It is a large annual festival originating in the city of Puri. Most of the city's society is based around the worship of Lord Jagannath with the ancient temple being the fulcrum of the area. Usually the deities-Jagannath (Krishna), Baladeva and Subhadra are worshipped within the temple, but on this one day they are taken through the streets so that everyone can have the fortune of seeing them.This commemorates the annual journey of Lord Jagannath, Lord Balabhadra and their sister Subhadra to their aunt' s temple which is situated at a distance of 2 kilometres from their temple.

This is the only day when devotees who are not allowed in the temple premises such as non-Hindus and foreigners, can get their glimpse of the deities openly. The Rath carts themselves are some 50-60 feet high and are pulled by the thousands of pilgrims who turn up for the event. Millions of people congregate at Puri for this annual event from all over the country and abroad.

The festival commemorates Krishna's return to His home in Vrindavan after a long period of separation from the people there.

A look at the several stories associated with its origins throws light on the sentiments underlying the festival:

1. Kansa, the maternal uncle of Lord Krishna, invited Krishna and Balram to Mathura with the malicious intention of killing them. The evil Kamsa sent Akrur with a chariot to Gokul. Lord Krishna and Balram climbed onto the chariot with Akrur, taking leave of the Gopis to proceed to Mathura. This day of departure is celebrated by the devotees as Rath Yatra.
2. Jubilant devotees celebrated the day when Lord Krishna, having vanquished the evil Kamsa, gave them darshan in Mathura in a chariot with his brother, Balaram.
3. Devotees in Dwarika celebrated the day when Lord Krishna, accompanied by Balaram, took Subhadra-his sister, for a ride on a chariot to show the city's beauty.
4. Once in Dwarka, Lord Krishna's eight queens requested mother Rohini to narrate the divine episodes of Lord Krishna with the Gopis while he was in Vraj. For a

while Rohini dithered. Finally, after a lot of insistence she relented. However, considering it unbecoming of Subhadra to hear such episodes (Leela), she sent her to guard the palace doorway. Yet the Vrajkatha soon absorbed Subhadra. Soon, Lord Shri Krishna and Balaram arrived at the doorway. With arms wide apart, she stood between the two, preventing them from entering. However, from where they stood, Rohini's katha soon engrossed them all! Just then sage Narad arrived. Seeing the siblings standing together like murtis, he humbly prayed, "May the three of you grant darshan in this manner forever." The Lord granted the boon. And the three eternally reside in the Jagannath Mandir in Puri.

5. There is an interesting story of Lord Krishna becoming the Sarathi-driver of Arjuna's chariot, during the eighteen-day battle of the Mahabharat.
6. Finally, a story which has been passed on from mouth to mouth, concerns about what happened after the cremation of Lord Krishna's mortal body.

When Shri Krishna was being cremated in Dwarika, Balaram, overcome with grief, dashed into the ocean with Shri Krishna's partially cremated body. Subhadra too, followed both the brothers. At the same time, on the eastern shore of India, King Indradyumna of Jagannath Puri had a dream that the Lord's body would float up to the shores of Puri. He should build a huge mandir in the city and consecrate the wooden murtis of Shri Krishna, Balaram and Subhadra. The bones (asthi) of Lord Krishna's body should be placed in the hollow in the back of the murti.

The dream came true. He found the splinters of bone (asthi) and took them. But the question was who would carve the murtis. It is said that the architect of the gods-Vishwakarma-arrived as an old carpenter. He stipulated that while carving the murtis nobody should disturb him and if anybody did, he would stop work and leave. A few months elapsed. Driven with impatience, Indradyumna opened the door of Vishwakarma's room, who vanished instantly as he had stipulated. Despite the incomplete murtis, the king consecrated them, placing the holy cinders of Lord Krishna in the hollow of the murti and installed them in the mandir. Every year a grand procession is carried out with the murtis of Lord Krishna, Balaram and Subhadra in three gigantic floats. The floats are pulled by devotees from Janakpur to the mandir in Jagannath Puri. The murtis are changed every twelve years, the new ones being incomplete too.

The Jagannath Mandir in Jagannath Puri is one of the four most sacred mandirs in the four directions of the Indian sub-continent. The other three are: Rameshwar in South, Dwarka in West and Badrinath in the Himalayas. Probably the mandir in Jagannath Puri is the only mandir in the world housing murtis of three deities who are siblings-Lord Krishna, Balaram and Subhadra.

Mahabharat-The Life Rath: Shri Krishna becomes his devotee, Arjun's Sarathi, leading him and the Pandavas to victory.

Shri Krishna says in the Gita (18/78) that, where there is Krishna and Arjuna, there's wealth, victory, power and immutable morality. This was borne out during the battle when the mighty warrior Bhishma vowed to kill Arjuna on the tenth day. Lord Krishna anxiously searched for Arjuna and found him asleep. Bewildered, Lord Krishna asked him how he could sleep with such a pledge looming over his life. To his astonishment Arjuna answered, "Because you are awake!"

The ultimate essence of the chariot stories is that the Jiva should unwarrantedly surrender to the supreme Sarathi-God or the God-realised Sadhu, if he wishes to successfully traverse the yatra of life, Samsara.

Rath Yatra Festival in Gujarat : In many cities of Gujarat like Ahmadabad, Surat, Bhavnagar, etc, glorious processions are carried out annually with devotional fevour and joy. The Jagannath Mandir in Ahmadabad organises a yatra through the walled areas of the city. People make kaleidoscopic Raths and floats of various materials mounted on trucks. This year many youth and religious organizations in the city of Ahmadabad constructed ninety-eight Raths, which followed the Jagannath Mandir's fifteen decorated elephants. Onlookers and devotees thronged the narrow alleys, buildings and balconies, patiently awaiting up to three hours for the 5-km-long colorful procession to pass by at a sedate pace. When the chariots with the murtis arrived, people ritually sprinkled rice and gulal powder as a form of puja.

The participants sitting in these raths liberally handed out fistfuls of prasadam of raw, sprouted mung beans. Children were given sweets and confectionery. Finally, at the rear were three raths of Subhadra, Balaram and Lord Krishna. These were all hand-drawn and pushed by devotees. The flurry and festive excitement was enhanced by the jubilant chanting of 'Jai Ranchhod Makhan Chor'. Indra, the god of rain, too arrived to participate! It has been noted that sometime during the Rath Yatra, usually late afternoon or early evening, he sprinkles a light shower, never a heavy downpour, sanctifying the occasion.

The festival of Rath Yatra is celebrated at all the Swaminarayan Mandirs of the BAPS. Every year the center in Calcutta celebrates it on a large scale with colorful floats pulled by devotees and dignitaries. This year the Satsang center in Surat carried out a procession of eight floats with 15,000 devotees joyously chanting the Lord's name. The 1.5 km long procession inspired reverence and devotion in thousands of bystanders and pedestrians.

The Rath Yatra is a festival suffused with devotional sentiments for the Lord. For over five thousand years, Hindus have celebrated this spectacular festival. Gathering together, they earnestly pray to the Lord to steer the chariots of their mundane lives through the vicissitudes of Samsara.

This spectacular chariot festival celebrated for 8 days is held at the famous Jagannath Temple at Puri (Orissa). Thousands of devotees flock to Puri during the occasion, as they believe that a glimpse of Lord Jagannath in his chariot gives salvation. Images of Lord Jagannath-the Lord of the Universe, his sister Subhadra and brother Balbhadra are taken out in a procession in three immense chariots. The main chariot is 14 meters high and 10 meters square with 16 wheels.

Thousands of devotees pull these chariots to Gundicha Mandir, a temple 3 km away. After a week, on 'Ashadha Sukla Dasami', the 10th day of the bright fortnight of Ashadha (June-July), return journey or 'Bahuda Yatra' of the deities commences in the same manner from Gundicha temple to the main temple like Rath Yatra. When two months of Ashadha fall in one year, Rath Yatra is observed as the festival of 'Nabakalebar' the old deities are buried within the temple premises ('Koilibaikuntha') and are replaced by new deities, carved out of Margosa trees for which there are set procedures. Double Ashadha occurs at intervals of 8 to 19 years. Construction of the chariots begin as early as April. Jagannath Rath Yatra or the 'chariot journey of Lord Jagannatha', observed in the month of Ashadha (June-July), is a festival that celebrates the annual visit of the God to his birthplace.

The Jagannath Temple at Puri, Orissa is the venue for all celebrations. Several lakh people converge at Puri for this festival. An atmosphere of almost hysterical devotion prevails on this day and in earlier years; devotees were known to have thrown themselves under the wheels of the rath in the hope of obtaining instant salvation. Images of Jagannath, as Lord Krishna is known, his brother Balabhadra and sister Subhadra, are taken in giant chariots to Gundicha Ghar.

They stay there for a week and then return to the temple. On their journeys they are accompanied by a huge procession of people, singing and celebrating. The Legends behind the Yatra. The festival has been celebrated since ancient times. According to a legend about its origin, Jagannatha is said to have expressed his desire to visit his birthplace every year for a week. Accordingly, the deities are taken to the Gundicha Mandir every year. According to another legend, Subhadra wanted to visit Dwarka, her parent's home, and her brothers took her there on this day.

The Yatra is a commemoration of that visit. According to the Bhagavad Purana, it is believed that it was on this day that Krishna and Balarama went to Mathura to participate in a wrestling competition, at Kansa's invitation. Some Hindus believe that Jagannatha is an incarnation of Vishnu. Since

Vishnu has four arms, Balabhadra, Subhadra and Sudarshana represent Vishnu's four arms. Each deity has its own massive chariot, which are replicas of the temple. Jagannatha's chariot, Nandighosha, is yellow in colour, 45 ft high and has 16 wheels, each one seven feet in diameter.

About 4,200 devotees draw the chariot. Balabhadra's chariot is called Taladhvaja, is blue in colour and has 14 wheels. Subhadra's chariot is the smallest, with 12 wheels and is called Deviratha. Origin of the chariot ride According to a legend, when a poisonous arrow accidentally killed Krishna, his body was left under a tree. Later, someone cremated him and placed the ashes in a box. Directed by Vishnu, Indradyumna requested the divine artisan Vishvakarma to mould an image from the holy relics.

Vishvakarma agreed to undertake the task, provided that he was left undisturbed till its completion. When several years passed, Indradyumna became impatient and went to see how work was progressing. Enraged, Vishvakarma left the image incomplete. Indradyumna had ordered the construction of a temple to house the statue. So he ordered his chariot to transport the statue, as it was, to the temple. There, Brahma breathed life into the image.

The Rituals On the day of the journey, people get up early and offer prayers to Jagannatha. The chariots are lined up in front of the Puri temple. The King of Puri with great pomp and ceremony then brings the deities to their respective chariots. Devotees offer prayers to the deities. Descendants of the King, heralded by gaily-caparisoned elephants sweep the chariot platforms with a gold-handled broom and sprinkle scented water to demonstrate that in the eyes of God, all men are equal. Devotees also hurl obscenities and profane abuses at the God. Locals believe that there existed an incestuous relationship between Jagannatha and his sister Subhadra, which provoked abuses when the images were out in public.

The entire yatra is a symbolic humanization of God and an attempt to bring God down from his pedestal of glory to a more human level. Only the King of Puri and the King of Nepal are allowed to touch the idols as they belong to the Chandravanshi dynasty, the same as Krishna. Then the teeming pilgrims line up and pull the chariot. When the chariots reach the summerhouse, the idols are installed. The journey back, a week later, consists of another ritual, known as Phera Rath Yatra. Every year, the chariots are broken down, its wood sold as relics and a replica made. However the images of the deities are preserved. It is only when two Ashadha months occur one after the other that the images are changed. This happens once in 12 or 24 years.

The ceremony, Naba Kalebar, consists of burying the old images inside the temple. Then new images are created. This practice stems from the belief that in such a year, everything in the universe changes form, and therefore Jagannatha receives the same treatment. Celebrations This day is a public holiday in the state. Children are seen on the streets carrying miniature versions of the chariots with tiny idols installed on them. Shops and houses are decorated with flowers, lights and rangoli. Special dishes and sweets are prepared. Most people refrain from eating non-vegetarian food. As this festival falls during the monsoon season, people also thank the Gods for their mercy and bounty, by participating in the procession. Nowhere else is a deity, once consecrated, taken out of the temple. The Jagannatha Temple at Puri is the sole exception to this general rule. In fact during the Ratha Yatra, the chariots become mobile temples, which sanctify the city.

One of the four most famous holy pilgrimages of the Hindus in India is the Jagannath Temple of Puri. The festival of Rath Yatra celebrated here, is world famous for the enormous crowd of devotees that gathers to witness Lord Jagannath's yearly journey in his huge chariot. Perhaps the only deity to be brought out of the temple every year, Lord Jagannath, with his brother Balabhadra and sister Subhadra, goes to his garden house for five days, visiting his aunt on the way. At the end of the five days, the three siblings are brought back to the Jagannath temple in a procession called the Ultarath.

As the preparations for the procession begin, all routine activity in the town comes to a standstill. The temple kitchen – the largest in the world – serves more than 75 quintals of rice everyday along with 55 other dishes. These are offered to the gods in the temple and later distributed as Mahaprasad to the devotees.

Every year in July, the sacred coastal town of Puri comes alive to celebrate the Rath Yatra of Lord Jagannath, one of the biggest festivals during the monsoon season. According to the Indian solar calendar, it falls two days after the new moon day of the month of Asadh.

Amidst the resounding clash of cymbals, and the tumultuous thundering of drums, the three gods, Jagannath, his brother Balabhadra and sister Subhadra leave their abode, the Jagannath temple, to journey to the Gundicha Mandir, three kilometers away. Millions of devotees flock to the town to watch the trinity ride in their elaborate chariots through the streets of Puri. On all auspicious occasions, special ceremonies and rituals are performed replete with pomp and splendor in the temples of Puri, but nothing matches that of the Rath Yatra.

Since the portals of the Jagannath temple allow entry only to Hindus, one of the gods, Maitri Devta, who symbolizes universal brotherhood, steps outside during this time so people of all religions and castes can pay obeisance. A spiritual ambience pervades the whole scene as bells chime; conch shells blow and the saffron robed sadhus dance with abandon. It is fascinating to watch the delirious masses paying homage to the Lord as the chariots move on almost as if propelled by a divine force.

A fortnight before the Rath Yatra, the three deities are given a holy bath on an open platform – the Snana Vedi. Since the images become discolored as a result of the bath, they are kept away from the public. At this time, the deities are said to be ill and are left to rest in isolation.

A day before the procession, three gigantic chariots are exquisitely decorated and lined up outside the temple gates. Lord Jagannath's chariot, the red and yellow Nandighosh, is about 45 feet in height with 16 massive wheels and a gold dome on top. The red and green Taladhwaj is only slightly smaller and belongs to Balabhadra. The smallest, Dev Datan belongs to Subhadra, who travels between the chariots of her two brothers. These grandiose structures, with brightly colored canopied tops, resemble the 12th century Jagannath temple in shape. Embellished and decorated with tinsel and ancient accessories, each of the chariots has a large platform covered with huge flower umbrellas.

On the morning of the Yatra, the rhythmic clang of metal gongs, blowing of conch shells and trumpets and chanting of holy men fill the air as priests called Daityas vbring out the bedecked idols to their raths. Lord Jagannath makes his appearance first, amidst ecstatic cries of 'Jai Jagannath'. The overwhelmed jubilant crowds work themselves into a state of devotional frenzy, as if hypnotized by the large eyes of their beloved Lord.

The procession then awaits the arrival of the Gajapati or the King of Puri. The king comes in a traditional pamaquin, following a procession of decorated elephants and horses. The King of Puri is a descendant of the royal family of Orissa and has complete control over the management and property of the Jagannath temple.

He performs the Chhera Paharna, to express his humility before God. He sweeps the chariots with a gold broom and sprinkles holy water on them. There is a deafening roar of cheer as the procession inches ahead. Balabhadra the eldest brother takes the lead followed by Subhadra and Jagannath. The chariots are drawn by 50-metre long ropes attached to their front. Devotees surge ahead for an opportunity to give a hand in pulling the ropes, as it is believed that this will absolve them of all their sins and help them attain salvation.

One of the unique rituals of this procession is the Lord's visit to his aunt's house. It is said that the three siblings do not like visiting their aunt who is said to be mean. However, the three go to the mashibari after being ritually scolded by the head priest.

Legands: According to tradition and folklore, the origin of the Jagannath cult is tribal, where the god was symbolized as a log of wood signifying growth, procreation and tolerance. The Vedic period saw him emerge with a wooden stump-like structure for a body and large round eyes representing the sun and the moon-the ultimate sources of life and light. Even today the mystique of Jagannath lies in its shape. It is portrayed as a stumpy body with large prominent eyes on a shield-like face.

There is an interesting story about how Lord Jagannath, one of the various forms of Krishna, came to take this shape. The image of Lord Jagannath is said to have been created by Vishwakarma himself. Commissioned by Lord Vishnu to create this idol, Vishwakarma promised he would dazzle the gods by his creation but only if he was able to work alone unseen. When many months passed by, Lord Vishnu got impatient and forced open the doors. The image was ready but the arms were incomplete. Even today Lord Jagannath stands in the temple with two stumps for arms.

Many believe that dying under the wheels of the chariot of Lord Jagannath would give them instant Moksh. Even today, the police keep an eye for those wanting to take this route to salvation. Tracing its origin to this belief is the English word juggernaut, which denotes a huge vehicle that would crush anything that comes in its way. However, the name Jagannath, from which juggernaut has been derived, means 'the Lord of the world'.

2

Festivals of Hindus

Makar Sankaranti

The great diversity of Indian religious beliefs is projected through the various festivals that are celebrated in our country.

They arise from the innate desire of man to seek diversion from humdrum activities and they help in symbolising, reflecting and enriching social life in a specific cultural setting.

The festival of Makar Sankrant traditionally coincides with the beginning of the Sun's northward journey (the *UTTARAYAN*) when it enters the sign of Makar (the *CAPRICORN*). It falls on the 14th of January every year according to the Solar Calendar. This day has a very special significance because the day and night on Makar Sankrant are of exactly of equal hours. This day is celebrated as a festival right from the times of the Aryans and is looked upon as the most auspicious day by the Hindus.

The evidence of this festival being lucky is found in our great epic Mahabharat wherein it is told that the great warrior-hero, Bhishma Pitamaha even after being wounded and lying on the bed of arrows, lingered on till Uttarayan set in, to breathe his last.

It is believed that the person who dies on this auspicious day of Sankrant escapes the cycle of birth and re-birth and that his soul mingles with the Almighty.

This festival is celebrated differently in different parts of the country yet the use of til that is sesame is found everywhere.

Til or sesame seed contain lot of oil and they therefore have a quality of softness in them. Therefore, firstly the use of til in sweets is good for health and secondly being soft their exchange means exchange of love and tender feelings.

In Maharashtra on the Sankranti day people exchange multi-coloured tilguds made from til (sesame seeds) and sugar and til-laddus made from til and jaggery. Til-polis are offered for lunch and these are specialities of Maharashtra. Maharashtrian women are proud of their excellence in preparing these delicacies. While exchanging tilguls as tokens of goodwill people greet each other saying-"til-gul ghya, god bola" meaning "accept these tilguls and speak sweet words". The underying thought in the exchange of tilguls is to forget the past ill-feelings and hostilities and resolve to speak sweetly and remain friends. This is a special day for the women in Maharashtra when married women are invited for a get-together called "Haldi-Kumkoo" and given gifts of any utensil, which the woman of the house purchases on that day.

In Gujarat Sankrant is observed more or less in the same manner as in Maharashtra but with a difference that in Gujarat there is a custom of giving gifts to relatives. The elders in the family give gifts to the younger members of the family. The Gujarati Pundits on this auspicious day grant scholarships to students for higher studies in astrology and philosophy. This festival thus help the maintenance of social relationships within the family, caste and community.

In Punjab where December and January are the coldest months of the year, huge bonfires are lit on the eve of Sankrant and which is celebrated as *"LOHARI"*. Sweets, sugarcane and rice are thrown in the bonfires, around which friends and relatives gather together. The following day, which is Sankrant is celebrated as *MAGHI*. The Punjabi's dance their famous Bhangra dance till they get exhausted. Then they sit down and eat the samptions food that is specially prepared for the occasion.

In Bundelkhand and Madhya Pradesh this festival of Sankrant is known by the name *"SUKARAT"* or *"SAKARAT"* and is celebrated with great pomp merriment accompanied by lot of sweets.

In South Sankrant is known by the name of *"PONGAL"*, which takes its name from the surging of rice boiled in a pot of milk, and this festival has more significance than even Diwali. It is very popular particularly amongst farmers. Rice and pulses cooked together in ghee and milk is offered to the family deity after the ritual worship. In essence in the South this Sankrant is a "Puja" (worship) for the Sun God.

In Uttar Pradesh, Sankrant is called *"KICHERI"*. Having bath on this day is regarded as most important. A mass of humanity can be seen bathing in the Sangam at Prayagraj where the rivers Ganga, Jamuna and Saraswathi flow together. At the confluence of these holy rivers every year Kumbh Mela is held for full one month.

In Bengal every year a Mela is held at Ganga Sagar where the river Ganga is believed to have dived into the nether region and vivified the ashes of the sixty thousand ancestors of King Bhagirath. This mela is attended by a large number of pilgrims from East India. The tribals in our country start their New Year from the day of Sankrant by lighting bonfires, dancing and eating their particular dishes sitting together. The Bhuya tribals of Orissa have their Maghyatra in which small home-made articles are put for sale.

There is also a fair in the Western Ghats at a place called Shabari Mala, where the temple of the Community Goddess is decorated with dazzling lights. The Goddess is worshipped by touchables and untouchables both and the "bhog" to the Goddess is cooked in the touchables and untouchables both. These tribals participate in the Mela and enjoy all together as if they belong to one single family. May be therefore, the experts pine that this festival of Makar Sankrant comes to us from those olden times when the caste system did not exist in India as it emphasises or communal harmony.

Thus we see that this festival occupies a significant place in the cultural history of our country and symbolises the victory of ORDER over CHAOS and of Love over Hate.

These are specially prepared for the Sankrant festival because a mixture of til (sesame) and jaggery contribute to the health if eaten during cold season.

Sankranti means to go from one place to another place (to change direction). It also means one meets another. The time when the sun changes direction from one constellation (of the zodiac) to another is known as Sankranti.

Transition of the Sun from Sagittarius to Capricorn during the winter solstice in the northern hemisphere (Uttarayana) is known as Makar Sankranti.

Maha-Shivratri

Maha Shivratri is celebrated throughout the country; it is particularly popular in Uttar Pradesh. Maha Shivratri falls on the 13th (or 14th) day of the dark half of 'Phalgun' (February-March). The name means "the night of Shiva". The ceremonies take place chiefly at night. This is a festival observed in honour of Lord Shiva and it is believed that on this day Lord Shiva was married to Parvati. On this festival people worship 'Shiva-the Destroyer'. This night marks the night when Lord Shiva danced the 'Tandav'.

In Andhra Pradesh, pilgrims throng the Sri Kalahasteshwara Temple at Kalahasti and the Bharamarambha Malikarjunaswamy Temple at Srisailam. About *The Lord Shiva*-the word meaning auspicious-is one of the Hindu Trinity, comprising of Lord Brahma, the creator, Lord Vishnu, the preserver and Lord Shiva or Mahesh, the Destroyer and Re-Producer of life. Shiva is known by many names like "Shankar", "Mahesh", "Bholenath", "Neelakanth", "Shambhu Kailasheshwar", "Umanath", "Nataraj" and others.

For few people, Shiva is "Paramatman", "Brahman", the Absolute, but many more prefer to see Shiva as a personal God given to compassion for his worshippers, and the dispenser of both spiritual and material blessings. Related to the Absolute concept is Shiva as "Yoganath" meaning the Lord of Yoga, wherein he becomes teacher, path and goal. As such he is the "Adi Guru" or the Highest Guru of 'Sannyasins' who have renounced the world to attain the Absolute. He is the most sought-after deity amongst the Hindus and they pray to him as the god of immense large-heartedness who they believe grants all their wishes. Around him are weaved many interesting stories that reveal His magnanimous heart. Not only this, but these stories and legends also enrich the Indian culture and art. Time is invisible and formless.

Therefore Mahakal Shiva, as per the Vedas, manifested himself as "LINGUM" to make mankind aware of the presence of Eternal Time. That day when Shiva manifested himself in the form of "Lingum" was the fourth day of the dark night in the month of 'Magha' *i.e.* February-March. Maha Shivratri continues to be celebrated forever and ever. The Story of king Chitrabhanu in the Shanti Parva of the Mahabharata, Bhishma, whilst resting on the bed of arrows and discoursing on Dharma, refers to the observance of Maha Shivaratri by King Chitrabhanu. The story goes as follows-Once upon a time King Chitrabhanu of the Ikshvaku dynasty, who ruled over the whole of Jambudvipa, was observing a fast with his wife, it being the day of Maha Shivaratri.

The sage Ashtavakra came on a visit to the court of the king. The sag asked the king the purpose of his observing the past. King Chitrabhanu explained that he had the gift of remembering the incidents of his previous birth. The king said to the sage that in his previous he was a hunter in Varanasi and his name was Suswara. His only livelihood was to kill and sell birds and animals. One day while roaming through forests in search of animals he was overtaken by the darkness of night. Unable to return home, he climbed a tree for shelter. It happened to be a Bael tree. He had shot a deer that day but had no time to take it home. So he bundled it up and tied it to a branch on the tree. As hunger and thirst tormented him, he was kept awake throughout the night. He shed profuse tears when he thought of his poor wife and children who were starving and anxiously waiting for his return. To pass away the time that night he engaged himself in plucking the Bael leaves and dropping them down onto the ground.

The next day he returned home and sold the deer and then bought some food for himself and his family. The moment he was about to break his fast a stranger came to him, begging for food. He served the food first to stranger and then had his own. At the time of his death, he saw two messengers of Lord

Shiva. They were sent down to conduct his soul to the abode of Lord Shiva. He learnt then for the first time of the great merit he had earned by the unconscious worship of Lord Shiva during the night of Shivaratri.

The messengers told him that there was a Lingam at the bottom of the tree. The leaves I dropped fell on the Lingam. His tears, which had shed out of pure sorrow for his family, fell onto the Lingam and washed it and he had fasted all day and all night. Thus, he unconsciously worshiped the Lord. As the conclusion of the tale the King said that he lived in the abode of the Lord and enjoyed divine bliss for long ages and now he has reborn as Chitrabhanu. People observe a strict fast on this day. Some devotees do not even take a drop of water and they keep vigil all night.

The Shiva Lingam is worshipped throughout the night by washing it every three hours with milk, curd, honey, rose water, etc., whilst the chanting of the Mantra "Om Namah Shivaya" continues. Offerings of Bael leaves are made to the Lingam as Bael leaves are considered very sacred and it is said that Goddess Lakshmi resides in them. Hymns in praise of Lord Shiva, such as the "Shiva Mahimna Stotra" of Pushpadanta or Ravana's "Shiva Tandava Stotra" are sung with great fervor and devotion. People repeat the 'Panchakshara' Mantra, "Om Namah Shivaya". He, who utters the names of Shiva during Shivratri, with perfect devotion and concentration, is freed from all sins. He reaches the abode of Shiva and lives there happily. He is liberated from the wheel of births and deaths. Many pilgrims dock to the places where there are Shiva temples.

On the day of Shivratri, the lingam is bathed with the five sacred offerings of a cow, called the panchagavya-milk, sour milk, urine, butter and dung. Thereafter the five foods of immortality-milk, clarified butter, curd, honey and sugar-are placed before the lingam. Dhatura and jati, though poisonous fruits, are believed to be sacred to Shiva and thus offered at his temple. Eleven is considered to be the sacred number of the Lord. Devotees keep a fast (vrat) on Shivratri and observe strict rules, for vardan (boon). Special celebration are held at important Shiva temples at Chidambaram, Kalahasi Khajuraho and Varanasi. Worship of Shiva is to release the worship perform the cycle of birth and rebirth. In Kashmir, the festival is held for 15 days; the thirteenth day is observed as Hearth, a day of fast followed by a family feast.

During the samudra manthan by the gods and demons, haalaa-hala, a poison came out of the ocean. It was so toxic, that it effects would have wiped out the entire creation. At this juncture, as per the advice of Vishnu, gods approached Mahadev and prayed him to protect life by consuming this poison. Pleased with their prayers, out of compassion for living beings, Lord Shiva drank this poison and held it in his throat by binding it with a snake. The throat became blue due to the poison (Thus Lord Shiva is also know as Neelakantha) and Shiva remained unharmed. The doctors advised gods to keep Lord Shiva awake during the night as part of the therapy. To amuse Shiva and to keep him awake, the gods took turn performing various dances and playing music. A vigil was thus kept by the gods in contemplation of Shiva. As the day broke out, Shiva, pleased with their devotion blessed them all. Since then, on this day and night-devotees fast, keep vigil, sing glories of Lord and meditate.

After creation was complete, Parvati asked Shiva of which rituals pleased him the most. The Lord replied that the 14th night of the new moon, during the month of Phalgun, is my most favourite day. It is known as Shivaratri. Parvati repeated these words to her friends, from whom the word spread over all creation. Once upon a ti me, a hunter worshipped Lord Shiva unknowingly on Shivaratri. He did this by dropping bheel leaves on a shiva linga at the base of a bheel tree from its branches where he was hiding and fasting all night. For this he was forgiven of all his sins. This forms the basis behind the offerings of bheel to the Lord on Shivaratri.

Holi

The festival of Holi is celebrated on the day after the full moon in early March every year. Originally a festival to celebrate good harvests and fertility of the land, Holi is now a symbolic commemoration of a legend from Hindu Mythology. The story centres around an arrogant king who resents his son Prahlada worshipping Lord Vishnu. He attempts to kill his son but fails each time. Finally, the king's sister Holika who is said to be immune to burning, sits with the boy in a huge fire. However, the prince Prahlada emerges unscathed, while his aunt burns to death. Holi commemorates this event from mythology, and huge bonfires are burnt on the eve of Holi as its symbolic representation.

This exuberant festival is also associated with the immortal love of Krishna and Radha, and hence, Holi is spread over 16 days in Vrindavan as well as Mathura-the two cities with which Lord Krishna shared a deep affiliation. Apart from the usual fun with coloured powder and water, Holi is marked by vibrant processions which are accompanied by folk songs, dances and a general sense of abandoned vitality.

Today Holi is an excuse for Indians to shed inhibitions and caste differences for a day of spring fever and Big Fun. Teenagers spend the day flirting and misbehaving in the streets, adults extend the hand of peace, and everyone chases everyone else around, throwing brightly colored powder (gulal) and water over each other.

The festival's preamble begins on the night of the full moon. Bonfires are lit on street corners to cleanse the air of evil spirits and bad vibes, and to symbolize the destruction of the wicked Holika, for whom the festival was named. The following morning, the streets fill with people running, shouting, giggling and splashing. Marijuana-based bhang and thandai add to the uninhibited atmosphere.

Promptly at noon, the craziness comes to an end and everyone heads to either the river or the bathtub, then inside to relax the day away and partake of candies. In the afternoon an exhausted and contented silence falls over India. Although Holi is observed all over the north, it's celebrated with special joy and zest at Mathura, Vrindavan, Nandgaon, and Barsnar. These towns once housed the divine Krishna.

Each area celebrates Holi differently; the Bhil tribesmen of western Madhya Pradesh, who've retained many of their pre-Hindu customs, celebrate Holi in a unique way. In rural Maharashtra State, where the festival is known as *Rangapanchami* it is celebrated with dancing and singing. In the towns of Rajasthan — especially Jaisalmer — the music's great, and clouds of pink, green, and turquoise powder fill the air. The grounds of Jaisalmer's Mandir Palace are turned into chaos, with dances, folk songs, and colored-powder confusion.

Holi or Holika, also called holikotsava, is an extremely popular festival observed throughout the country (India). It is especially marked by unmixed gaiety and frolics and is common to all sections of the people.

This festival is very ancient. Known originally as *'Holika'* it has been mentioned in very early religious works such as Jaimini's Purvamimamsa-sutras and Kathaka-grhya-sutras. It must have therefore existed several centuries before Christ. It was at first actually a special rite performed by married women for the happiness and well-being of their families and the full moon (Raka) was the deity worshipped by them.

There are two ways of reckoning a lunar month: *Purnimanta* and *Amanta*. In the former, the first day starts after the full moon; and in the latter, after the new moon. Though the latter reckoning is more common now, the former was very much in vogue in the earlier days. According to this purnimanta reckoning, Phalguna purnima was the last day of the year and the new year heralding the Vasanta-ritu (with spring starting from next day). Thus the full moon festival of Holika gradually became a festival of merrymaking, announcing the commencement of the spring season. This perhaps explains the other names of this festival: Vasanta-Mahotsava and Kama-Mahotsava.

According to the stories in the Puranas and various local legends, this day is important for three reasons.

- It was on this day that Lord Siva opened his third eye and reduced Kamadeva (the god of love, Cupid or Eros) to ashes.
- It was on this day that Holika, the sister of the demon king Hiranyakasyapu, who tried to kill the child devotee

Prahlad by taking him on her lap and sitting on a pyre of wood which was set ablaze. Holika was burnt to ashes while Prahlad remained unscathed!

- It was again on this day that an ogress called Dhundhi, who was troubling the children in the kingdom of Prthu (or Raghu) was made to run away for life, by the shouts and pranks of the mischievous boys. Though she had secured several boons that made her almost invincible, this-noise, shouts, abuses and pranks of boys-was a chink in her armour due to a curse of Lord Siva. The day itself came to be called 'Adada' or 'Holika' since then.

There are practically no religious observances for this day like fasting or worship. Generally a log of wood will be kept in a prominent public place on the Vasantapanchami day (Magha Sukla Panchami), almost 40 days before the Holi Festival. An image of Holika with child Prahlada in her lap is also kept on the log. Holika's image is made of combustible materials whereas Prahlada's image is made of non-combustible ones. People go on throwing twigs of trees and any combustible material they can spare, on to that log which gradually grows into a sizable heap.

On the night of Phalguna Purnima, it is set alight in a simple ceremony with the Raksoghna Mantras of the Rgveda (4.4.1-15; 10.87.1-25 and so on) being sometimes chanted to ward off all evil spirits. (Coconuts and coins are thrown into this bonfire).The next morning the ashes from the bonfire are collected as prasad (consecrated material) and smeared on the limbs of the body. Singed coconuts, if any are also collected and eaten.

In some houses the image of Kamadeva is kept in the yard and a simple worship is offered. A mixture of mango blossoms and sandalwood paste is partaken as the prasad.

The day-Phalgun krsna pratipad-is observed as a day of revelry especially by throwing on one another gulal or coloured water or perfumed coloured powder. Throwing of mud or earth dust was prevalent in the earlier days also, but among the low culture groups.

Instead of the gay and frenzied celebrations that are witnessed elsewhere in the country, Bengal observes this festival in a quiet and dignified manner as Dolapurnima or Dolayatra (the festival of the swing). The festival, said to have been initiated by the king Indradyumna in Vrndavana, is spread over 3 or 5 days, starting from the sukla Chaturdasi of Phalguna. A celebration in honour of Agni and worship of Govinda (Krsna) in image on a swing are the important features. The fire kindled on the first day is to be preserved till the last day. The swing is to be rocked 21 times at the end of the festival.

The day is also celebrated as the birthday of Sri Krsna Chaitanya (A.D. 1486-1533), mostly in Bengal, as also in Puri (Orissa), Mathura and Vrndavan (in Uttar Pradesh).

Holi or *Phagwah* (Bhojpuri), is an annual and popular Hindu spring festival. It takes place over two days in the latter part of March or early April. As per the Hindu calendar, it falls on the Phalgun Purnima (or Pooranmashi, Full Moon). It is also called the Festival of Colours.

On the first day, a bonfire is lit at night to signify burning Holika. On the second day, known as *Dhulandi*, people go around until afternoon throwing coloured powder and water at each other, although the powder stings the eyes. A special drink called 'thandai' or bhang is also consumed sometimes, which actually contains small amounts of marijuana (*Cannabis sativa*). People invite each other to their houses for feasts and celebrations later in the evening. *Rangapanchami* occurs a few days later on a Panchami (fifth day of the full moon), marking the end of festivities involving colours.

This festival occurs at the onset of spring. This period, during which the weather changes, is prone to cause viral fever and cold. Thus, the playful throwing of the coloured powders has a medicinal significance as the coloured powders are made of Neem, Kumkum, Haldi, Bilva, and other medicinal herbs prescribed by Ayurvedic doctors.

Amongst India's innumerable festivals, Holi ranks as the most colourful. It celebrates the arrival of spring and death of demoness Holika, it is a celebration of joy and hope. Holi provides a refreshing respite from the mundane norms as people from all walks of life enjoy themselves. In a tight knit community, it also provided a good excuse for letting off some steam and settling old scores, without causing physical injury.

Holi continues to be celebrated with great vigour through out India. Countless Hindi films have brought the vibrant colours of the festival to the screen. Indians all over the world eagerly await the Festival of Colours, as bonfires are lit to banish the cold dark nights of winter and usher in warmer spring. Dhuleti, day after Holi, is the actual festival of colours, when everything in sight is covered in a riot of colours.

Twin towns of Nandagow (where Lord Krishna grew up) and Barsana (where Shri Radha grew up), near Mathura, are the epicentre of the celebrations. Lord Krishna, while growing up in Vraj, popularised the festival with his ingenious pranks. Gopies of Vraj responded with equal enthusiasm and the festivities have continued ever since. Role reversal, feminism etc. are accepted customs for the duration of the festival! Men and women of Vraj clash in a colourful display of battle of the sexes.

Celebrations start a week earlier than rest of India. Men of Nandagow raid Barsana with hopes of raising their flag over Shri Radhikaji's temple. They receive a thunderous welcome as the women of Barsana greet them with long wooden sticks. The men are soundly beaten as they attempt to rush through town to reach the relative safety of Shri Radhikaji's temple. Men are well padded as they are not allowed to retaliate. In this mock battle the men try their best not to be captured. Unlucky captives can be forcefully lead away, thrashed and dressed in female attire before being made to dance!!

Rush through Barsana is far more lethal than running with the bulls in Spain, at least you don't have to marry them one day! Famous poets like Surdas, Nand-das, Kumbhan-das and others, have written beautifully as to how Lord Krishna was similarly received and forced to wear a sari, forced to wear makeup and made to dance before being released by the gopies of Vraj.

Ram Navami

The birthday of Lord Rama, the celebrated hero of the famous epic, 'Ramayana', is enthusiastically celebrated all over India. Lord Vishnu is worshipped in his human incarnation as Rama, the divine ruler of Ayodhya.

Celebrations begin with a prayer to the Sun early in the morning. At midday, when Lord Rama is supposed to have been born, a special prayer is performed. Temples of Rama are decorated, religious discourses are held and the Ramayana is recited for ten days. People sing devotional songs in praise of Rama and rock, images of him in a cradle to celebrate his birth. Rathyatras or chariot processions of Rama, his wife Seeta, brother Lakshmana and devotee Hanuman are held from many temples. The chariot is accompanied by several devotees dressed up in ancient costumes as Rama's soldiers. The procession is a gusty affair with the participants shouting praises echoing the happy days of Rama's reign. People gather in thousands on the banks of the sacred river Sarayu for a dip. Some observe a strict fast on this day.

Ayodhya is the focus of great celebrations. Devotees throng the temples of Ayodhya and Pondicherry, two places closely connected with the events of the Ramayana to participate in Ramnavami festivities.

Ramanavami celebrates the birth of Rama or Ramachandra. On the ninth day of the first fortnight of Chaitra the birth of Rama is commemorated. The story of Rama was first written by Vaalmeeki in about the 4th century B.C. Rama is supposed to have lived during the 8th or 7th century B.C. The epic known as the Ramayana. In some parts of India, it is a nine-day festival, coinciding with the Vasanta Navaratri.

The public worship starts with morning ablutions, chanting Vedic mantras dedicated to Vishnu, and offering flowers and fruit to the god. People keep a fast throughout the day, breaking it only at midnight with fruit. In some parts of India, especially Bihar and Uttar Pradesh, public gatherings called satsangs are organised to commemorate the birth of Rama. Excerpts from the Ramacharitamanas, extolling the glory of Rama, are recited.

People of all castes and creeds participate in these gatherings to listen to the stories and their explanations offered by the learned.

Krishna Janmashtami

Shravan vad 8 celebrates the birth of Lord Shri Krishna, one of the most venerated incarnations in the Hindu Dharma. Five thousand years ago, he incarnated, at the end of the third cosmic phase, 'Dwapar Yuga' and the beginning of the present, 'Kali Yuga'.

Purpose of Incarnation: In the Gita (4/78) the Lord has ordained:

"Yadaa yadaa hi dharmasya glanir bhavati Bharat;

Dharma sansthaapanaarthaaya sambhaavami yuge yuge."

In the Bhavishyottara Puran Shri Krishna himself extols the celebration of Janmashtami to Yudhishtir, the eldest of the five Pandavas.

He incarnated in Mathura (Uttar Pradesh) to vanquish the evil King Kansa and other evil elements who were harassing pious people. His second reason was to fulfil the pledge he had given to Vasudev and Devki. When they married Kansa heard a divine proclamation that the couple's eighth son would be his nemesis. To obviate this, Kansa imprisoned the couple and killed the first seven sons born to Devki. When Shri Krishna was born Vasudev placed him in a cradle and took the baby child through the river Yamuna. Thus the Lord survived and eventually vanquished Kansa and other evil elements.

Festival Sentiments: The first importance of Janmashtami is to observe dharma. Since we humans are all imprisoned in samsara, the Lord incarnates in this prison with us, establishes dharma and redeems us from maya. We can only win over maya if we seek the Lord's aid, as did Arjuna during the battle of Mahabharat. As sage Ved Vyas ordains:

"Yato Krishnastato dharmaha,. Yato dharmastato Jayaha."

I.e. Where there is Krishna, there is dharma, where there is dharma, there is victory. Since Duryodhana, leader of the Kauravs did not observe dharma, he did not have Krishna. No Krishna, no victory.

Surrenderance-'Sharnaagati': During the battle Shri Krishna uttered 700 shloks in the form of the 'Bhagvad Gita' to convince the reluctant Arjun to fight. The Lord finally uttered the essence of his sermons in the following verse (18/66):

"Sarva dharmaan parityajya maamekam sharanam vraja,
aham twaa sarvapaapebhyo mokshayishyaami maa shuchaha."

I.e. O Arjun! Forsake all your personal beliefs and surrender to me. Do not lament for I shall deliver you from all sins.

Therefore a true spirit of Janmashtami is for devotees to implicitly surrender at the Lord's lotus-feet, while staunchly observing dharma.

Ideal Devotee: In the Gita (18/54), the Lord stipulates:

"Brahma bhootaha prasannaatmaa na shochati na kaankshati,
Samaha sarveshu bhuteshu madbhaktim labhate param."

I.e. One who becomes 'Brahmarup' and offers devotion to Parabrahma (God), he forever remains blissful and attains the highest glory of God. 'Brahmarup' simply means to become the ideal devotee like Arjun who represents 'Nar' to then worship Krishna-Narayan. Hence the murtis of Nar-Narayan. Similarly, Shri Krishna played the 'Maha Raas' traditional (stick folk dance) with the Gopis of Vrindavan because of their unalloyed love for him. Radha was the foremost among them. Therefore devotees should develop 'Gopi-bhav', to become Radha-rup (like Radha) to worship Shri Krishna. Hence devotees everywhere also consecrate murtis of 'Radha-Krishna' in mandirs, worshipping the Lord with his consort or choicest devotee. In addition to such surrenderance, how should the devotee strive to attain 'Gopi-bhav' to please the Lord?

Satsang: In the Srimad Bhagwat (11/12/1,2), Shri Krishna himself propounds 'Satsang', which is another important principle in celebrating Janmashtami.

"I am not as pleased by endeavors such as: Yoga, Sankhya, scriptural study, austerities, renunciation, altruistic social deeds, donation, fasting, yagna, study of Vedic scriptures, observance of the laws of Dharma and Yama (part of yoga), as I am by Satsang."

'Satsang' means associating with a God realised Sadhu. This was exemplified by King Parikshit when he was cursed to die in seven days, by surrendering to Shukdevji, who was a God-realised sadhu.

Finally, after Shri Krishna's departure from earth, how did the Lord continue his manifestation? This question was posed by Shaunak and other rishis to Suta Purani (in the Bhagwat). He replied, "Dharma resided in the Lord's true sadhu who is the true beholder of Dharma." In the Bhagwat, Shri Krishna supports this when he revealed to Uddhavji: "O Uddhav! You are not any the lesser than me." Thus the Lord revealed Bhagwat Dharma to Uddhavji and since then propagated it through him. The true spirit then, in celebrating Janmashtami is for devotees to do Satsang through the Satpurush who is the beholder of Bhagwat Dharma-in order to realize God within.

Ganesh Chaturthi

Ganesh Chaturthi is one of the most popular of Hindu festivals. This is the birthday of Lord Ganesha. It is the day most sacred to Lord Ganesha. It falls on the 4th day of the bright fortnight of Bhadrapada (August-September). It is observed throughout India, as well as by devoted Hindus in all parts of the world.

Clay figures of the Deity are made and after being worshipped for two days, or in some cases ten days, they are imnersed into water.

Lord Ganesha is the elephant-headed God. He is worshipped first in any prayers. His Names are repeated first before any auspicious work is begun, before any kind of worship is begun.

He is the Lord of power and wisdom. He is the eldest son of Lord Shiva and the elder brother of Skanda or Kartikeya. He is the energy of Lord Shiva and so He is called the son of Shankar and Umadevi. By worshipping Lord Ganesha mothers hope to earn for their sons the sterling virtues of Ganesha.

The following story is narrated about His birth and how He came to have the head of an elephant:

Once upon a time, the Goddess Gauri (consort of Lord Shiva), while bathing, created Ganesha as a pure white being out of the mud of Her Body and placed Him at the entrance of the house. She told Him not to allow anyone to enter while she went inside for a bath. Lord Shiva Himself was returning home quite thirsty and was stopped by Ganesha at the gate. Shiva became angry and cut off Ganesha's head as He thought Ganesha was an outsider.

When Gauri came to know of this she was sorely grieved. To console her grief, Shiva ordered His servants to cut off and bring to Him the head of any creature that might be sleeping with its head facing north. The servants went on their mission and found only an elephant in that position. The sacrifice was thus made and the elephant's head was brought before Shiva. The Lord then joined the elephant's head onto the body of Ganesha.

Lord Shiva made His son worthy of worship at the beginning of all undertakings, marriages, expeditions, studies, etc. He ordained that the annual worship of Ganesha should take place on the 4th day of the bright half of Bhadrapada.

Without the Grace of Sri Ganesha and His help nothing whatsoever can be achieved. No action can be undertaken without His support, Grace or blessing.

In his first lesson in the alphabet a Maharashtrian child is initiated into the Mantra of Lord Ganesha, *Om Sri Ganeshaya Namah.* Only then is the alphabet taught.

The following are some of the common Names of Lord Ganesha: Dhoomraketu, Sumukha, Ekadantha, Gajakarnaka, Lambodara, Vignaraja, Ganadhyaksha, Phalachandra, Gajanana, Vinayaka, Vakratunda, Siddhivinayaka, Surpakarna,

Heramba, Skandapurvaja, Kapila and Vigneshwara. He is also known by many as Maha-Ganapathi.

His Mantra is *Om Gung Ganapathaye Namah.* Spiritual aspirants who worship Ganesha as their tutelary Deity repeat this Mantra or *Om Sri Ganeshaya Namah.*

The devotees of Ganesha also do Japa of the Ganesha Gayatri Mantra. This is as follows.

Tat purushaaya vidmahe
Vakratundaaya dheemahi
Tanno dhanti prachodayaat.

Lord Ganesha is an embodiment of wisdom and bliss. He is the Lord of Brahmacharins. He is foremost amongst the celibates.

He has as his vehicle a small mouse. He is the presiding Deity of the Muladhara Chakra, the psychic centre in the body in which the Kundalini Shakti resides.

He is the Lord who removes all obstacles on the path of the spiritual aspirant, and bestows upon him worldly as well as spiritual success. Hence He is called Vigna Vinayaka. His Bija Akshara (root syllable) is *Gung,* pronounced to rhyme with the English word "sung". He is the Lord of harmony and peace.

Lord Ganesha represents Om or the Pranava, which is the chief Mantra among the Hindus. Nothing can be done without uttering it. This explains the practice of invoking Ganesha before beginning any rite or undertaking any project. His two feet represent the power of knowledge and the power of action. The elephant head is significant in that it is the only figure in nature that has the form of the symbol for Om.

The significance of riding on a mouse is the complete conquest over egoism. The holding of the *ankusha* represents His rulership of the world. It is the emblem of divine Royalty.

Ganesha is the first God. Riding on a mouse, one of nature's smallest creatures and having the head of an elephant, the biggest of all animals, denotes that Ganesha is the creator of all creatures. Elephants are very wise animals; this indicates that Lord Ganesha is an embodiment of wisdom. It also denotes the process of evolution—the mouse gradually evolves into an elephant and finally becomes a man. This is why Ganesha has a human body, an elephant's head and a mouse as His vehicle. This is the symbolic philosophy of His form.

He is the Lord of Ganas or groups, for instance groups of elements, groups of senses, etc. He is the head of the followers of Shiva or the celestial servants of Lord Shiva.

The Vaishnavas also worship Lord Ganesha. They have given Him the name of Tumbikkai Alwar which means the divinity with the proboscis (the elephant's trunk).

Lord Ganesha's two powers are the Kundalini and the Vallabha or power of love.

He is very fond of sweet pudding or balls of rice flour with a sweet core. On one of His birthdays He was going around house to house accepting the offerings of sweet puddings. Having eaten a good number of these, He set out moving on His mouse at night. Suddenly the mouse stumbled—it had seen a snake and became frightened—with the result that Ganesha fell down. His stomach burst open and all the sweet puddings came out. But Ganesha stuffed them back into His stomach and, catching hold of the snake, tied it around His belly.

Seeing all this, the moon in the sky had a hearty laugh. This unseemly behaviour of the moon annoyed Him immensely and so he pulled out one of His tusks and hurled it against the moon, and cursed that no one should look at the moon on the Ganesh Chaturthi day. If anyone does, he will surely earn a bad name, censure or ill-repute. However, if by mistake someone does happen to look at the moon on this day, then the only way he can be freed from the curse is by repeating or listening to the story of how Lord Krishna cleared His character regarding the Syamantaka jewel. This story is quoted in the *Srimad Bhagavatam*. Lord Ganesha was pleased to ordain thus. Glory to Lord Ganesha! How kind and merciful He is unto His devotees!

Ganesha and His brother Lord Subramanya once had a dispute as to who was the elder of the two. The matter was referred to Lord Shiva for final decision. Shiva decided that whoever would make a tour of the whole world and come back first to the starting point had the right to be the elder. Subramanya flew off at once on his vehicle, the peacock, to make a circuit of the world. But the wise Ganesha went, in loving worshipfulness, around His divine parents and asked for the prize of His victory.

Lord Shiva said, "Beloved and wise Ganesha! But how can I give you the prize; you did not go around the world?"

Ganesha replied, "No, but I have gone around my parents. My parents represent the entire manifested universe!"

Thus the dispute was settled in favour of Lord Ganesha, who was thereafter acknowledged as the elder of the two brothers. Mother Parvati also gave Him a fruit as a prize for this victory.

In the *Ganapathi Upanishad,* Ganesha is identified with the Supreme Self. The legends that are connected with Lord Ganesha are recorded in the Ganesha Khanda of the *Brahma Vivartha Purana.*

On the Ganesh Chaturthi day, meditate on the stories connected with Lord Ganesha early in the morning, during the Brahmamuhurta period. Then, after taking a bath, go to the temple and do the prayers of Lord Ganesha. Offer Him some coconut and sweet pudding. Pray with faith and devotion that He may remove all the obstacles that you experience on the spiritual path. Worship Him at home, too. You can get the assistance of a pundit. Have an image of Lord Ganesha in your house. Feel His Presence in it.

Don't forget not to look at the moon on that day; remember that it behaved unbecomingly towards the Lord. This really means avoid the company of all those who have no faith in God, and who deride God, your Guru and religion, from this very day.

Take fresh spiritual resolves and pray to Lord Ganesha for inner spiritual strength to attain success in all your undertakings.

May the blessings of Sri Ganesha be upon you all! May He remove all the obstacles that stand in your spiritual path! May He bestow on you all material prosperity as well as liberation!

Ganesha — the elephant-deity riding a mouse — has become one of the commonest mnemonics for anything associated with Hinduism. This not only suggests the importance of Ganesha, but also shows how popular and pervasive this deity is in the minds of the masses.

The Lord of Success: The son of Shiva and Parvati, Ganesha has an elephantine countenance with a curved trunk and big ears, and a huge pot-bellied body of a human being. He is the Lord of success and destroyer of evils and obstacles. He is also worshipped as the god of education, knowledge, wisdom and wealth. In fact, Ganesha is one of the five prime Hindu deities (Brahma, Vishnu, Shiva and Durga being the other four) whose idolatry is glorified as the *panchayatana puja*.

The devotees of Ganesha are known as 'Ganapatyas', and the festival to celebrate and glorify him is called Ganesh Chaturthi.

Significance of the Ganesha Form: Ganesha's head symbolizes the *Atman* or the soul, which is the ultimate supreme reality of human existence, and his human body signifies *Maya* or the earthly existence of human beings. The elephant head denotes wisdom and its trunk represents Om, the sound symbol of cosmic reality. In his upper right hand Ganesha holds a goad, which helps him propel mankind forward on the eternal path and remove obstacles from the way. The noose in Ganesha's left hand is a gentle implement to capture all difficulties.

The broken tusk that Ganesha holds like a pen in his lower right hand is a symbol of sacrifice, which he broke for writing the *Mahabharata*. The rosary in his other hand suggests that the pursuit of knowledge should be continuous. The *laddoo* (sweet) he holds in his trunk indicates that one must discover the sweetness of the *Atman*. His fan-like ears convey that he is all ears to our petition. The snake that runs round his waist represents energy in all forms. And he is humble enough to ride the lowest of creatures, a mouse.

How Ganesha Got His Head: The story of the birth of this zoomorphic deity, as depicted in the *Shiva Purana*, goes like this: Once goddess Parvati, while bathing, created a boy out of the dirt of her body and assigned him the task of guarding the entrance to her bathroom. When Shiva, her husband returned, he was surprised to find a stranger denying him access, and struck off the boy's head in rage. Parvati broke down in utter grief and to soothe her, Shiva sent out his squad (*gana*) to fetch the head of any sleeping being who was facing the north. The company found a sleeping elephant and brought back its severed head, which was then attached to the body of the boy. Shiva restored its life and made him the leader (*pati*) of his troops. Hence his name 'Ganapati'. Shiva also bestowed a boon that people would worship him and invoke his name before undertaking any venture.

However, there's another less popular story of his origin, found in the *Brahma Vaivarta Purana*: Shiva asked Parvati to observe the *punyaka vrata* for a year to appease Vishnu in order to have a son. When a son was born to her, all the gods and goddesses assembled to rejoice on its birth. Lord Shani, the son of Surya (Sun-God), was also present but he refused to look at the infant. Perturbed at this behaviour, Parvati asked him the reason, and Shani replied that his looking at baby would harm the newborn. However, on Parvati's insistence when Shani eyed the baby, the child's head was severed instantly. All the gods started to bemoan, whereupon Vishnu hurried to the bank of river Pushpabhadra and brought back the head of a young elephant, and joined it to the baby's body, thus reviving it.

Ganesha, the Destroyer of Pride: Ganesha is also the destroyer of vanity, selfishness and pride. He is the personification of material universe in all its various magnificent manifestations. "All Hindus worship Ganesha regardless of their sectarian belief," says D N Singh in *A Study of Hinduism*. "He is both the beginning of the religion and the meeting ground for all Hindus."

During the festivals, a household worships an idol of Shri Ganesha. The worship happens for 1 day in South India, but in western states of Maharashtra and Goa, the worship may last from 2 to 10 days.

The main sweet-dish during the period are modaks, also known as modagam [kozhakottai] in South India and karanjis. A modak is a sort of dumpling made from rice flour with a stuffing of coconut, jaggery and some other condiments. It can be either steam-cooked or fried and the coconut can be fresh-grated or dried-grated. A karanji is similar but has the shape of the 4th day moon.

There are also public celebrations of the festival, with local communities (*mandals*) vying with each other to put up the biggest idol. The festival is the time for a lot of cultural activities like songs, dramas and orchestra.

Legends say that Lord Ganapati (contraction of Ganesh pati-"Father Ganesh") was created by goddess Parvati, wife of Lord Shiva. Parvati created Ganesha out of the sandalwood paste that she used for her bath and breathed life into him. Letting him stand guard at the door she went to have her bath. However, while Parvati was taking her bath, Lord Shiva happened to come there and as Ganesha didn't know him, he didn't allow him to enter the house. As a result, Lord Shiva got angry and severed the head of the child and entered his house. But after realizing that he had beheaded his own son, Lord Shiva fixed the head of an elephant in place of Ganesha's head. In this way, Lord Ganesha acquired the image of the elephant-headed God.

According to the historian Shri Rajwade, records reveal that Ganesh Chaturthi was celebrated even during the reigns of Satavahana, Rashtrakuta and Chalukya. There are also references in historical records to similar celebrations during Peshwa times, Lord Ganapati being the family deity of the Peshwas. After the end of Peshwa rule, from 1818 to 1892 Ganesh Festival remained a family affair in Maharashtra.

It was around 1893, during the growth of nascent Indian nationalism, that the radical nationalist Bal Gangadhar Tilak began to organize the Ganesh Utsav as a social and religious function. Since then, Ganesh Chaturthi has been celebrated throughout Maharashtra with great community enthusiasm and participation.

Rooted in Tradition: From then onwards, this festive occasion has grown in acceptance and today, commands the respect of millions of citizens all over Maharashtra. Lokmanya Bal Gangadhar Tilak brought Ganesha as a deity out on the streets. It was a unique move by this freedom fighter, which he achieved with the Ganpati visarjana or immersion procession, wherein the mass output of several Ganesh mandals is taken out on a parade on the final day of the Ganesh festival and taken to be immersed. This process was started in 1892 and is now prevalent virtually all over Maharashtra, with special emphasis on Bombay and Pune. Lokmanya Tilak attached this mass celebration to increase national awareness about the Freedom movement. Herein, neighbourhood Ganeshas are worshipped and brought to immersion sites, where huge crowds gather to bid him an emotional and frenzied farewell.

In Pune, as the sun sets over darkening rivers, the images are taken out in boats and as each one is immersed, a cry is raised asking him to return the next year. It is an emotional and public farewell to their beloved god as parthiva (of the earth), who like the Phoenix, will rise once again the following year.

A special puja is performed for Ganesha. The worship of the deity involves getting a corner ready to receive the god. Ganesha is invited with a special phrase and with material and verbal offerings, the puja begins. It involves the Panchamrit (five nectars), which includes milk, curd, ghee, honey and jaggery, with which the god's icon is bathed, cleansing in between with water.

Ganesha is then given a red garment and the sacred thread-saying it is silver. He is then smeared with red sandal paste and offered red or yellow flowers. A lamp is lit, bells chime and food is offered in six symbolic mouthfuls-not to the god's body, but to his five panchapranas or 'vital breaths' and the one beyond-the absolute.

During the festival, puja is performed twice every day-once in the morning and again in the evening. Ganesha is offered special leaves and flowers, 21 of each and white durva grass.

The idol is formally installed on the first day and given life in the presence of Brahma, Vishnu and Shiva, and the Vedas. Touching the idol with blades of durva grass, he is brought to life step by step and made to go through 15 of the 16 rites of passage that each Hindu goes through in his lifetime. (The sixteenth one, which is for death, is omitted.)

The Ganesha mantra is chanted, followed by a Ganesha prayer. The last puja done, the family or congregation gathers around and rice grains are placed on the head of the idol, which is moved, symbolically unseating him.

As a matter of interest there are about 91 different figures of Ganesha according to research done by several scholars. The details of their make up may vary from figure to figure, but with no change in the main set-up. It is the enigma of certain striking variations in details that the sublime in the figures of Ganesha has to be sought for.

Some figures are seen sitting with their trunks turned towards the left side, invariably reaching a bowl of modaks (a sweet edible and festive preparation), while in some figures, the trunks are seen turning towards the right and in yet others, the trunk is straight, hanging down, with or without a pot of nectar in the curve of their trunks.

In some images, Ganesha is seen standing, resting his right foot on a lion and his left foot on a mouse (his chosen mode of transport), while in some other images, his left foot is found resting on a mouse and his right foot lifted in an effort to touch the serpent girdle-his mount carrying a jewel in its mouth.

Environmentalists too have questioned the dumping of the idols made increasingly with chemicals which pollute the lakes and seas. On September 2004, the Chennai High Court imposed a temporary ban on such immersions. Every year there are at least a couple of casualties associated with accidents (while dumping the idols) or clashes associated with this.

On the day of the festival, it is placed on raised platforms in homes or in elaborately decorated outdoor tents for people to view and pay their homage. The priest, usually clad in red silk dhoti and shawl, then invokes life into the idol amidst the chanting of mantras. This ritual is the pranapratishhtha. After this the shhodashopachara (16 ways of paying tribute) follows. Coconut, jaggery, 21 modakas (rice flour preparation), 21 durva (trefoil) blades and red flowers are offered. The idol is anointed with red unguent (rakta chandan). Throughout the ceremony, Vedic hymns from the Rig Veda and Ganapati Atharva Shirsha Upanishad, and Ganesha stotra from the Narada Purana are chanted.

Swami Sivananda Recommends : On the Ganesh Chaturthi day, meditate on the stories connected with Lord Ganesha early in the morning, during the Brahmamuhurta period. Then, after taking a bath, go to the temple and do the prayers of Lord Ganesha. Offer Him some coconut and sweet pudding. Pray with faith and devotion that He may remove all the obstacles that you experience on the spiritual path. Worship Him at home, too. You can get the assistance of a pundit. Have an image of Lord Ganesha in your house. Feel His Presence in it.

Don't forget not to look at the moon on that day; remember that it behaved unbecomingly towards the Lord. This really means avoid the company of all those who have no faith in God, and who deride God, your Guru and religion, from this very day.

Take fresh spiritual resolves and pray to Lord Ganesha for inner spiritual strength to attain success in all your undertakings.

May the blessings of Sri Ganesha be upon you all! May He remove all the obstacles that stand in your spiritual path! May He bestow on you all material prosperity as well as liberation!

The Visarjan (immersion) Processions and Ceremony: The festival ends with the ceremony of immersion of the idols in the sea or rivers and wells. This ceremony which is called Ganesha-Visarjan which means immersion of Ganesha is as popular as the festival proper. During the immersion ceremony huge crowds move in a procession carrying idols of Ganesha towards the places of immersion. These processions which take place with great fanfare, begins in the afternoon and continue till the late hours of the night.

Ganesh Chaturthi is celebrated as the birthday of Lord Ganesh on the fourth day (Chaturthi) of the bright fortnight of Bhadrapada month of Hindu calendar. It is among the most celebrated of the festivals in India, and perhaps the only one involving general public (others only involve families and friends and are celebrated privately).

It is interesting to note that the festival was not celebrated until the times of Lokamanya Bal Gangadhar Tilak, who used it a great means to unite Hindus all over India and educate them the evils of colonization.

The festivities include fund-raising, building all kinds of innovative forms Ganesh idols, organizing public performances of music and dance, cooking grand feasts and making a lot of noise. The festivities end when the idol of the year is immersed in water (*visarjan*), accompanied by loud shouts of *Ganapati Bappa Moraya*!

Lokamanya Tilak (portrait-biography) visualized the cultural importance of this diety and brought in Ganesha Chaturthi as National Festival. It was an important festival during Peshwa rule in Maharashtra, but acquired more organized from all over India during the *Swaraj* movement (see Tryst with Destiny— The story of India's struggle for freedom remains as a guiding light for resolving the various conflicts around the globe). It made way for learned discourses, dance dramas, poetry recital, musical concerts bringing together all castes and communities who vied with enthusiasm in organizing this public festival. The all-pervading Gajanana (another name of Ganesh) has countless temples all over India and is worshipped with more affection than awe in every Hindu home.

Ganesha, the elephant-headed son of Shiva and Parvati is widely worshipped as the munificent god of wisdom. Ganesh Chaturthi is a festival in his honour and is celebrated in the states of Maharashtra, Tamil Nadu, Karnataka and Andhra Pradesh.

On the day of the Chaturthi, *i.e.* the last of the days dedicated to the elephant-headed god, thousands of processions converge on the beaches of Mumbai to immerse the holy idols in the sea.

This immersion is accompanied by drum beats, devotional songs and dancing.

There is a curiously interesting tale about the birth of Ganesha. It is believed that once while Parvati was bathing, she created a human figure from some unguent and balm, gave him life and asked him to guard the door while she bathed. After a long period of meditation on Mountain Kailash (Shiva's abode), Shiva chose that very moment to drop by to see his better half, but was abruptly stopped by the man-god Parvati had posted at the door. Outraged by the cheek of this stranger, Shiva cut off his head only to discover that he had killed Parvati's son! For fear of enraging his wife, Shiva immediately dispatched his ganas (attendants) to get him the head of the first living creature they could find. Well, the first living creature happened to be an elephant.

As instructed, the head was chopped off and brought back to Shiva, who placed it on Parvati's son's body, bringing him back to life. This elephant-headed god was welcomed into the first family of the Hindu heavens and named Ganesha or Ganapati, which literally means the chief of the ganas, or the attendants of Shiva. Ganesha is the foremost god of the Hindu pantheon. This brave guardian of the door to Parvati's bath is beheld today as the most auspicious God of new beginnings. He is worshipped during every festival and before people undertake a journey or embark upon a new venture. You will also see him carefully guarding entrances to temples and homes, peeping out of calendars and happily gracing marriages and other such occasions.

Vinayaka (Ganesha) drives away all sorrows, difficulties, and miseries. He is the enemy of all obstacles. He will not allow any obstacles to come in the way. He is the destroyer of obstacles. He confers happiness and peace (on his devotees). He is the master of all these powers (intellect (buddhi) and fulfillment (siddhi, self-realization). What is this siddhi? When there is purity of mind, you achieve peace (which is siddhi). Vinayaka is thus the Lord of the intellect and self-realization. Hence, every human being should acquire control over the mind....

Vinayaka is the Lord of all learning (vidya). Does learning mean bookish scholarship? No. Everything pertaining to the cosmos is included in the term learning (vidya). Walking, talking, laughing, sitting, eating, strolling, thinking —every kind of activity is related to learning. Vinayaka is the master of every kind of learning. Today, learning is identified with acquisition of information. But apart from knowledge of the physical world, we have many other kinds of knowledge, relating to chemistry, the fine arts and other skills.

Vinayaka is the master of every kind of knowledge. Learning is related to the intellect (buddhi). It is not mere scholarship. Familiarity with books is not knowledge. One's entire life is a continuous process of learning. Any process of inquiry is related to learning. But basically our inquiry should be concerned with finding out what is transient and what is permanent. This is true knowledge.

Hence, today, students worship Vinayaka with zeal. Vinayaka is not the one who merely comes to the aid of those who read their books. He helps everyone at every step in life's journey.

In the verse (sloka) beginning with the words Suklaambara-dharam Vishnum, only the form of the deity is described. But there is another inner meaning for the name Vinayaka. Suklaambaradharam means one who is clad in white. Vishnum means he is all-pervading. Sasivarnam means his complexion is grey, like that of ash. Chathurbhujam means he has four arms. Prasannavadanam means he has always a pleasing mien. Sarvavighnopasaanthaye means for the removal of all obstacles. Dhyaayeth means meditate (on him). Vinayaka is the deity who removes all bad qualities, instills good qualities, and confers peace on the devotee who meditates on him. However, the Vinayaka-principle has only one meaning, which is relevant to everyone regardless of whether he is a believer or a non-believer. Vinayaka means that he is totally master of himself. He has no master above him. He does not depend on anyone. He is also called Ganapathi. This term means he is the lord of the ganas —a class of divine entities. This term also means that he is the master of the intellect and discriminating power in man. He possesses great intelligence and knowledge. Such knowledge issues from a pure and sacred mind. This knowledge leads to wisdom (vijnaana). Because he is the master of intelligence (buddhi) and wisdom or realisation (siddhi), he is described as the Lord of Buddhi and Siddhi. Buddhi and Siddhi are referred to as the consorts of Vinayka.

The mouse is the vehicle of Vinayaka. What is the inner significance of the mouse? The mouse is considered as the embodiment of the sense of smell. The mouse is a symbol of the attachment to worldly tendencies (vaasanas). It is well known that if you want to catch a mouse, you place a strong-smelling edible inside the mouse-trap. The mouse also symbolises the darkness of night. The mouse can see well in the dark. As Vinayaka's vehicle, the mouse signifies an object that leads man from darkness to light. Thus, the Vinayaka-principle means that which removes all the bad qualities, bad practices, and bad thoughts in men and inculcates good qualities, good conduct and good thoughts.

Another name for Vinayaka is Vighneswara. Easwara is one who is endowed with every conceivable form of wealth — riches, knowledge, health, bliss, beauty, etc. Vighneswara is the promoter of all these forms of wealth and removes all obstacles to their enjoyment. He confers all these forms of wealth on those who worship him. Vinayaka is described as "the first deity who should be worshipped (prathama vandana)". ASinceeveryone in the world desires wealth and prosperity, everyone offers the first place for worship to Vighneswara.

Where are the ganas? What is their form? When you investigate this, you find that the five organs of perception and the five organs of action (jnaanendriyas and karmendriyas) are the ganas. The mind is the master over these ten organs. The intellect (buddhi) is the discriminating faculty above the mind. The ten senses, the mind, and the intellect together constitute the ganas.

In the word "gana", "ga" stands for intellect (buddhi) and "na" means "Vaijnaana (the higher knowledge or wisdom)". Ganapathi is the Lord of the intellect and higher knowledge.

The question may be asked, Are the intellect and higher knowledge present in the external world, or are they to be found within man? The answer is that he is present within each human being. There is no need to seek for him in the outside world. Ganapathi dwells in every human being in the form of intellect and wisdom.

When Ganapathi is described as "Parvathee thanaya", who is this Parvathee? Parvathee signifies Prithvi, Mother Earth. Everyone is a child of Mother Earth.

The meaning of "son of Parvathee (Parvatheethanaya)" is that Ganapathi, who is the Lord of the Ganas, is the son of Parvathee, who symbolizes the divine energy (sakthi).

The adoration of Parvathieeand Ganapathi is not of recent origin. Ganapathi is lauded at several places in the *Rig Veda*. This clearly shows that Ganapathi is as ancient as the *Vedas*.

In several places, Ganapathi is mentioned both in the *Vedas* and the *Upanishaths*. Many prayers are addressed to Ganapathi in the *Narayanopanishath*. There are also prayers to him in the *Thaithiriya Upanishath*. The Ganapathi Gayathri Mantra also figures in the *Upanishath*.

Ganapathi is called Vinayaka because there is no master above him. He is all powerful and independent. Without recognizing the esoteric significance of the Vinayaka Principle, people look only at the external form and offer worship in mundane terms.

What is the inner significance of worshipping the elephant-faced deity? The elephant is a symbol of might and magnitude. The elephant's foot is larger than that of any other animal. The elephant can make its way through the densest jungle. In this way, it signifies the quality of a leader who shows the way for others. The elephant is also known for its fidelity and gratitude. In any circumstance, it will not forget its master. Even in its last moments, if it hears the voice of its master, it will open its eyes and look for him. It will sacrifice its life for its master. These are the lessons man should learn from the elephant. Intelligence without gratitude is valueless. Every man should be grateful to those who have helped him.

Ganesh's Birth: Once Lord Shiva left his usual dwelling on Mt.Kailas in the Himalayas, to meditate in one of the caves in the same mountain. Two friends of Parvati, his consort, suggested that she should have a 'gana'-attendant of their own, since they were not too happy with Shivaji's 'ganas'. Parvati agreed. Soon after, using her divine powers, she created a son, naming him Vinayak. She instructed him to guard their home.

When Shivaji returned Vinayak prevented him from entering. After some bickering, Shivaji beheaded Vinayak with his 'trishul' (trident). When Parvati heard of this she lamented intensely. Shivaji realised his error. To set things right he sent his men to the forest to fetch the head of the first living thing they met. They encountered a baby elephant and returned with its head. With his divine power, Shivaji placed the head over his son's body. Instantly Vinayak sprung to life. Henceforth Vinayak also earned the name of Gajaanan. 'Gaja' means elephant. Shivaji blessed him with a boon that people would first worship and offer him dedication in all their auspicious activities. Those who didn't would not attain success. Bhadarva Sud 4th is the day Parvati was offering the final pujan to the dead Ganeshji, when he resurrected.

Ganapati Vivaha (Marriage): When Shiva and Parvati decided to have their sons, Kartikeya and Ganesh married, they stipulated that he who circumambulated the earth first would be considered the best deity and would be married first. Kartikeya flew off on his vehicle-a peacock. Poor Ganapati's vehicle was a mouse which was no match for a peacock. Being the choicest devotee of God, Parvatiji consoling him showed Ganeshji a simpler and quicker way. She advised him to cicumambulate the cow since she also symbolically represents another earth and he had reap the same benefit as going round the earth. Another reference cites him circumambulating his parents.Consoling him, Parvati showed a short cut. She divulged that it was ordained in the scriptures that he who offered pujan to his parents and then circumambulated them received the same merit as he who went around the earth. Ganapati hence married first showing that one who obeys the wish of the choicest devotee of God or his parents attains his desired wishes.

Hence Ganeshji is invoked first in all auspicious events, rites and rituals such as marriage, opening ceremonies, ground-breaking ceremonies, yagnas and so on.

The Shiva Puran cites another story. Prajapati had two daughters, Siddhi (wealth) and Buddhi (intellect). He approached Parvati and Shivaji for the girls' marriage to Kartikeya and Ganeshji. However both girls wished to marry only the latter. Thus they married him. Siddhi gave birth to a son named 'Shubh' (auspiciousness) and Buddhi to 'Labh' (merit).

Therefore when businessmen and merchants offer pujan to Ganeshji and Lakshmiji they write 'Shubh' and 'Labh' inside their account ledgers to invoke the two deities.

Sentiments: The first person to observe the 'vrat' (vow) of Ganesh Chaturthi was Chandra-the moon. After Ganeshji's fame as leader ('pati') of Shiva's 'ganas', hence Ganapati, he was travelling through the heavens. As he passed Chandra-who prided on his attractive features, he slighted Ganeshji's peculiar form. In return, Ganeshji cursed him, "You shall bear the fruit of your karma. Whenever somebody does your darshan he will be cursed too." Chandra begged for forgiveness. Ganeshji then advised him to observe the Ganesh Chaturthi vrat and was freed from the curse.

By being aware of the detrimental effects of false pride one should cultivate humility. The Skanda Purana mentions this sentiment of the festival.

The Vayu Puran advocates the observance of this festival by listening to the following relevant episode of Shri Krishna, to be relieved from false accusation:

When Shri Krishna was falsely accused of pilfering the Syamantak Mani (gem) he observed Ganesh Chaturthi and was freed from the false charge.

This festival also inspires devotees to inculcate two virtues; obeying the commands of God and His choicest devotee, and consolidating faith in them, just as Ganeshji had faith and trust in Parvati regarding circumambulating his parents.

Names of Ganeshji : *Ekadant (one-toothed)*

- To scribe the Mahabharat Katha Ganeshji removed one of his tusks to carve a quill from it. He then scribed the epic on palm leaves as the sage Ved Vyas recited it. The scribing took three years!
- In south India there is a belief that when ploughing first began on earth, it was Lord Ganeshji who first ploughed using one of his tusks.
- In the Uttar Ramayan, Brahmand Puran and Padma Puran there is a reference of a battle between Ganeshji and Parshuram. During the duel, the latter's axe fractured one of Ganeshji's tusks According to the Brahmand Puran, it was his left tusk.

There are other names related to his body and virtues. A few commonly known are listed below:

- Lambodar-from the long-'lambo', tummy-'udar'.
- Gajkarna-from the large elephant 'Gaja' ears-'karna.'
- Kapil-from his ruddy complexion.
- Vikat-heavy-bodied.
- Bhalchandra-having a Chandra (moon) on his forehead-'bhal.'
- Dwaimatur-one who has 'dwi'-two, 'mata'-mother; Parvati-who gave birth to him and Malini-a demoness who nurtured him.
- Vakratund-one who breaks the ego of he who behaves anti-socially ('Vakra').
- Mudgal-In south India, a special 'Mudgal Puran' extols Ganapati's glory. It cites 32 names, while 'Shardatilak' lists 51 names.
- Vigneshwar-One who removes mayic obstacles-'vignas'

Symbolism and Import

Since Ganeshji represents auspiciousness, his whole being has symbolic imports for devotees:

Large ears-signify listening to God's katha with great zeal.

Small eyes-to do the Lord's darshan minutely.

Large forehead-to develop great intellect to realise God.

Large stomach-depicts his great capacity to empathise with the woes of devotees.

Short legs-depicts patience.

Long trunk-symbolic of his deep scriptural wisdom.

Mouse as vehicle-a hyperactive creature, symbolic of our indriyas. Therefore Ganesh sitting on such a vehicle represents a deity of control over the indriyas.

Four arms-which hold: 'ankush'-symbol for control over the mind

'ladu'-for happiness

'pash'-axe to punish the indriyas and antahkaran

'ashirvad mudra'-blessings for the well being of humanity

Depending on the role of Ganapati, the number of arms varies, as do the type of objects.

Ganesha is the god of wisdom and prosperity and is invoked before the beginning of any auspicious work by the Hindus. It is believed that for the fulfillment of one's desires, his blessing is absolutely necessary. According to the mythology, he is the son of Shiva and Parvati, brother of Kartikeya-the general of the gods, Lakshmi-the goddess of wealth and Saraswati-the goddess of learning. There are numerous stories in Hindu mythology, associated with the birth of this elephant-headed god, whose vehicle is the Mooshak or rat and who loves Modaks (droplet shaped Indian sweet). Legend has it that Parvati created Ganesha out of the sandalwood dough that she used for her bath and breathed life into him. Letting him stand guard at the door she went to have her bath. When her husband, Shiva returned, the child who had never seen him stopped him.

Shiva severed the head of the child and entered his house. Parvati, learning that her son was dead, was distraught and asked Shiva to revive him. Shiva cut off the head of an elephant and fixed it on the body of Ganesha. Another tale tells of how one day the Gods decided to choose their leader and a race was to be held between the brothers-Kartikeya and Ganesh. Whoever took three rounds of the earth first would be made the Ganaadhipati or the leader. Kartikeya seated on a peacock as his vehicle, started off for the test.

Ganesh was given a rat, which moved swiftly. Ganesh realised that the test was not easy, but he would not disobey his father. He reverently paid obeisance to his parents and went around them three times and thus completed the test before Kartikeya. He said, "my parents pervade the whole universe and going around them, is more than going round the earth." Everybody was pleasantly surprised to hear Ganesha's logic and intelligence and hence he came to be known as the Ganaadhipati or leader, now referred to as Ganpati.

There is also a story behind the symbolic snake, rat and the singular tusk. During one of his birthdays, His mother, Parvati, cooked for him twenty-one types of delicious food and a lot of sweet porridge. Ganesha ate so much that even his big belly could not contain it. Mounting his little mouse, he embarked on his nightly rounds. His mouse suddenly stumbled upon seeing a huge snake. To adjust His belly, Ganesha put the snake on as a belt around his stomach. All of a sudden, he heard laughter emanating form the sky.

He looked up and saw the moon mocking him. Ganesha infuriated, broke off one of his tusks and hurled it at the moon. Parvati, seeing this, immediately cursed the moon that whoever looks at it on Ganesh Chaturthi will be accused of a wrong doing. The symbology behind the mouse and snake and Ganesha's big belly and its relationship to the moon on his birthday is highly philosophic.

The whole cosmos is known to be the belly of Ganesha. Parvati is the primordial energy. The seven realms above, seven realms below and seven oceans, are inside the cosmic belly of Ganesha, held together by the cosmic energy *(kundalini)* symbolized as a huge snake which Ganesha ties around Him. The mouse is nothing but our ego. Ganesha, using the mouse as a vehicle, exemplifies the need to control our ego. One who has controlled the ego has Ganesha consciousness or God-consciousness.

Ganapathi's position in the Hindu Pantheon: The Supreme Being manifested Himself as the holy Trinity of Brahma, Vishnu and Maheswara to undertake the functions of creation, sustenance and dissolution respectively of the entire universe. Their divine consorts respectively are Saraswathi, Mahalakshmi and Maheswari, Goddesses of learning, wealth and activity. All the above manifestations of Divinity have blessed Lord Ganesa, granting Him all their powers and attributes. They have also conceded to Him the first priority in any worship. In fact, the Gods themselves pray to Ganesa to bring success in their all endeavours.

Ganesa Tattwa or the Principle of the Manifestation: It is necessary that the devotee tries to grasp the significance of the system of his worship to improve his concentration and to avoid dissipation of his energy. The entire creation is made up of five elements, namely, ether, air, fire, water and earth and they have emerged in that order from the Absolute Reality. These elements operate in the human body from the five spiritual centres of Muladhara, swadhisthana, Manipura, Anahata and Visudhi in the reverse order of their emergence. These spiritual centers along with the sixth centre "Ajna" form the "shadchakra" (six energy points) in the sushumnanadi inside the backbone.

The lower centre, Muladhara, situated near the hip, is the seat of earth element (prithvi), the controlling deity being Ganapathy. The remaining higher centers are controlled by Brahma, Vishnu, Rudra, Jivatma and Paramatma, (Their seats being Swadhisthana, Manipura, Anahata, Vishudhi, and Ajna respectively. By constant sadhana and the grace of the respective deities starting from Ganesa, the individual soul is raised to higher levels in the realm of the Spirit, in the above order, enabling him to finally merge with the Ultimate Reality, dwelling in Brahmarandhra at the crown of his head in the form of Sadasiva.

Mantrajapa Sadhana: Ganesa Mantras are very powerful and they confer success to devotees, chanting them with deep faith and regularity.

On the 4th day of the bright half of Bhadrapad, the great festival of Ganesh or Ganpati is celebrated. This festival marked the birthday of Lord Ganesh. Ganpati is one of the most popular deities. He is worshipped by both Shaivites and Vaishnavites. Even Buddhists and Jains have respect for Ganpati. He is considered to be an avatar of both Shiva and Vishnu. To appreciate this occasion, one must go to Mumbai where preparations begin months in advance. Images of Ganesha are installed within homes as well as in places of assembly. Elaborate arrangements are made for lighting and decoration and Ganesha is fervently worshipped for about 7-10 days.

On the day of the Chaturthi, the last of the days dedicated to the elephant-headed god, thousands of processions converge on the beaches of Mumbai to immerse the holy idols in the sea. This immersion is accompanied by drum beats, devotional songs and dancing. Every year, the largest Ganesh idol is installed at Khairatabad in Hyderabad, which is more than 30 ft tall.The Ganapati Mahotsav or the Grand Festival of Ganesha is the principle festival in Bombay, the financial capital of India. In Bombay the largest of the 6000 or so Ganeshas are commissioned collectively by factories. Each of these idols can be upto 10 metres in height and are paraded on lorries decorated with multi-coloured lights. At the other end of the scale, little Ganeshas are placed in nukkads or street corners and in homes, and pujas are performed daily.

The festival was started by Shivaji, the great Maratha ruler, to promote culture and a feeling of nationalism amongst his subjects who were fighting against the Mughals. After his death the festival was celebrated but on a smaller scale. In 1894 when the British banned public assemblies the festivalwas revived by Lokmanya Bal Gangadhar Tilak who felt that this was way of spreading the freedom message through a legitimate religious festival. On full moon day every idol is taken down to the Chowpatty beach accompanied by hordes of people singing and dancing and is immersed in the Arabian Sea.

How the Brahma-Madhwa Vaishnava's observe Ganesh Chaturthi: The icon of Ganapati made of clay by artists of Udupi is brought to badage maalige during an auspicious period on that day. The entire area is decorated artistically with different kinds of decorations. A huge rangavalli of Ganesha is constructed in front of the icon. This is a feast to the eyes for the next four days.

After worshipping the special Ganapati icon for four days the icon is taken out in procession and then immersed in the Madhva-Sarovara.

At the entrance of the shrine also there is a small icon of Ganapati. Special worship is arranged there to the Lord Vishnu in the form of Sri Vishvambhara. The priests perform a sacrifice known as ganahoma. The Swamiji offers prasaada of Lord Vishvambhara to Ganapati and performs aarati.

A special icon of Ganapati made of five metals is present at Ananteshwara and is worshipped every day. Here also, the festival of Ganesha is celebrated with pomp.

I was going to mention it in the chapter containing the initial reference to Ananteshwara but because of incomplete memory of the story I didn't. It goes along the lines — the icon had been worshipped in a fort (can't remember where) and when the fort was attacked by marauding Muslims the icon was removed and eventually placed in the Ananteshwara temple for safe keeping. Even after the Muslims had been driven back, the icon remained in the Ananteshwara temple.

During Ganesha-chaturthi, special festivals are held here during the night and it is a magnificent sight. The whole of the temple is lit up with oil lamps and the people queue up to view the icon. Because of all the oil lamps this is the best time to view the icon.

Dusshera

This festival is observed twice a year, once in the month of Chaitra and then in Aswayuja. It lasts for nine days in honour of the nine manifestations of Durga. During Navaratri (the word literally means "nine nights") devotees of Durga observe a fast. Brahmins are fed and prayers are offered for the protection of health and property.

The beginning of summer and the beginning of winter are two very important junctions of climatic and solar influence. These two periods are taken as sacred opportunities for the worship of the Divine Mother. They are indicated respectively by the Rama-Navaratri in Chaitra (April-May) and the Durga Navaratri in Aswayuja (September-October). The bodies and minds of people undergo a considerable change on account of the changes in Nature. Sri Rama is worshipped during Ramnavmi, and Mother Durga during Navaratri.

The Durga Puja is celebrated in various parts of India in different styles. But the one basic aim of this celebration is to propitiate Shakti, the Goddess in Her aspect as Power, to bestow upon man all wealth, auspiciousness, prosperity, knowledge (both sacred and secular), and all other potent powers. Whatever be the particular or special request that everyone may put before the Goddess, whatever boon may be asked of Her, the one thing behind all these is propitiation, worship and linking oneself with Her. There is no other aim. This is being effected consciously or unconsciously. Everyone is blessed with Her loving mercy and is protected by Her.

Durga Puja or Navaratri commences on the first and ends on the tenth day of the bright half of Aswayuja (September-October). It is held in commemoration of the victory of Durga over Mahishasura, the buffalo-headed demon. In Bengal Her image is worshipped for nine days and then cast into water. The tenth day is called Vijaya Dasami or Dussera (the "tenth day"). Processions with Her image are taken out along the streets of villages and cities.

The mother of Durga (that is, the wife of the King of the Himalayas) longed to see her daughter. Durga was permitted by Lord Shiva to visit her beloved mother only for nine days in the year. The festival of Durga Puja marks this brief visit and ends with the Vijaya Dasami day, when Goddess Durga leaves for Her return to Mount Kailas. This is the view of some devotees.

In Bengal, Durga Puja is a great festival. All who live away from home return during the Puja days. Mothers reunite with their sons and daughters, and wives with their husbands.

The potter shows his skill in making images, the painter in drawing pictures, the songster in playing on his instrument, and the priest in reciting the sacred books. The Bengalis save money throughout the year only to spend everything during the Puja days. Cloth is freely distributed to the Brahmins.

The woman of Bengal welcomes the Goddess with a mother's love and sends away the image on the last day, with every ceremony associated with a daughter's departure to her husband's home and with motherly tears in her eyes. This signifies the parting of Durga from Her beloved mother.

Durga Puja is the greatest Hindu festival in which God is adored as Mother. Hinduism is the only religion in the world which has emphasised to such an extent the motherhood of God. One's relationship with one's mother is the dearest and the sweetest of all human relations. Hence, it is proper to look upon God as mother.

Durga represents the Divine Mother. She is the energy aspect of the Lord. Without Durga, Shiva has no expression and without Shiva, Durga has no existence. Shiva is the soul of Durga; Durga is identical with Shiva. Lord Shiva is only the silent witness. He is motionless, absolutely changeless. He is not affected by the cosmic play. It is Durga who does everything.

Shakti is the omnipotent power of the Lord, or the Cosmic Energy. The Divine Mother is represented as having ten different weapons in Her hands. She sits on a lion. She keeps up the play of the Lord through the three attributes of Nature, namely, Sattwa, Rajas and Tamas. Knowledge, peace, lust, anger, greed, egoism and pride, are all Her forms.

You will find in the Devi Sukta of the *Rig Veda Samhita* that Vak, symbolising speech, the daughter of the sage Anbhirna, realised her identity with the Divine Mother, the Power of the Supreme Lord, which manifests throughout the universe among the gods, among men and beasts and among the creatures of the deep ocean.

In the *Kena Upanishad*, you will find that the Divine Mother shed wisdom on Indra and the gods and said that the gods were able to defeat the demons only with the help of the power of the Supreme Lord.

The worship of Devi, the universal Mother, leads to the attainment of knowledge of the Self. The story in the *Kena Upanishad* known as the "Yaksha Prasna", supports this view. It tells how Uma, the Divine Mother, taught the Truth to the gods. Goddess Shakti thus sheds wisdom on Her devotees.

Devi worship is, therefore, worship of God's glory, of God's greatness and supremacy. It is adoration of the Almighty. It is unfortunate that Devi is ignorantly understood by many as a mere blood-thirsty Hindu Goddess. No! Devi is not a vicious demoness nor is She the property of the Hindus alone. Devi does not belong to any religion. Devi is that conscious power of God. The words Devi, Shakti, etc., and the ideas of different forms connected with these names are concessions granted by the sages due to the limitations of the human intellect; they are by no means the ultimate definitions of Shakti.

The original or Adi Shakti is beyond human comprehension. Bhagavan Krishna says in the *Gita*: "This is only My lower nature. Beyond this is My higher nature, the life-principle which sustains the universe".

The *Upanishad* also says: "The supreme power of God is manifested in various ways. This power is of the nature of God, manifesting as knowledge, strength and activity".

Truly speaking, all beings in the universe are Shakti-worshippers, whether they are aware of it or not, for there is no one who does not love and long for power in some form or other. Physicists and scientists have now proved that everything is pure, imperishable energy. This energy is only a form of divine Shakti which exists in every form. A child is more familiar with the mother than with the father, because the mother is very kind, loving, tender and affectionate and looks after the needs of the child. In the spiritual field also, the aspirant or the devotee—the spiritual child—has an intimate relationship with the Mother Durga, more than with the Father Shiva. Therefore, it behoves the aspirant to approach the Mother first, who then introduces Her spiritual child to the Father for his illumination.

The Mother's Grace is boundless. Her mercy is illimitable; Her knowledge infinite; Her power immeasurable; Her glory ineffable; and Her splendour indescribable. She gives you material prosperity as well as spiritual freedom.

Approach Her with an open heart. Lay bare your heart to Her with frankness and humility. Be as simple as a child. Kill ruthlessly the enemies of egoism, cunningness, selfishness and crookedness. Make a total, unreserved, and ungrudging self-surrender to Her. Sing Her praise. Repeat Her Name. Worship Her with faith and unflinching devotion. Perform special worship on the Navaratri days. Navaratri is the most suitable occasion for doing intense spiritual practices. These nine days are very sacred to the Divine Mother. Plunge yourself in her worship. Practise intense repetition of the Divine Name, having a regular "quota" of repetitions per day, and the number of hours spent on it.

Devi fought with Bhandasura and his forces for nine days and nine nights. This Bhandasura had a wonderful birth and life. When Lord Shiva burnt Cupid with the fire of His "third eye", Sri Ganesha playfully moulded a figure out of the ashes, and the Lord breathed life into it! This was the terrible demon Bhandasura. He engaged himself in great penance and on account of it obtained a boon from Lord Shiva. With the help of that boon, he began harassing the worlds. The Divine Mother fought with him for nine nights (the demons have extraordinary strength during the night), and killed him on the evening of the tenth day, known as the Vijaya Dasami. The learning of any science is begun on this highly auspicious day. It was on this day that Arjuna worshipped Devi, before starting the battle against the Kauravas on the field of Kurukshetra.

Sri Rama worshipped Durga at the time of the fight with Ravana, to invoke Her aid in the war. This was on the days preceding the Vijaya Dasami day. He fought and won through Her Grace.

In days of yore, kings used to undertake ambitious expeditions on the day of the Vijaya Dasami. Those kings who did not go on such expeditions used to go out hunting in the deep forests. In Rajputana, India, even up to this date, people arrange mock attacks on some fort on Vijaya Dasami.

This day, however, has much to do with the life of Sri Rama. Nowhere in the history of the world can we find a parallel to the character of Sri Rama as a man, son, brother, husband, father or king. Maharishi Valmiki has exhausted the entire language in describing the glory of Sri Rama. And, we shall be rightly celebrating the Dussera if we make honest efforts to destroy the demon of our ego, and radiate peace and love wherever we go. Let us all resolve to become men of sterling character. Let us resolve and act. The story of Sri Rama is known in almost all parts of the globe, and if we but succeed in following even a hundredth part of His teachings, we shall make our lives more fragrant than the rose and more lustrous than gold!

Dusshera can also be interpreted as "Dasa-Hara", which means the cutting of the ten heads of Ravana. So, let us resolve today to cut the ten heads—passion, pride, anger, greed, infatuation, lust, hatred, jealousy, selfishness and crookedness—of the demon, Ego, and thus justify the celebration of Dussera.

Religious observances, traditional worship and observances at times have more than one significance. Apart from being the adoration of the Divine, they commemorate stirring events in history, they are allegoric when interpreted from the occult standpoint and, lastly, they are deeply significant pointers and revealing guides to the individual on his path to God-realisation.

Outwardly, the nine-day worship of Devi is a celebration of triumph. This nine days' celebration is offered to the Mother for Her successful struggle with the formidable demons led by Mahishasura. But, to the sincere spiritual aspirant, the particular division of the Navaratri into sets of three days to adore different aspects of the Supreme Goddess has a very sublime, yet thoroughly practical truth to reveal. In its cosmic aspect, it epitomises the stages of the evolution of man into God, from Jivahood (the state of individualisation) to Shivahood (the state of Self-realisation). In its individual import, it shows the course that his spiritual practice should take.

Let us, therefore, examine in detail the spiritual significance of Navaratri.

The central purpose of existence is to recognise your eternal identity with the supreme Spirit. It is to grow into the image of the Divine. The supreme One embodies the highest perfection. It is spotless purity. To recognise your identity with That, to attain union with That, is verily to grow into the very likeness of the Divine. The aspirant, therefore, as his initial step, has to get rid of all the countless impurities, and the demoniacal elements that have come to cling to him in his embodied state. Then he has to acquire lofty virtues and auspicious, divine qualities. Thus purified, knowledge flashes upon him like the brilliant rays of the sun upon the crystal waters of a perfectly calm lake.

This process demands a resolute will, determined effort, and arduous struggle. In other words, strength and infinite power are the prime necessity. Thus it is the Divine Mother who has to operate through the aspirant.

Let us now consider how, on the first three days, the Mother is adored as supreme power and force, as Durga the Terrible. You pray to Mother Durga to destroy all your impurities, your vices, your defects. She is to fight with and annihilate the baser animal qualities in the spiritual aspirant, the lower, diabolical nature in him. Also, She is the power that protects your spiritual practice from its many dangers and pitfalls. Thus the first three days, which mark the first stage or the destruction of impurity and determined effort and struggle to root out the evil tendencies in your mind, are set apart for the worship of the destructive aspect of the Mother.

Once you have accomplished your task on the negative side, that of breaking down the impure propensities and old vicious habits, the next step is to build up a sublime spiritual personality, to acquire positive qualities in place of the eliminated demoniacal qualities. The divine qualities that Lord Krishna enumerates in the Gita, have to be acquired. The aspirant must cultivate and develop all the auspicious qualities. He has to earn immense spiritual wealth to enable him to pay the price for the rare gem of divine wisdom. If this development of the opposite qualities is not undertaken in right earnest, the old demoniacal nature will raise its head again and again.

Hence, this stage is as important in an aspirant's career as the previous one. The essential difference is: the former is a ruthless, determined annihilation of the filthy egoistic lower self; the latter is an orderly, steady, calm and serene effort to develop purity. This pleasanter side of the aspirant's Sadhana is depicted by the worship of Mother Lakshmi. She bestows on Her devotees the inexhaustible divine wealth or Deivi Sampath. Lakshmi is the wealth-giving aspect of God. She is purity itself.

Thus the worship of Goddess Lakshmi is performed during the second set of three days. Once the aspirant succeeds in routing out the evil propensities, and develops Sattwic or pure, divine qualities, he becomes competent to attain wisdom. He is now ready to receive the light of supreme wisdom. He is fit to receive divine knowledge. At this stage comes the devout worship of Mother Saraswathi, who is divine knowledge personified, the embodiment of knowledge of the Absolute. The sound of Her celestial *veena* awakens the notes of the sublime utterances of the *Upanishads* which reveal the Truth, and the sacred monosyllable, Om. She bestows the knowledge of the supreme, mystic sound and then gives full knowledge of the Self as represented by Her pure, dazzling snow-white apparel. Therefore, to propitiate Saraswathi, the giver of knowledge, is the third stage.

The tenth day, Vijaya Dasami, marks the triumphant ovation of the soul at having attained liberation while living in this world, through the descent of knowledge by the Grace of Goddess Saraswathi. The soul rests in his own Supreme Self or Satchidananda Brahman. This day celebrates the victory, the achievement of the goal. The banner of victory flies aloft. Lo! I am He! I am He!

This arrangement also has a special significance in the aspirant's spiritual evolution. It marks the indispensable stages of evolution through which everyone has to pass. One naturally leads to the other; to short-circuit this would inevitably result in a miserable failure. Nowadays many ignorant seekers aim straight at the cultivation of knowledge without the preliminaries of purification and acquisition of the divine qualities. They then complain that they are not progressing on the path. How can they? Knowledge will not descend until the impurities have been washed out, and purity is developed. How can the pure plant grow in impure soil?

Therefore adhere to this arrangement; your efforts will be crowned with sure success. This is your path. As you destroy one evil quality, develop the virtue opposite to it. By this process you will soon bring yourself up to that perfection which will culminate in identity with the Self which is your goal. Then all knowledge will be yours: you will be omniscient, omnipotent and you will feel your omnipresence. You will see your Self in all. You will have achieved eternal victory over the wheel of births and deaths, over the demon of worldliness. No more pain, no more misery, no more birth, no more death! Victory, victory be yours! Glory to the Divine Mother! Let Her take you, step by step to the top of the spiritual ladder and unite you with the Lord!

At the Sivananda Ashram, Rishikesh, the following are the regular features during the Durga Puja celebrations:

1. A special ritualistic worship of the Mother is conducted daily, which includes the recitation of the *Durga Saptashati*.
2. Laksharchana for the Mother in the temple, with recitation of the *Sri Lalita Sahasranama*, is also conducted.
3. All are exhorted to do the maximum number of Japa of the Navarna Mantra, *Aim hreem kleem chaamundaayai vichche*, or the Mantra of their own tutelary Deity.
4. An elaborately decorated altar is set up for the evening Satsangs, with the picture of Mother Durga for the first three days, Mother Lakshmi for the next three days, and Mother Saraswati for the last three days. Many sacred verses from the scriptures are recited and many Kirtans are sung. The *Durga Saptashati* or the *Devi Mahatmya* is recited and explained in discourses. The function concludes with the formal floral worship and Arati. Sometimes scenes from the *Devi Mahatmya* are also enacted.

5. Earnest spiritual aspirants fast with milk and fruits only on all the nine days, or at least once in each of the three three-day periods.
6. Besides the books representing Saraswathi, all instruments and implements like typewriters, printing machinery, etc., are also worshipped on the ninth day.
7. On the Vijaya Dasami day, all aspirants *en masse* are given initiation into various Mantras according to their tutelary Deities. Deserving aspirants are initiated into the holy order of Sannyas. Initiation in the study of the alphabets is given to young children, and to the old children also! New students commence their lessons in music, etc. During the morning Satsang the books which were worshipped on the ninth day are again worshipped and a chapter from each of the principal scriptures like the *Gita, Upanishads, Brahma Sutras, Ramayana,* and *Srimad Bhagavatam* is recited.
8. On the Vijaya Dasami day, there is Kanya Puja also. Nine girls below the age of ten are worshipped as the embodiment of the Divine Mother. They are fed sumptuously and, amongst other things, presented with new clothes.
9. On this last day a grand *havan* is conducted in the temple, with recitation of the *Durga Saptashati* and other verses in praise of the Divine Mother.

Durga, in Sanskrit means "She who is incomprehensible or difficult to reach." Goddess Durga is a form of Shakti worshiped for her gracious as well as terrifying aspect. Mother of the Universe, she represents the infinite power of the universe and is a symbol of a female dynamism.

Dushaharaa is the festival of Kshatriya. Right after Pitra Paksh of sixteen days, starts the second Nav Ratri of the year in Aashwin Maas. First Nav Raatri was in Chaitra Maas. This Nav Raatri is celebrated in the same way as it was celebrated in Chaitra Maas. Except that After the Chaitra Nav Raatri comes Ram Navamee, Lord Raam's birthday, and after this Nav Raatri comes Dushaharaa, the day Lord Raam killed Raavan the great demon.

During this Nav Raatri in every village, town, city, Ramleelaa drama is played in which the whole story of Ramaayan is retold. The tenth day, on the day of Dushaharaa (10th day) Lord Raam kills Raavan. Large fairs are arranged, and during the late evening (about after 5.00 pm) a life-like image of Raavan is built with wood, paper etc material and some fireworks are burned to depict the victory of Good on Evil.

In houses, Dushaharaa an image is drawn on the floor with cow dung, people worship it around noon, then take good food, take a nap, and then go to Dushaharaa fair. Kshatriya worship their weapons and Vaishya write the current prices of main items in a new book.

This day is important for farmers also. Farmers go out in their farms and try to see a bird called Neelkanth (a bird with blue throat). If they can find this bird in their farms, they feel lucky, because if this bird is there, they need not to worry about many kinds of natural worms and insects which may destroy their crop.

The Essentials of Durga Puja: The decorated puja platform with all the required essentials. Specific items are needed for each day of Durga Puja. There is a detailed method to worshiping Goddess Durga that are mentioned in the scriptures. Items which are needed for the ritual worship of the goddess should be collected beforehand so that the ritual is performed smoothly. The list of essentials of Durga Puja are:

Items needed for Kalparambho, the ritual performed before the commencement of the puja and Mahasna:

Food Offerings : Panchashasha (grains of five types-rice, mung or whole green gram, til or sesame, mashkalai or any variety of whole black leguminous seed, job or millet), panchagobbo (five items obtained from the cow-milk, ghee or clarified butter, curd, cow dung and gomutra), curd, honey, sugar, three big noibiddos, one small noibiddo, three bowls of madhupakka (a mixture of honey, curd, ghee and sugar for oblation), bhoger drobbadi (items for the feast), aaratir drobbadi mahasnan oil, dantokashtho, sugar cane juice, an earthen bowl of atop (a type of rice), til toilo (sesame oil).

Water Offerings: Ushnodok (lukewarm water), coconut water, sarbooushodhi, mahaoushodhi, water from oceans, rain water, spring water, water containing lotus pollen.

Puja Items: Sindur (vermillion), panchabarner guri (powders of five different colours-turmeric, rice, kusum flowers or red aabir, rice chaff or coconut fibre burnt for the dark colour, bel patra or powdered wood apple leaves), panchapallab (leaves of five trees-mango, pakur or a species of fig, banyan, betal and Joggodumur or fig), pancha ratna (five types of gems-gold, diamond, sapphire, ruby and pearl), panchakoshay (bark of five trees-jaam, shimul, berela, kool, bokul powdered in equal portions and mixed with water), green coconut with stalk, three aashonanguriuk (finger ring made of kusha).

Cloth Offerings: Gamcha or a piece of cloth to cover the pot, a dhoti for Vishnu, a sari each for bodhon and Chandi.

Decorative Items : Ghat or a pot, kundohari, a mirror, four arrows, tekatha or a triangular frame of wood, horitoki flowers (myrobalan), chandmala (garland with circular decorations), aashon (a mattress of jute or hay).

Other Items : Water camphor and perfumed sandal wood paste. soil-extracted from elephant tusks, from the teeth of the pig, from the horns of the ox, from the bank of rivers Ganga and Saraswati, from both the banks of a river, from a place where four roads intersect, from palaces, from the ant hill, from the mountains, Vishnu toilo.

Origin of Durga-The Mythology: Durga, a beautiful warrior seated upon a tiger.

Devi is the great goddess of the Hindus,the consort of Shiva and she is worshiped in various forms corresponding to her two aspects: benevolence and fierceness. She is Uma, "light"; Gauri, "yellow or brilliant"; Parvati, "the mountaineer"; and Jagatmata, "the-mother-of-the-world" in her milder guise. The terrible emanations are Durga "the inaccessible"; Kali, "the black"; Chandi, "the fierce"; and Bhairavi, "the terrible."

Descent of the Goddess: Durga, a beautiful warrior seated upon a tiger, was the first appearance of the great goddess. The circumstance of her miraculous arrival was the tyranny of the monster-demon Mahishasur, who through terrific austerities had acquired invincible strength. The gods were afraid of this water-buffalo bull because neither Vishnu nor Shiva could prevail against him. It seemed that the joint energy of Shakti was only capable of vanquishing Mahisha, and so it was the eighteen-armed Durga who went out to do battle.

Battlefield : She went to battle on her ferocious mount lion, armed with the weapons given to her by the other Gods. Durga is one of the angry and aggressive aspects of the goddess Shakti, whose role in Hindu mythology was to fight and conquer demons and also personify the Sakti or female aspect of any male deity. In the battle, she fought and killed the evil Mahishasura and restored heaven to the Gods. Since then the goddess is invoked for protection from the powers of evil. Durga Puja is observed in her honour, to celebrate her victory over evil.

Revered Mother: She has been worshiped from about 400 AD, but probably earlier, to the present. Her literary references are chiefly the Ramayana and Mahabharata, epic and Puranic texts, and she is mentioned by name in Vedic literature. In general, Durga is regarded in northern India as the gentle bride epitomizing family unity while in southern India she is revered more in her warrior aspect.

Navratri: Dandiya, the most awaited traditional dance festival of India.

Navratri, the festival of nights, lasts for 9 days with three days each devoted to worship of Ma Durga, the Goddess of Valor, Ma Lakshmi, the Goddess of Wealth and Ma Saraswati, the Goddess of Knowledge. During the nine days of Navratri, feasting and fasting take precedence over all normal daily activities amongst the Hindus. Evenings give rise to the religious dances in order to worhip Goddess Durga Maa.

1st-3rd day of Navratri: On the first day of the Navaratras, a small bed of mud is prepared in the puja room of the house and barley seeds are sown on it. On the tenth day, the shoots are about 3-5 inches in length. After the puja, these seedlings are pulled out and given to devotees as a blessing from god.

These initial days are dedicated to Durga Maa, the Goddess of power and energy. Her various manifestations, Kumari, Parvati and Kali are all worshipped during these days. They represent the three different classes of womanhood that include the child, the young girl and the mature woman.

4th-6th day of Navratri: During these days, Lakshmi Maa, the Goddess of peace and prosperity is worshipped. On the fifth day which is known as Lalita Panchami, it is traditional, to gather and display all literature available in the house, light a lamp or 'diya' to invoke Saraswati Maa, the Goddess of knowledge and art.

7th-8th day of Navratri: These final days belong to Saraswati Maa who is worshipped to acquire the spiritual knowledge. This in turn will free us from all earthly bondage. But on the 8th day of this colourful festival, yagna (holy fire) is performed. Ghee (clarified butter), kheer (rice pudding) and sesame seeds form the holy offering to Goddess Durga Maa.

Mahanavmi: The festival of Navratri culminates in Mahanavami. On this day Kanya Puja is performed. Nine young girls representing the nine forms of Goddess Durga are worshiped. Their feet are washed as a mark of respect for the Goddess and then they are offered new clothes as gifts by the worshiper. This ritual is performed in most parts of the country.

Mahalaya: People offering 'tarpan' in memory of their deceased forefathers. Mahalaya ushers in the aura of Durga Puja. The countdown for the Durga Puja begins much earlier, from the day of 'Janmastami'. It is only from the day of Mahalaya that the preparations for the Durga Puja reaches the final stage. The midnight chants of various hymns of 'Mahishasura Mardini' reminds one of the beginning of Durga Puja.

Mahalaya is an auspicious occasion observed seven days before the Durga Puja, and heralds the advent of Durga, the goddess of supreme power. It's a kind of invocation or invitation to the mother goddess to descend on earth-"Jago Tumi Jago". This is done through the chanting of mantras and singing devotional songs.

The day of Mahalaya is also the day of remembrance. On this day, people offer 'tarpan' in memory of their deceased forefathers. The banks of River Ganga becomes a sea of humanity. Priests are seen busy performing 'Tarpan' for devotees in groups. The rituals start from early down and end during the midday. Devotees and worshipers buy clothes and sweets to offer to their forefathers. 'Tarpan' is to be performed in empty stomach. After offering 'tarpan', people eat at the same place.

The festival of Dassehra, also known as Vijayadashmi, is one of the fascinating festivals of India and is celebrated with joy and enthusiasm. According to the great Hindu scripture, the Ramayana, Lord Rama performed chandi-puja (holy prayer). This was carried out in order to invoke the blessings of Durga Maa for the killing of Ravana, the ten-headed demon king of Sri Lanka who had abducted Seeta, wife of Lord Rama.

Durga Maa divulged the secret to Rama on how he could slay the great Ravana. Hence upon vanquishing the demon Ravana, Lord Rama with Sita and younger brother Laxmana, returned victorious to his kingdom of Ayodhya on the day which is called 'Diwali'. Revelers across northern India re-enact the legend at sundown in a performance called the Ramlila, featuring actors dressed as Rama shooting flaming arrows at effigies stuffed with firecrackers.

Dassera day is considered a most auspicious day. It is a time-honored belief that if any new venture is started on this day, it is bound to be successful. Hence, all the undertakings be it laying-in of foundation of a new building, opening of a new commercial establishment or even initiating a child into the world of learning-are started on this day. Also on this day implements of agriculture, manufacturer's machines, the intellectuals pens, the household articles, the children's school books are placed before the idol of Durga and worshiped.

The Beautiful Bengali Decoration Surrounding the Majestic Warrior: Sati, the consort of Shiva was the daughter of Daksha Prajaapati a descendant of Bhrama. Sati had married Shiva against the wishes of her father. Daksha was sponsoring a sacrifice and attendees came from various parts of the universe. He invited all of the gods and goddesses except his son in law Shiva. Against Shiva's wishes, Sati attended this sacrifice and was insulted by her father. Unable to bear this insult, Sati immolated herself.

Enraged at the insult and the injury, Shiva destroyed Daksha's sacrifice, cut off Daksha's head and when pleaded by other gods, replaced it with that of a goat and restored him to life. Still berserk with grief, he picked up the remains of Sati's body, and danced the dance of destruction throughout the Universe. The other gods intervened to stop this dance, and the disk of Vishnu cut through the corpse of Sati, whose various parts of the body fell at several spots all through the Indian subcontinent and formed the sites of what are known as Shakti Peethas today.

Shiva was finally pacified when the last piece fell off from his shoulder. Narayana revived sati as Uma for a new life. Ever since peace was restored, Uma, with her children, Ganesh and Kartick, and with her two 'sakhis'-Jaya and Bijaya, comes to visit her parent's home each year during the season of 'Sharat' or autumn when Durga Puja is celebrated.

The worship of Devi Durga in the month of Ashwin is called 'Akalbodhan'-an uncustomary time for commencement of the worship. It is so called since the period of this worship differs from the conventional period (during the spring-'Basanta'). Ramayana says that when Rama was engaged in the fierce battle with Ravana, he wanted to secure the blessings of victory from Devi Durga. He held the puja to evoke the goddess during autumn to his dire plight, thereby worshiping Durga untimely (in Akal). Hence this puja is called Akalbodhon.

It was customary to worship Durga with 100 neel kamals (blue lotuses). Rama could gather only 99 of them; he offered one of his eyes as a substitute of the 100th lotus. Pleased with his devotion Durga blessed him. The battle started on Shaptami and Ravana was killed at the Shandhikshan (in between) Ashtami and Navami; he was cremated on Dashami. Therefore the four days of the puja that we celebrate ends in the triumph of the good over evil.

Region: West Bengal, Bihar, Uttar Pradesh, Delhi & Madhya Pradesh : During Durga puja or Durga Puja (commonly called in West Bengal), the idols of Goddess Durga are worshipped for nine days in beautifully decorated 'pandaals'. It is a public festival. On the tenth day, the 'Visarjan' or immersion of idols in sea waters is performed. During this time, in various parts of India, the 'Ram-Leela' is performed. Ram-Leela is a stage inaction of Ramayana, the story of Lord Rama. Durga puja has come to be associated with a grand exhibition of cultural functions.

In towns and villages, the evenings are replete with jatra, theatre, song, music, dance programmes, sports, physical and cultural competitions etc which everyone is free to attend. Community feasts are held. The immersion ceremony (vijaya), provides an impressive finale.

Region: Gujarat, Punjab and Maharashtra: Navratri is a festival of worship, dance and music celebrated over a period of nine nights. Devotees perform the 'devi-sthaapna' in their homes wherein they invite the Goddess and perform 'pooja-path' for nine days. Gujaratis perform their traditional dances 'Garba' & 'Dandiya-Raas' during Navratri. The women-folk dance in a circle, singing 'Garbas' or traditional songs.

'Dandiya-Raas' is played with wooden sticks or 'dandiyas'. Apart from Gujrat, Garbas are performed in other states & cities like Mumbai. Young men-women wear colourful traditional dresses and play Garba with great enthusiasm.The mood of Navratri is very colourful & unique.

Region: Kullu Valley, Himachal Pradesh : The annual mela or festival takes place in the Kullu Valley-also known as the Valley of the Living Gods, in North India. The festival celebrates the triumph of the God Ram over evil. The Rath Yatra of the idol of Lord Ragunath is led by the Kullu Raja and village deities, and is known as the running of the Gods. The procession starts a week of religious ceremonies, cultural activities, socializing and shopping at the huge bazaar, or market, that comprises most of the mela ground.

Dusshera at Kullu: commences on the tenth day of the rising moon, *i.e.* on 'Vijay Dashmi' day itself and continues in seven days. The birth of Dusshera in Kullu lay in royal fads and it nourished on religious, social and economic factors and ultimately came to be well established, because of the inborn love of the hill-men for fun, frolic, displayed in community singing and dancing. Numerous stalls offer a verity of local wares. This is also the time when the International Folk Festival is celebrated.

Region: Mysore, Karnataka: In Mysore, Dusshera is easily the most popular festival. It is celebrated on a grandiose scale here. Elephants are decked up with robes and jewelery and taken in processions through the streets of the city. In fact, many people visit Mysore from all over the country to watch this colorful event. There is also a floating festival in the temple tank at the foot of Chamundi Hill and a procession of chariots around the temple at the top.

The Dusshera of Mysore or Mysore Dassara as it is famously called is a 10-day long festival. On the day of Dussehra, a procession of caparisoned elephants carrying the idol of goddess Chamundi is taken through the city. The festival is celebrated in a grand style with scores of cultural performances in the great Durbar Hall of the Maharaja's Palace. On Vijaydashami, the 10th day of the festival, a colorful procession featuring caparisoned elephants winding through the gaily-decorated streets of the city, mark the occasion.

Region: Tamil Nadu, Karnataka and Andhra Pradesh: Bommai Kolu is traditionally a women's festival that Tamilians celebrate during Dusshera. Every year, a series of steps is set up and kolu bommai or dolls are displayed. These dolls typically depict gods or village scenes and weddings. A kolu can be as simple or as elaborate as one likes. The woman of the house invites other women to come inspect the kolu, eat a few snacks, exchange a little gossip and go home with a couple of small goodies.

During this time, the girls and women make rounds from house to house during those nine days of Navrathri. Sundal is a delicious confection made from bean sprouts and coconut that is traditionally served at kolu. Women set up decorated planks in a corner and place on it all the dolls in the house. This beautiful clay figurines of gods and goddesses are worshipped during Navaratri, viewing art as Divinity. Women traditionally exchange gifts of coconuts, clothes and sweets.

The ninth day is also the day of the Ayudha Puja. After the slaying of Mahisasura and other demons by Chamundeswari, there was no more use for her weapons. So the weapons were kept aside and worshipped. This Ayudha puja is being celebrated since ancient times. The importance of Ayudha Puja on this occasion may also be due to the fact that on the Vijayadasami day, Arjuna took back his weapons which he had hidden in a Vani tree in order to lead a life in disguise for the promised period of exile. It is believed that one who begins or renovates his learning to work on the Vijayadasami day will secure a grand success as Arjuna did in Kurukshetra war.

The Ayudha Puja is a worship of whatever implements one may use in one's livelihood. On the preceding evening, it is traditional to place these implements on an altar to the Divine. If one can make a conscious effort to see the divine in the tools and objects one uses each day, it will help one to see one's work as an offering to God. It will also help one to maintain constant remembrance of the divine. In India it is customary for one to prostrate before the tools one will use before starting one's work each day; this is an expression of gratitude to God for helping one to fulfil one's duties.

The tenth day or Vijayadasami is also the day of Vidyaramba or beginning of study when children usually begin to learn the alphabets. On the Vijayadasami day after a Puja in the morning, the Books and implements are removed from the room and this ceremony is called 'Puja Eduppu'. The time for the break up of the puja marks the beginning of learning and work. Learning and work commence at this auspicious moment.

Literates, in general write the alphabets on sand and read a few sentences from sacred books. Similarly the craftsmen and other skilled workers do some work using their implements. At this auspicious moment the children for the first time are given instructions to write the first few alphabets on rice or sand. They are thus initiated into the world of knowledge. This is called 'Ezhuthinu Iruthu' and according to custom only after this ceremony child becomes entitled to write or read.

The Goddess Saraswathi is worshipped as the Goddess of Learning, the deity of Gayathri, the fountain of fine arts and science, and the symbol of supreme vedantic knowledge. On the Durgashtami day, a ceremony called Poojavaipu is performed in the evening in Kerala. In a village, generally, it is done only in certain households, in temples and also sometimes in the village schools. The Brahmin houses and the houses which enjoy reputation for learning, mainly take the lead in celebrating the festival. The members of other houses in the village attend the ceremony performed in these houses or institutions.

In a well-decorated room, books and grandhas (holy books) are tastefully arranged with a picture or an image of Goddess Saraswathi in front. In certain poaches weapons and implements are kept by the side of books and garandhas. Then a Puja is performed to Saraswathi during which fruits, beaten rice, roasted paddy (malar), jaggery etc, are offered to Her. These offerings are distributed among those present when the Puja is over. Just before the Pujavaipu, all studies and work which mainly require skill, are suspended. The following day is known as Mahanavami and it is totally devoted to the worship of Saraswathi. Pooja is performed both in the morning and in the evening. Many more items such as rice, payasam, thirali, etc are also offered to Devi.

The ten-day Saraswati festival, also known as Dussehra or Navaratri, is held September-October. It's celebrated throughout India but takes on special significance in Kerala. Young children are taken to the temples and, before an image of a goddess-celebrated in Kerala as Saraswati, the goddess of wisdom and learning-they are introduced to the letters of the alphabet.

Region: Maharashtra : In ancient times kings used the feast of Dasara to cross the frontier and fight against their neighboring kingdoms. This border crossing is known as "Simollanghan". Thus Dasara also marks the beginning of the war season.

This was also the day to worship the weapons. According to legend, Pandav went to dwell in the forest. On the way he hid his weapons in the hole of a "shami" tree. After one year he returned from the forest and on Dussehra day he took again his weapons and worshipped the shami tree and the weapons. Hence the custom of worshipping weapons on this feast.

People decorate the entrances of their homes with torans, flower studded strings, and worship the tools of trade, vehicles, machinery, weapons and even books. As the evening falls, the villagers cross the border, and worship the Shami tree. The leaves of the Apta tree are collected and exchanged among friends and relatives as gold.

Durgá's mode of journey to the earth is detailed in scriptures. The modes, an elephant, a horse, palanquin, boat all signify luck or omen which influence the life on earth.Goddess Durga visits the earth for only four days but seven days prior to puja starts the Mahalaya. From this day starts 'Devipaksha' when people pray for their demised relatives and take holy dip in the Ganges. This ritual is known as 'Tarpan'. Puja Rule according to Bengali calender. Days are counted based on sunrise and sunset while 'Tithi' depends on the rising and setting of the moon. Sandhi Puja is performed counting 'Tithi'. Sasthi, Saptami, Nabami and Dashami pujas are performed after sunrise even if they fall in the previous evenings.This year the goddess arrives on a boat and departs on an elephant. Goddess Durga's arrival on a boat signifies good harvest, growth and prosperity while her departure on an elephant indicates greenery and prosperity through out the year. Dates : Festivities commence on the first night in the month of Ashwin (September/ October). Nine nights are spent in worship and the tenth day is devoted to goddess Durga, who occupies a special position in the Hindu pantheon of gods and goddesses.

Durga is Shakti, the cosmic energy that animates all beings. According to a Puranic legend attached to this day, demon Mahishasur vanquished the gods and their king, Indra, who approached the Holy Trinity, Brahma, Vishnu and Shiva. They in turn sought the help of the divine mother Durga who, equipped with lethal weapons, riding a ferocious lion, in all her awesome majesty, killed Mahishasur. This day, thus, also celebrates the magnificence and omnipotence of Goddess Durga. Practice : Durga pooja is celebrated extensively in North India where beautiful idols of the Mother Goddess are worshipped in elaborate pandals for nine days, and on the tenth day, these are carried out in procession for visarjan (immersion) in a river or pond. The face of the goddess remains covered until the bodhon (unveiling) ritual is performed on Sasthi-the sixth day of the moon. It is Sarat, or autumn, and Nature adorns herself to welcome the advent of the Mother Goddess, Durga. Rabindra Sangeet, dances and various programmes form a part of the celebrations.

The Goddess is worshipped as a kumari or young girl, and reveals herself in her true form Mahasaptami (the seventh day of the moon). On Mahastami (eighth day) and Mahanavami (ninth day) the celebrations reach a fever pitch. On Dashami (tenth day) the idol of Durga is immersed in water. The ten-armed goddess dazzles the devotees with her splendour and appearance of fiery valour during her short stay every year. In the older days of zamindars (landed aristocracy) there used to be a Barwari pooja financed by the local zamindar who usually had a huge Nat Mandir or Mandap (out-hall) for pooja purposes, where the entire village congregated. All found employment of some kind-from the Brahmins performing the rites to various artisans of lower castes. Even women had their share of work in the preparations. The time of immersion is a sad occasion and the Devi is repeatedly requested to return to shower bliss on devotees whenever invoked.

The festival sees a boom in pre-pooja sales. All trade and commerce gears up to meet the challenge of coping with the frenetic shopping spree. Whole communities of artisans spend their busiest time to ensure the netting of a sizeable income that will sustain them for several months to come. It is a time of activity and employment for all. Artisans build the mammoth pandal (a pandal constructed in 1994 as a replica of the Belur Math, was almost 90 ft high, required 3500 bamboo poles, 5000 planks of wood and over 2000 metres of cloth and cost Rs 5 lakh.). Weavers are kept busy, as are the craftsmen who model the exquisitely chiseled features and limbs of each figure in the pooja tableau from clay; electricians who ingeniously devise the decorative illuminations (everything of topical interest from the dinosaurs of Jurassic Park to World Cup football, to nuclear testing is portrayed); the dhaakis whose unsurpassed virtuosity finds expression in frenzied pounding on huge barrel-shaped drums, invoking an almost hypnotic rapture. Everybody is involved, and there is profit and fun for all.It is a time of prosperity also for publishing houses-the pooja Editions capitalize on the festive mood of the reading public. From big established dailies to little magazines, all thrive this season.

There is also a big demand for audiocassettes, which are Pooja Hits. Today pooja pandals seem to sprout like mushrooms-practically one every 100 yards. Apart from loudspeakers blaring forth pop and Hindi film music and other forms of entertainment (there are also cultural programmes), there is a fierce competition among organisers to compete with and outdo each other in the extravagant and lavish show they put up. Pooja committees are known to spend in lakhs on attractive pandal decor. Galaxies of twinkling lights make Technicolor pageants out of the dingiest lanes.

The para poojas become grander still each year, as the poojas are an occasion people look forward to. Money is not a constraint, as people donate generously. Poojas are a convenient occasion for fun-loving denizens to forget their cares and let their hair down. Multitudes throng the streets-people from all communities are agog-shopping, gorging themselves or gazing on Durga who is a shimmering vision-power personified-tresses streaming, a flickering tongue of flame. Durga Pooja is celebrated with more fervour by Bengalis than any other community in India. With the Bengali, Bijoya evokes sentiment. It is a time of renewal of ties of kinship with friends and relatives. Thus Kolakuli echoes the Id embrace among Muslims. Durga Pooja is a festival Bengalis celebrate without religious inhibition. The nine days of pooja are synonymous with the Navratras and the tenth day is celebrated as Vijayadashmi in some parts of India.

Rituals: Durga pooja is celebrated extensively in North India where beautiful idols of the Mother Goddess are worshipped in elaborate pandals for nine days, and on the tenth day, these are carried out in procession for visarjan (immersion) in a river or pond. The face of the goddess remains covered until the bodhon (unveiling) ritual is performed on Sasthi-the sixth day of the moon.

The Goddess is worshipped as a kumari or young girl, and reveals herself in her true form Mahasaptami (the seventh day of the moon). On Mahastami (eighth day) and Mahanavami (ninth day) the celebrations reach a fever pitch. On Dashami (tenth day) the idol of Durga is immersed in water. The ten-armed goddess dazzles the devotees with her splendour and appearance of fiery valour during her short stay every year.

It is the time of the Durga Puja, celebrating the ten-armed goddess of fertility and the third embodiment of the Devi, Durga. It was Durga who vanquished the buffalo-demon Mahishasura. The festivities start with the first day called Mahalaya. It is also the day of the beginning of the countdown to the Durga Puja, which is celebrated in most households apart from the gaily-decorated puja mandaps that are erected in almost every locality. It is a common belief that Ma Lakshmi brings peace and prosperity to the households that celebrate the puja.

Goddess Durga is called by various names on each day of the Navaratri festival:

Day 1: Shaila Putri

Day 2: Brahmacharini

Day 3: Chandraghanta

Day 4: Kooshmanda

Day 5: Scandamaata

Day 6: Kaatyayini

Day 7: Kaalaraatri

Day 8: Mahagowri

Day 9: Siddhidaatri

She is worshipped on all the days with special pooja. The fifth day, Lalithapanchami is considered a very auspicious day.

On this day, Sharada pooja is done, where everyone worships his or her books and anything connected to learning. On Durgashtami, Durga Havana is performed, and on Mahanavami, Ayudha Pooja is performed. On this day, people worship their respective tools of work, and their vehicles too.

It is believed that if Goddess Durga is worshipped during Navaratri with devotion and dedication, the devotee will be bestowed with Her blessings, which will bring about prosperity in all that he/she does.

The various kinds of Poojas conducted during Navaratri are:

- Sharada Pooja
- Pustaka Pooja
- Lalitapanchami Vrata
- Durga Pooja
- Durgadeeta Namaskara
- Chandika Parayana
- Navadurga Poojane
- Durga Havana
- Chandika Havana
- Laxminarayana Hradaya Parayana
- Kumkumarchane
- Ayudha Pooja
- Yantra Vaahana Pooja

The story of the creation of this goddess is also very interesting. The gods in heaven decided to create an all-powerful being to kill the demon king Mahishasur who was ready to attack them. At that very moment a stream of lightning dazzled forth from the mouths of Brahma, Vishnu and Mahesh and it turned into a beautiful, magnificent woman with ten hands. Then all the gods furnished her with their special weapons. Those weapons and armour are very artistically carved in the ancient sculptures of this goddess in Java. The image of Durga, the Eternal Mother destroying the demon, Mahishasur on Chamundi Hills near Mysore is symbolic of the final confrontation of the spiritual urge of man with his baser passions. This goddess Durga as Lord Shiva's Consort represents two forms of female energy-one mild and protective and the other fierce and destructive. Dassera festival is also known as Durgotsav and during the ten days, the many splendoured goddess Durga is worshipped in one of her many forms differently in different regions.

With religious rituals and chantings of mantras followed by "KATHA" or story-telling told by Pandits who by reading passages from religious texts awaken religious fervour in the minds of the listeners. In Bengal and the neighbouring states of Assam and Orissa Durga devi is worshipped by name of Kali as a symbol of Shakti before whom animal sacrifices were made. Her dance of conquest is famous in our ancient texts. As per the orthodox Hindu conceptions, the personality of one deity cannot be entirely separated from that of another. As such in some regions all the three principal goddesses-Durga, Lakshmi and Saraswati are worshipped during this festival, each for 3 days of the Navaratri.

As per our great epic Mahabharat, Pandavas after wandering in the forest for 12 years, hung their weapons on a Shami tree before entering the court of king Virat to spend the last one year in disguise. After the completion of that year on Vijayadashmi the day of Dassera they brought down the weapons from the Shami tree and declared their true identity. Since that day the exchange of Shami leaves on Dassera day became symbols of good, will and victory.

The founder of the Hindu Swarajya Chatrapati Shivaji before any military expedition always invoked the blessings of Durga in the form of his goddess Bhawani. The Sikh guru Gobind Singh introduced the worship of Durga into his cult of the sword. This festival has immense mythological significance. As per Ramayan, Ram did "chandi-puja and invoked the blessings of Durga to kill Ravana, the ten-headed king of Lanka who had abducted Seeta and had charmed life. Durga divulged the secret to Ram how he could kill Ravana. Then after vanquishing him, Ram with Seeta and Laxman returned victorious to his kingdom of Ayodhya on Dassera day. Therefore, the festival of Durgotsava and Dassera is celebrated more in honour of Prabhu Ramchandra than Durgadevi in many regions of India and recitations from Ramayan and dances and dramas depicting the exploits of Ram assume great importance.

These Ramlila shows are very popular in Uttar Pradesh, Madhya Pradesh and to an extent in Maharashtra and effigies of king Ravana, his brother, Kumbhakarna and his son, Meghnath are burnt. During the pre-British period, the powerful Hindu rulers used to celebrate Dassera in right royal fashion and start military expeditions on this Dassera day against their enemies or recalcitrant vassals. With the arrival of the British, Hindu rulers could not indulge in military activities yet Dassera was celebrated with the old pomp and pageant of full military parades of all arms in the capitals of Hindu states when the Rajas and Maharajas personally took the salute, Trumpets blared militant notes, war drums sounded their loudest and soldiers looked martial.

The procession of Dassera taken out in Mysore is always remembered for its grandeur. With independence and the disappearance of princely states these ancient pageants are dying out and Dassera is becoming more democratic than regal. Dassera day is considered a most auspicious day. It is a time-honoured belief that if any new venture is started on this day, it is bound to be successful. Hence, all the undertakings be it laying-in of foundation of a new building, opening of a new commercial establishment or even initiating a child into the world of learning-are started on this day. Also on this day implements of agriculture, manufacturer's machines, the intellectuals pens, the household articles, the children's school books are placed before the idol of Durga and worshipped.

The revolutionaries who followed the "CULT OF THE BOMB" to free their motherland from the slavery of the British imperialism looked up to Durgadevi for success in their mission. Even to-day in free India, Durga's blessings are invoked and Dassera is celebrated all over the country. These celebrations involve inter-Asia visits to temples like Meenakshi at Madras, Kamakshi at Conjivaram, Annapurna at Benares, Mumbadevi and Mahalaxmi at Mumbai and signify the triumph of good, of piety and devotion over all the forces of evil. Following is the recipe for preparing MALPUAS Ingredients: 3 cups of fine wheat flour1 cup fine semolina (Suji) 2 cups grated jaggery (gur)2 Tablespoons ghee 1 Tablespoon peppercorns 2 cups milk1 Lime 1 Tablespoon curd Pinch each of salt and soda. Method: 1. Place the flour & the semolina in a dekchi along with the milk, curds, jaggery and the pinch of salt. 2. Beat at least for 5 to 7 minutes so that the mixture becomes light and fluggy. 3. Pound the peppercorns coarsely & add to the mixture. 4. Heat 2 tablespoons of ghee and pour over the mixture. 5. Mix well, cover the dekchi and let stand for 7/8 hours in a warm place. 6. The mixture would have risen by this time. Stir it well. If it is thick, add a little milk or water to bring it to the pouring consistency. 7. Add and blend in it the pinch of soda and juice lime. 8. Place a deep frying pan with lot of ghee in it, when it is heated lower the fire, gently put in 1 tablespoon of the ready balter into the heated ghee. 9. Fry to a golden brown colour on both sides. 10. While frying splash to make it porous and crisp. 11. Take out with a slotted spoon & place in a strainer so that the extra ghee drips down. 12. Thus fry all the Malpuas. They can be stored for a week or so.

The worship of Durga in the autumn (*Shôrot*) is the year's most major festival in Bengal, Orissa, Tripura and other parts of East India as well as in Bangladesh. *Puja* means "worship," and Durga's Puja is celebrated from the sixth to tenth day of the waxing moon in the month of *Ashshin*, which is the sixth month in the Bengali calendar. Occasionally however, due to shifts in the lunar cycle relative to the solar months, it may also be held in the following month, *Kartik*. In the Gregorian calendar, these dates correspond to the months of September/ October.

In the Krittibas Ramayana, Rama invokes the goddess Durga in his battle against Ravana. Although she was traditionally worshipped in the spring, due to contingencies of battle, Rama had to invoke her in the autumn (akaal bodhan). Today it is this Rama's date for the puja that has gained ascendancy, although the spring puja, known as Basanti Puja, is also present in the Hindu almanac. Since the season of the puja is *Shôrot* (autumn), it is also known as *Sharodia*.

The pujas are held over a five-day period, which is traditionally viewed as the coming of the married daughter, Durga, to her father, Himalaya's home. It is the most important festival in Bengal, and Bengalis celebrate with new clothes and other gifts, which are worn on the evenings when the family goes out to see the *pandals* (temporary structures set up to venerate the goddess). Although it is a Hindu festival, many religious groups participate in the ritual. In Kolkata alone more than a thousand *pandals* are set up, all clamouring for the fickle attention of the populace. Across the world, Durga Puja serves as a community gathering and a connection to roots for the widespread Bengali diaspora. Tokyo has nearly ten Pujas, and North America has several hundred. Bangladesh, with its 10% Hindu population celebrate the puja in many temples, with more than 100 pujas taking place in the capital Dhaka alone.

History: A considerable literature exists around Durga in the Bengali language and its early forms, including *Durgotsavnirnaya* (11th century), *Durgabhaktitarangini* by Vidyapati (14th century), etc. Durga Puja was popular in Bengal in the medieval period, and records exist of it being held in the courts of Rajshahi (16th century) and Nadia (18th century). It was during the 18th century, however, that the worship of Durga became popular among the landed elite of Bengal. Prominent Pujas were conducted by the banyans enriched by British rule, including Nabakrishna Deb, translator for Robert Clive, who initiated an elaborate Puja at his Shobhabazar residence. Today, the culture of Durga Puja has shifted from the princely houses to *Sarvojonin* (literally, "involving all") forms.

Durga puja mood starts off with the Mahalaya. Bengalis traditionally wake up at 4:00 AM in the morning listening to the enchanting voice of Birendra Kishore Bhadra on All India Radio.

During the week of Durga Puja, in the entire state of West Bengal as well as in large enclaves of Bengalis everywhere, life comes to a complete standstill. In play grounds, traffic circles, ponds—wherever space may be available—elaborates structures called *pandals* are set up, many with nearly a year's worth of planning behind them. The word *pandal* means a temporary structure, made of bamboo and cloth, which used to be the venue of the worship of the goddess.

Durga Puja Pandal in Kolkata: Somewhere inside these complex edifices is a stage on which Durga reigns, standing on her lion mount, wielding ten weapons with her ten hands. This is the religious center of the festivities, and the crowds gather to offer flower worship on the mornings, of the sixth to ninth days of the waxing moon fortnight. Ritual drummers, carrying large leather-strung *dhaaks* show off their skills during ritual dance worships called *aarati*. On the tenth day, Durga the mother returns to her husband, Shiva, ritualized through her immersion into the waters.

Today's Puja, however, goes far beyond religion. In fact, visiting the *pandals* recent years, one can only say that Durgapuja the largest outdoor art festival on earth. In the 1990s, a preponderance of architectural models came up on the *pandal* exteriors, but today the art motif extends to elaborate interiors, executed by trained artists, with consistent stylistic elements, carefully executed and bearing the name of the artist.

The sculpture of the idol itself has evolved. The worship always depicts Durga with her four children, and occasionally two attendant deities and some banana-tree figures. In the olden days, all five idols would be depicted in a single frame, traditionally called *pata*. Since the 1980s however, the trend is to depict each idol separately.

At the end of six days, the idol is taken for immersion in a procession amid loud chants and drumbeats to the river or other water body, and it is cast in the waters symbolic of the departure of the deity to her home with her husband in the Himalayas. After this, in a tradition called *Vijaya Dashami*, families visit each other and sweetmeats are offered to visitors (*Dashami* is literally "tenth day" and *Vijay* is "victory").

Kerala: In Kerala, Durga Puja signifies the beginning of formal education for every child aged 3-5 years. While puja goes on in the temple for all ten days, it is only the concluding three days which are really important. Ashtami is the day of Ayudya Puja, when all the tools at home are worshiped. Custom dictates that no tools be used on this day. On navami, day, Goddess Saraswati is honored by worshiping the books and records at home.Thousands throng the Saraswati temple at Kottayam during this period to take a dip in the mysterious holy pond whose source is yet unknown. Large gatherings are also seen at the famous temples at Thekkegram (Palghat), in which there are no idols— only huge mirrors. A devotee finds himself bowing before his own reflection which indicates that God is within us.

Kashmir: Hindus are a minority in Jammu and Kashmir but they celebrate their festivals with pomp and show. These days, festivities are subdued, though. The favourite deities of Kashmir are Lord Shiva and Serawali Ma Durga, the one who rides the tiger. Pundits and Muslims alike vouch that Navratri is important. No big pandals here, each Hindi house-hold does the pooja at home. All the adult members of the household fast on water. In the evenings, fruit may be taken. As elsewhere, Kashmiris grow barley in earthen pots. They believe that if the growth in this pot is good, there is prosperity all year. The most important ritual for Kashmiri Pandits is to visit the temple of guardian goddess Kheer Bhawani on all nine days. On the last day of Navratri, an aarti is held at the temple after which people break their fast. On Dussehra day, Ravana's effigy is burnt.

Durga Pooja has some fond memories related to childhood. Initial ones are those of my native place. Later, we were not so frequent in visiting the village during Durga Pooja and it had not remained that interesting either. But at one point of time, it was almost a custom in our family that almost everyone would gather in our village during this time. Needless to say the place looked really cheerful then. Even the married daughters of the families would not stay at their in-laws place during Durga Pooja. They will come there with their children and stay here, most of the times accompanied by their husbands too all along. And it was not the case with just our family, but almost all the families in the locality. The Pooja of our village was quite famous in the villages nearby. We were usually the ones to reach the last, since my father's job would not give him break before *saptami* or *ashtami*, unlike the jobs of many of our relatives.

And usually, this was the only time in the year when I would visit the village. So, to me, the picture of always elucidates the picture of a place filled with people. I woud not glamourize it and be honest, being the shy and introvert person I was as child, the experience was not usually a very interesting one for me. But today, sitting here in the hostel, wondering what to do with this occasion called Durga Pooja, I can not help but feel nostalgic about those days, which probably will never come back. People have scattered all around, the aspirations of lives have changed (not that I bemoan it!) and things won't even be the same again.

There was this tradition (familiar to people almost all over India) of inviting young girls to eat. The feast is called "Kumari Bhoj" (Feast for virgin girls). Now, unfortunately for me, most of the families would have this feast for all the 10 days of Puja. Since, I would always reach late, I was not in the regular list of people :(. Sometimes, when people increased the number on *Ashtami* or *navami*, I may also end up getting an invitation. At other times, it would be out of sheer consideration and formality-"Oh! So Jaya has also come. Bring her along." Being the person I am, loss of the opportunity to eat was not really a loss (was more a relief, given the choosy nature I had with respect to what I did and did not eat), but when on *Dashami*, all my cousin sisters would return with the money and sometimes clothes they get after *Kumari Bhoj*, I did not used to feel a pang of envy. Not that I ever said anything.

Dahsami was a good day even for me. All the elders of the family (those who are earning) would give all the kids money for visiting the fair. And here, there even a late-comer like me was not at a disadvantage. In fact, this town-bred, shy, out-of-place girl was often at an advantage because she won't pressurize anyone. So, people used to get more generous at times, I would receive some amount secretly too. (Blame me for not being ethical) Especially from *kakka* (tau jee-dad's elder brother). The system was such that older children will get more money. There would usually be groups according to the age. And those on the border would try their best to get counted in the upper group so that they will be eligible for a higher amount!

Even before *Dashami*, we would go to the *Durga Sthan* (the temple of Goddess Durga) daily. Now, most of the things at the place and in the fair was hardly of any interest to me. My cousin sisters would go mad after the posters, song-books etc. I would usually end up spending very little, except on some the story books that were available. The normal ice cream that was available was not something I felt like eating (I had no qwality walls-upbringing then, but even for my small-town-taste, it was not up to the mark). However, there was a higher priced curd ice cream, which tasted quite well. I would usually have that.

The village used to be a very quiet and safe place then. There would be these drama shows (done by the people of the village themselves) all night and everyone including women (even the newly wed daughter-in-laws, who would usually be under strict *parda*) and kids would go there. No need of the group of women being escorted by men.

Then there was *Nisha Pooja*. This would involve an offering of all 56 *vyanjans* (dishes) at the *Durga Sthan* and would go on for all night. Almost all the adults and the kids who could manage it, would be there in the temple for the whole night.

Even at our home, there used to be celebrate rituals of the worship for the 10 days. The eldest man of the family would preside over the rituals. The second one of the four siblings of my grand-father's generations, was an avid devotee of Durga. We, kids, used to call him *Pooja-Baba* (Pooja= Worship, Baba = Grandfather). In those early days, he wasthe one who would preside over the things. Those ringing of *ghantas* (do not know exactly what is the English name for this instrument) along with the chorus recitation of "*Na mantram, na yantram*" by the whole family is something that would overwhelm even someone who knows nothing about the whole celebration.

Several things have changed since then. The village was not as safe a place afterwards. The clash of unemployed-youth-turned-into-trouble-makers of two nearby villages had made things really scary at one point of time. Every other month we would hear of someone or the other getting killed. This appears to have improved over time, however. However, in that period, some charm was lost and lost for ever.

Now, more and more people are town and city bound. Several amongst those who would look at my discomforts in the village with skepticism, have themselves gone out to live in cities like Delhi and Mumbai and now find the lack of electricity in the village such a big trouble. Their kids are faring worse than I did! Again am not bemoaning the changes. Has led to at least some initiatives at personal level in the village to live in a better way. A proper toilet was never considered a necessity in the village in those days.

People can not manage to come every year now. Many have permanently settled outside and find it difficult to leave their homes for extended periods of times. The schools and homeworks and exams of the kids are big deterrents. It's good. The kids will aspire for a yet between life. However, as many people do not gather in my village now. Kids do not clout to be considered in the higher age-group, while getting money to go to the fair. Girls are no as crazy after the posters. The cheap clothes given during the *Kumari Bhoj* are not as attractive. People demand better fashion and aesthetics. Now, the sisters do not buy the clothes of the same pattern on any occasion, which was so common earlier.

It looks like a "band party". Those days people would go barefooted from the home to the temple. I found it very irritating as a child, but my mother would insist that I should not stand out. Last time when I went there, I followed the same practice and went out without a pair of slippers. Only to realize that everyone else was wearing it. A cousin sister took pity on my burning foot and offered me her slippers. Despite my protest she got me to wear it.

Several things have changed for better, yet several things still lag behind. And several things have changed for wors simplicity of the life is lost. I would not want the world to be exactly as it was then, still I do feel nostalgic about certain things.

The main temples of mother goddess that are visited by multitude of devotees during Navratri are the *shaktipithas*. One belief is that Lord Vishnu had to cut the body of Sati into fifty-two pieces to stop the destruction by Shiva who was perturbed by her death. The main temples are therefore where these pieces of her body were believed to have fallen. The nine nights are dedicated to the three main goddesses of Hinduism-Parvati, Lakshmi and Sarasvati.

The first three nights are dedicated to the goddess of action and energy. Her different manifestations Kumari, Parvati and Kali are worshipped during these days. They represent the three natures/ stages of womanhood-the innocent virgin young girl, caring wife/ mother and the angry old woman. Lakshmi is worshipped for the next three days in her various aspects as the goddesses of peace, plenty, fulfillment and bliss. Saraswati, the goddess of knowledge is worshipped during the final three days of the Navratri.

In various parts of India, the 'Ram-Leela' is performed during Navratri. Ram-Leela is a stage enaction of the *Ramayana,* the mythological book on Lord Rama. The day after Navratri, *i.e.* 'Dassera' (tenth day) or 'Vijayadashmi' is observed. It is believed that on this day, Lord Rama had killed the demon Ravana. So, on Vijayadashmi, effigies of Ravana are burnt all over India. It marks the victory of good over evil.

As the case with most festivals today, lots has been added and changed. It has also been seriously commercialised. So today it is a festival of religious, devotional, cultural and recreational activities. People enjoy this period's festivities by dancing them away to the blare of loud music and scant attention is given to the spiritual aspect of the festival. The Hindus of Gujarat perform their traditional dances 'Garba' & 'Dandiya-Raas' during Navratri. The women-folk, dresses in traditional clothing, dance in a circle, singing 'Garbas' (traditional songs and dance). 'Dandiya-Raas' (rhythmic dance with sticks) is played with 'dandiyas' (wooden sticks). Beautifully decorated 'mandaps' (stages) are set up for playing garba & dandiya and the mood is quite colourful.

In West Bengal, Navratri is celebrated as 'Durga-pooja' which is the most important festival in that part of India. Celebrations of Durga-pooja in Bengal are similar to celebration of Ganesh Chaturthi in Maharashtra. Idols of Goddess Durga are worshipped for nine days in beautifully decorated 'pandaals'. It is a public festival. On the tenth day, the 'Visarjan' or immersion of idols in the sea is performed.

This festival is a great holiday of the year, shared by Christians, Muslims and Hindus alike. It is connected with the autumnal equinox. Nominally, they commemorate the victory of Goddess Durga, wife of Lord Shiva over a buffalo headed demon (Mahisasur). The form under which she is adored is that of an image with ten arms and a weapon in each hand, her right leg resting on a lion and her left on the buffalo demon. This image is worshipped for nine days following on the sixteen sraddhas of the Pitri Paksh and then cast into the water.

According to Chandi Purana, Mahisasur, the buffalo headed demon, by his austere meditation compelled Brahma to grant him the boon of invincibility. Brahma announced that the demon would die at the hands of a woman. Deeming this an impossibility, Mahisasur terrorized earth and heaven. Vishnu and Shiva were enraged. Goddess Durga was created to massacre Mahisasur. On the advice of Brahma, Rama of Ayodhya, undertook an elaborate and dedicated worship of devi Goddess Durga. At the climax of the pooja, one out of 108 lotus flowers for pooja, was found missing. Rama offered to pluck out his eye to make up the missing flower. The goddess appeared and granted him victory over demon king Ravana. The victory day is thus celebrated as Dussehara and as Goddess Durga pooja, both festivals on the same day (Vijaya Dashmi). This festival creates a conviction that evil has been vanquished and a benevolent deity Trinayani Goddess Durga (Three eyed Goddess Durga) smiles upon the world. In this dew fresh season, the human soul bursts into celebrations.

Goddess Durga pooja or Nava Ratra (nine nights), commencing on the 1st and ending on the 10th day of the light half of Ashwin (September-October) are celebrated in various parts of India, specially Bengal. In Assam, the great festivity to invoke the blessings of Goddess Durga, the Mother goddess in her most benign and protective aspects, is celebrated with great I ceremony. Illumination, beautifully painted clay images of the deity, dances and plays, keep thousands entertained over the pooja holidays, until, the images are taken iri procession and immersed in the great river. ~ In Tripura, at Agartala, this festival of the mother goddess Goddess Durga in her benign and protective form, it celebrated as in Bengal. It is celebrated for four days with great enthusiasm and ends when images of the goddess are taken out in procession and immersed in the river.

In Imphal, this festival is known as Kwak Yatra when goddess Goddess Durga is propitiated with pomp and ceremony. Animal sacrifice used to be an obligatory requirement of Goddess Durga pooja (worship of warrior goddess Goddess Durga). This practice is now defunct all over India. At the poojas, now, symbolic slashing of pumpkins and sugarcane, is done. Formally pooja begins with the dawn recitation from the Chandi Puran on Mahalaya. The creation of Mahisasurmardine in these days is broadcast resoundingly over AIR and Doordarshan at 5 a.m. on shasti, the next day the goddess is invoked in bodhan ceremony. From saptami onwards, for three days, fasting worshippers offer pushpanjali.

On dashami, it all ends with the aforementioned sindoor khela and baran or aarti of the devi. Then, in a crescendo of shouting and dancing, the image is carried by bullock carts or trucks to the nearest river or pond and immersed. The worshippers return to the pooja pandal for shantijal, without which no religious ceremony is complete. Cultural activities during Goddess Durga pooja consist of Jatras, plays, songs and variety programmes to cater to needs of the modern public.

Night entertainments are norm. Show of films and videos on the occasion, has beeb discarded. The common people, in great distress have inevitable been drawn towards the source of life and enei the universal mother, Shakti Durga, who had delivered earth from Mahisasur, is worshipped increasingly to insp courage for the struggle against forces of evil. Devi Durga appears once in a year, to share her force and hearten her devotees to endure another year, till she descends from Kailash again.

During winter the popular Dusshera festival is celebrated. It lasts for ten days.

Like everybody else, Indians love celebrations and festivals. Most of the festivals in India are linked to the agricultural calendar. Many are actually harvest festivals or those signifying a change in the season. Each region has its own local festivals, besides the all India ones. One important festival celebrated all over India is Dasara or Dusshera. It is also called Navaratri or nine-nights festival.

The origin of this festival is not clearly known, but it would appear its roots reach back to staggeringly ancient times. It is essentially a mother goddess celebration.Traces of this festival are seen all the world over although they may be hidden under some other layers. Essentially it is a sort of thanksgiving to Nature in various forms.

The colour of Rajas is red, represented by that aspect of mother Durga we worship as goddess Lakshmi. She wears red. Rajas is of the nature of activity, passion and ambition, the source of thirst for physical enjoyment. Rajas binds fast one by attachment to action. (Gita Ch.14. Verse 7.)

The Rajasic person runs after power, position, name, fame and comforts, and involves himself in endless activities to acquire material wealth.

When we worship goddess Lakshmi for spiritual wealth, she bestows on her devotees the inexhaustible divine wealth or Daivi Sampat (which is described in the Gita, Ch.16, Verses 1,2. and 3). Divine wealth or the wealth of 26 divine qualities, brings with it material prosperity as well.

Tamas is black, represented by that aspect of mother Durga we worship as goddess Kali. She is sometimes depicted in dark blue.

Tamas is born of ignorance, deluding all embodied beings.

Tamas binds fast in heedlessness, sleep, indolence, laziness (Gita Ch.14 Verse 8). Tamas is that binding force with a tendency to lethargy (lack of energy, vitality), sloth and foolish actions. It causes non-discrimination or delusion. It binds one who associates the Self with the body. A tamasic person acts under the compulsion of the body. He has no power of judgment. His actions are not guided by reasons. His senses are dull.

These are all baser animal qualities, the lower diabolical nature in man.We pray to mother Kali, as Durga the terrible, as supreme power and force, to destroy all our impurities, our vices, our defects. She is to fight and annihilate these demons. This is the 'strength' aspect of shakti as mentioned in the Upanishad. Mother Kali is the power that guides and protects the devotee's spiritual practice from its many dangers and pitfalls. Mother Kali represents the ferocious and destructive aspect of TIME.

In contrast with creative force in nature, this power is ever active disintegrating forms and structures. It drives heavenly bodies back into their nebulous state.

In the Kenopanishad, part three, (Yaksha Prashna), 12th Mantra, the Divine Mother is described as a woman wondrously fair, daughter of the snowy mountain Himavat, her name Hemavati or Uma.

She is the energy aspect of the Lord. Her other name is Durga. This cosmic energy or shakti is the omnipotent power of the Lord. We call her Durga, the Divine Mother.

Lower states of ignorance and egoism are typified by or personified as demons with such names as Dhumralochan, Chanda and Munda, which should be destroyed by the sudden burst of energy and rough handling.

Dumralochan (the smoky-eyed, a person whose understanding is clouded by ignorance) stands for the grosser state of ignorance and egoism. Munda means the low. Munda is the low profile of our egoism. Chanda means fierce. Chanda is the more horrible and fierce side of it. Shumbha and Nishumbha signify more enlightened aspects of egoism. Shumbh means to shine.

Mahishasur stands for ignorance and stubborn egoism. Raktabij represents the more subtle states of desire which multiply endlessly to create more problems.

The following are the regular features of this festival:

A special ritualistic worship of the Mother Durga; this includes the recitation of Durga Saptashati or Devi Mahatmaya.

Recitation of Lalaitha Sahasrnama or Durga Sahasranama (Laksharchana 100,000 times too repeat the name of the Divine Mother).

Devotees are exhorted to do the maximum number of Japa of the Navaarna Mantra AIM HREEM KLEEM CHAAMUNDAAYAI VICHHE or the Mantra JAI SHRI DURGA.

Some devotees observe fasting with milk and fruits only on all these nine days or at least three days. Visiting Temples and participating in-group chanting and seeking the blessings of the Divine Mother is the common feature in all these nine days.

Let us celebrate Dasara in the right spirit by making honest efforts to destroy the demon

Ego, the ten headed *i.e.* passion, pride,anger,greed, infatuations, lust, hatred, jealousy, selfishness and crookedness) and radiate peace and love wherever we go, and get the blessings of the Divine Mother.

Three aspects of the eternal smother has been depicted in this Devi Sapta Shloki —The Goddess Lakshmi represents Iccha shakti (wealth) Goddess Saraswati represents Jnana Shakti (knowledge) and Goddess Kali represent Kriya Shakti (strength). All three merge in one form as Durga.

The glory of Durga is described in Markendeya Purana,. It is known as Devi Mahatmyam or Durga Sapta sati (700 Mantras). Allegorical representation of the constant war going on within all of us— between our divine and demonic natures. In the Saptasati legend every dominant passion and vice has its special Demon representative. Shumbha is the embodiment of Lust, Nishumbha is Greed and Mashishasura represents Anger.

We celebrate Victory of Good over the evil. Durga sapta shloki (the seven mantras) is the essence of the Durga Sapta sati (seven hundred mantras). It is very powerful to achieve Health, wealth and education...

Diwali

This is perhaps the most well-known of the Indian festivals: it is celebrated throughout India, as well as in Indian communities throughout the diaspora. It usually takes place eighteen days after Dusshera. It is colloquially known as the "festival of lights", for the common practice is to light small oil lamps (called *diyas*) and place them around the home, in courtyards, verandahs, and gardens, as well as on roof-tops and outer walls. In urban areas, especially, candles are substituted for diyas; and among the nouveau riche, neon lights are made to substitute for candles.

The celebration of the festival is invariably accompanied by the exchange of sweets and the explosion of fireworks. As with other Indian festivals, Diwali signifies many different things to people across the country. In north India, Diwali celebrates Rama's homecoming, that is his return to Ayodhya after the defeat of Ravana and his coronation as king; in Gujarat, the festival honors Lakshmi, the goddess of wealth; and in Bengal, it is associated with the goddess Kali. Everywhere, it signifies the renewal of life, and accordingly it is common to wear new clothes on the day of the festival; similarly, it heralds the approach of winter and the beginning of the sowing season.

Diwali (also called Deepavali) is a major Hindu festival. Known as the "Festival of Lights," it symbolises the victory of good over evil, and lamps are lit as a sign of celebration and hope for mankind. Celebrations focus on lights and lamps, particularly traditional diyas (as illustrated). Fireworks are associated with the festival in some regions of the country.

Deepavali is celebrated for five consecutive days in the Hindu month of Ashwayuja. It usually occurs in October/ November, and is one of the most popular and eagerly awaited festivals of India. Hindus, Jains and Sikhs alike regard it as a celebration of life and use the occasion to strengthen family and social relationships. For Jains it is one of the most important festivals, and beginning of the Jain year. It is also a significant festival for the Sikh faith.

Dates in Various Calendars: The date of Diwali is based on the Hindu calendar, which has solar sidereal years and lunar months. Although the festival is worshipped on exactly the same set of days across India, it falls in different months depending on the version of the Hindu calendar being used in the given region.

The *Amanta* ("ending on the no-moon") version of the Hindu Calendar has been adopted as the Indian national calendar. According to this calendar, which is prevalent in southern India and Maharashtra, Deepavali falls in the middle of the month of Ashwayuja. According to the *Purnimanta* ("ending on the full-moon") version prevalent in northern India, the 5-day celebration is spread over the last three days of the month of Ashwayuja and the first two days of the new month of Kartika. According to this calendar, the festival of Deepavali marks the new year's day of this calendar and is therefore an especially significant festival. Diwali is also known as festival of lights. Shown here is the view of Jaipur city on Diwali days.

The festival marks the victory of good over evil. The Sanskrit word Deepavali means array of lights that stands for victory of brightness over darkness. As the knowledge of Sanskrit diminished, the name was popularly modified to Diwali, especially in northern India. On the day of Diwali, many wear new clothes, share sweets and light firecrackers. The North Indian business community usually starts their financial new year on Diwali and new account books are opened on this day.

Hindus find cause to celebrate this festival for different reasons:

- As per sacred texts, according to Skandha Purana, the goddess Shakti observed 21 days of austerity starting from ashtami of shukla paksha (waxing period of moon) to get half part of the body of Lord Shiva. This vrata is known as kedhara vrata. Deepavali is the completion day of this austerity. This is the day Lord Shiva accepted

Shakti into the left half of the form and appeared as Ardhanarishvara. The ardent devotees observe this 21 days vrata by making a kalasha with 21 threads on it and 21 types of offerings for 35 days. The final day is celebrated as kedhara gauri vrata.

- Diwali also celebrates the return of the Lord Rama, King of Ayodhya, his wife Sita and brother Lakshmana to Ayodhya from a war in which he killed the demon king Ravana. It is believed that the people lit oil lamps along the way to light their path in the darkness. In North India, the festival is held on the final day of the Vikram calendar. The following day marks the beginning of the North Indian new year, and is called Annakut.
- It commemorates the killing of Narakasura, an evil demon who created havoc, by Lord Krishna's wife Sathyabhama. This happened in the Dwapara Yuga during this time of Lord Krishna's avatar. In another version, the demon was killed by Lord Krishna himself. In South India, Diwali does not coincide with the beginning of a new year as South Indians follow a different calendar, the Shalivahana calendar.
- In Bhavishyottara and Bramhavaivarta Purana, Diwali is associated with the Daitya king Bali, who is allowed to return to earth once a year.

The Five days of Diwali: Diwali is celebrated over five days in most of North India. All the days except Diwali are named using the designation in the Indian calendar. A lunar half-month is 15 days. Diwali as a new-moon day, marks the last day of a 15-day period. Diwali has emerged as one of the most famous Hindu festivals. An integral part of Diwali decorations, Rangoli is a colorful pattern drawn on the floor.

1. *Dhan-trayodashi* or *Dhan teras*: Dhan means "wealth" and Trayodashi means "13th day". Thus, as the name implies, this day falls on the 13th day of the first half of the lunar month. It is an auspicious day for shopping.
2. *Naraka Chaturdasi*: *Narak* means 'of a new era of Light and Knowledge'. *Chaturdasi* implies fourteenth day.

3. *Diwali*: the actual day of Diwali, is celebrated on the third day of the festival, when the moon completely wanes and total darkness sets in the night sky.
4. *Varsha-pratipada* or *Padwa*: Beginning of the New Year (Kartikadi Vikram). Pratipada means the first.
5. *Bhayiduj* (also Bhayyaduj, Bhaubeej or Bhayitika) — on this day, brothers and sisters meet to express their love and affection for each other.

The celebrations vary in different regions:

- In Southern India, *naraka chaturdashii* is the main day, with firecrackers at dawn.
- The main festival is on *Amavasya* evening with *Lakshmi Puja* which is followed by lighting of oil lamps around the house.

Diwali in Sikhism: Every year, thousands of Sikhs and Hindus celebrate Diwali at the Golden Temple in Amritsar, India. Sikhs also celebrate Diwali to commemorate the laying of the foundation stone for the Golden Temple in 1577. It is also known as Bandi Chhorh Divas. The Mughal emperor Jahangir arrested the Sikh Guru Hargobind and imprisoned him in Gwalior. Later Jehangir relented and released the Guru. The Guru asked that 52 rulers imprisoned with him should also be released. To the joy of the Sikhs the Guru returned to Amritsar on Diwali and it prompted the followers to celebrate the day with joy and happiness.

On Diwali the Sikhs illuminate their Gurdwaras and homesare with Deewé (earthen oil lamps) or candles. Early in the morning, Sikh pilgrims take a dip in the sacred tank while reciting Japji Sahib, and then pray at the Golden Temple. Circumambulation of the tank is done.

Diwali in Jainism: Lord Mahavira, the last of the Jain Tirthankaras, attained Nirvana on this day at Pavapuri. According to Jain tradition the chief disciple of Mahavira, Ganadhar Gautam Swami also attained complete knowledge on this very day, thus making Diwali a really special occasion for the Jains to celebrate.

Diwali is first mentioned in Jain books as the date of the nirvana of Lord Mahavira. The oldest use of the word "Diwali/ Dipavali" occurs in Harivamsha-Purana written by Acharya Jinasena, composed in Shaka Samvat 705. The sample of text containing the word Diwali is below:

The way Jains celebrate Diwali is different in many respects. There is a note of asceticism in whatever the Jains do, and the celebration of Diwali is not an exception. The Jains celebrate Diwali during the month of Kartik for three days. During this period, among the Shvetambaras, devoted Jains observe fasting and chant the Uttaradhyayan Sutra, which contain the final pravachans of Lord Mahavira, and meditate upon him.

Vira Nirvana Samvat: The Jain year starts with Pratipada following Diwali. Vira Nirvana Samvat 2532 starts with Diwali 2005. The Jain businessmen traditionally started their accounting year from Diwali.

Diwali in Other Parts of the World: Diwali is celebrated in various parts of the world, in countries such as Britain, The Netherlands, Suriname, Canada, Guyana, Mauritius, Fiji, Japan, Indonesia, Malaysia, Myanmar, Nepal, Singapore, Sri Lanka, South Africa, Trinidad and Tobago, Thailand, United Arab Emirates, Australia, much of Africa, and the United States. With more and more Indians now migrating to various parts of the world, the number of countries where Diwali is celebrated has been gradually increasing. While in some countries it is celebrated mainly by Indian expatriates, in others it has become part of the general local culture. In most of these countries Diwali is celebrated on the same lines as described in this article with some minor variations. Some important variations are worth mentioning.

In Malaysia, Diwali is known as "Hari Deepavali," and is celebrated during the seventh month of the Hindu solar calendar. It is a federal public holiday. In many respects it resembles the traditions followed in the Indian subcontinent.

In Nepal, Diwali is known as *Tihar* and celebrated during the October/November period. Here, though the festival is celebrated for five days, the traditions vary from those followed in India. On the first day, cows are given offerings, in appreciation of the food they have given and agricultural work they have performed. On the second day, dogs and all living animals are revered and offered special food. On the third day, celebrations follow the same pattern as in India, with lights and lamps and much social activity. On the fourth day Yama, the Lord of Death, is worshipped and appeased. On the fifth and final day, brothers and sisters meet and exchange pleasantries.

Diwali is celebrated in the Caribbean Islands as well. Especially in Trinidad and Tobago, Diwali is marked as a special occasion and celebrated with much fanfare. It is observed as a national holiday in this part of the world and some Ministers of the Government also take part in the celebrations publicly.

Economics of Diwali: Diwali is an annual stimulus for the Indian economy. Indians purchase gold, gifts, decorations, crackers and household appliances during this festival. Companies offer huge discounts during the Diwali season to attract customers, which helps the economy and also helps the poor. It also helps the community in hunger since this festival shares it food. It also brings tourists to the country.

Since Diwali period also marks school holidays in most parts of India, many Bollywood movies are released during this period.

This Diwali which leads us into Truth and Light is celebrated on a nation-wide scale on Amavasya-the 15th day of the dark fortnight of the Hindu month of Ashwin (Aasho) (October / November) every year. It symbolises that age-old culture of our country which teaches us to vanquish ignorance that subdues humanity and to drive away darkness that engulfs the light of knowledge. Diwali, the festival of lights even to-day in this modern world projects the rich and glorious past of our country and teaches us to uphold the true values of life.

The word "Diwali" is the corruption of the Sanskrit word "Deepavali"-Deepa meaning light and Avali, meaning a row. It means a row of lights and indeed illumination forms its main attraction. Every home-lowly or mightly-the hut of the poor or the mansion of the rich-is alit with the orange glow of twinkling diyas-small earthen lamps-to welcome Lakshmi, Goddess of wealth and prosperity. Multi-coloured Rangoli designs, floral decorations and fireworks lend picturesness and grandeur to this festival which heralds joy, mirth and happiness in the ensuring year.

This festival is celebrated on a grand scale in almost all the regions of India and is looked upon mainly as the beginning of New Year. As such the blessings of Lakshmi, the celestial consort of Lord Vishnu are invoked with prayers. Even countries like Gkyena, Thailand, Trinidad, Siam and Malaya celebrate this festival but in their own ways.

This Diwali festival, it is surmised dates back to that period when perhaps history was not written, and in its progress through centuries it lighted path of thousands to attain the ultimate good and complete ecstasy.

Diwali or more aptly Deepavali is very enthusiastically celebrated for five continuous days and each day has its significance with a number of myths, legends and beliefs.

The *First day* is called *DHANTERAS* or *DHANTRAYODASHI* which falls on the thirteenth day of the month of Ashwin. The word "Dhan" means wealth. As such this day of the five-day Diwali festival has a great importance for the rich mercantile community of Western India. Houses and Business premises are renovated and decorated. Entrances are made colourful with lovely traditional motifs of Rangoli designs to welcome the Goddess of wealth and prosperity. To indicate her long-awaited arrival, small footprints are drawn with rice flour and vermilion powder all over the houses. Lamps are kept burning all through the nights. Believing this day to be auspicious women purchase some gold or silver or at least one or two new utensils. "Lakshmi-Puja" is performed in the evenings when tiny diyas of clay are lighted to drive away the shadows of evil spirits. "Bhajans"-devotional songs-in praise of Goddess Laxmi are sung and "Naivedya" of traditional sweets is offered to the Goddess. There is a peculiar custom in Maharashtra to lightly pound dry coriander seeds with jaggery and offer as Naivedya.

In villages cattles are adorned and worshipped by farmers as they form the main source of their income. In south cows are offered special veneration as they are supposed to be the incarnation of Goddess Lakshmi and therefore they are adorned and worshipped on this day.

A very interesting story about this day is of the sixteen year old son of King Hima. As per his horoscope he was doomed to die by a snake-bite on the fourth day of his marriage. On that particular fourth day of his marriage his young wife did not allow him to sleep. She laid all the ornaments and lots of gold and silver coins in a big heap at the entrance of her husband's boudoir and lighted innumerable lamps all over the place. And she went on telling stories and singing songs.

When Yam, the god of Death arrived there in the guise of a Serpent his eyes got blinded by that dazzle of those brilliant lights and he could not enter the Prince's chamber. So he climbed on top of the heap of the ornaments and coins and sat there whole night listening to the melodious songs. In the morning he quietly went away. Thus the young wife saved her husband from the clutches of death. Since then this day of Dhanteras came to be known as the day of "YAMADEEPDAAN" and lamps are kept burning throughout the night in reverential adoration to Yam, the god of Death.

The *Second day* is called *NARKA-CHATURDASHI* or *CHOTI DIWALI* which falls on the fourteenth day of the month of Ashwin. The story goes that the demon king Narakasur ruler of Pragjyotishpur (a province to the South of Nepal) after defeating Lord Indra had snatched away the magnificent earrings of Aditi, the Mother Goddess and imprisoned sixteen thousand daughters of the gods and saints in his harem. On the day previous to Narakachaturdashi, Lord Krishna killed the demon and liberated the imprisoned damsels and also recovered those precious earrings of Aditi.

As a symbol of that victory Lord Krishna smeared his forehead with the demon king's blood. Krishna returned home in the very early morning of the Narakachaturdashi day. The womenfolk massaged scented oil to his body and gave him a good bath to wash away the filth from his body. Since then the custom of taking bath before sunrise on this day has become a traditional practice specially in Maharashtra.

In South India that victory of the divine over the mundane is celebrated in a very peculiar way. People wake up before sunrise prepare blood by mixing Kumkum in oil and after breaking a bitter fruit that represents the head of the demon King that was smashed by Krishna, apply that mixture on their foreheads. Then they have an oil bath using sandalwood paste.

In Maharashtra also, traditional early baths with oil and "Uptan" (paste) of gram flour and fragrant powders are a must. All through the ritual of baths, deafening sounds of crackers and fireworks are there in order that the children enjoy bathing. Afterwards steamed vermiceli with milk and sugar or puffed rice with curd is served.

Another legend is about King Bali of the nether world mighty power had become a threat to the gods. In order to curb his powers Lord Vishnu in the guise of a Batu Waman-a small boy-visited him and begged him to give him only that much land which he could cover with his three steps. Known for his philanthropy King Bali proudly granted him his wish. That very moment that small boy transformed himself into the all-powerful Lord Vishnu. With his first step Lord Vishnu covered the entire heaven and with the second step the earth and asked Bali where to keep his third step. Bali offered his head. Putting his foot on his head Vishnu pushed him down to the underworld. At the same time for his generosity Lord Vishnu gave him the lamp of knowledge and allowed him to return to earth once a year to light millions of lamps to dispel the darkness and ignorance and spread the radiance of love and wisdom.

Diwali is a five day Hindu festival which occurs on the fifteenth day of Kartika. Diwali means "rows of lighted lamps" and the celebration is often referred to as the Festival of Lights. During this time, homes are thoroughly cleaned and windows are opened to welcome Laksmi, goddess of wealth. Candles and lamps are lit as a greeting to Laksmi. Gifts are exchanged and festive meals are prepared during Diwali. The celebration means as much to Hindus as Christmas does to Christians.

Because there are many regions in India, there are many manifestations of the Diwali festival. In at least one area, the festival begins with Dhanteras, a day set aside to worship Laksmi. In the Indian culture, wealth is not viewed as a corruptive power. Instead, a wealthy person is considered to have been rewarded for good deeds of a past life.

The *Third day* of the festival of Diwali is the most important day of LAKSHMI-PUJA which is entirely devoted to the propitiation of Goddess Lakshmi. This day is also known by the name of "CHOPADA-PUJA". On this very day sun enters his second course and passes Libra which is represented by the balance or scale. Hence, this design of Libra is believed to have suggested the balancing of account books and their closing. Despite the fact that this day falls on an amavasya day it is regarded as the most auspicious.

The day of Lakshmi-Puja falls on the dark night of Amavasya. The strains of joyous sounds of bells and drums float from the temples as man is invoking Goddess Lakshmi in a wondrous holy "pouring-in" of his heart. All of a sudden that impenetrable darkness is pierced by innumerable rays of light for just a moment and the next moment a blaze of light descends down to earth from heaven as golden-footed Deep-Lakshmi alights on earth in all her celestial glory amidst chantings of Vedic hymns. A living luminance of Universal Motherhood envelopes the entire world in that blessed moment of fulfillment of a long-awaited dream of the mortal. A sublime light of knowledge dawns upon humanity and devotion of man finally conquers ignorance.

This self enlightenment is expressed through the twinkling lamps that illuminate the palaces of the wealthy as well as the lowly abodes of the poor. It is believed that on this day Lakshmi walks through the green fields and loiters through the bye-lanes and showers her blessings on man for plenty and prosperity. When the sun sets in the evening and ceremonial worship is finished all the home-made sweets are offered to the goddess as "NAIVEDYA" and distributed as "PRASAD". Feasts are arranged and gifts are exchanged on this day gaily dressed men, women and children go to temples and fairs, visit friends and relatives. Everything is gay, gold and glitter!

One of the most curious customs which characterises this festival of Diwali is the indulgence of gambling, specially on a large scale in North India. It is believed that goddess Parvati played dice with her husband, Lord Shiv on this day and she decreed that whosoever gambled on Diwali night would prosper throughout the ensuring year. This tradition of playing cards-flush and rummy with stakes on this particular day continues even today.

On this auspicious day Lord Shri Krishna around whom revolved the entire story of our great epic Mahabharat and the philosopher, who preached Karmayog through his Geeta to Arjun on the battlefield of Kurukshetra, discarded his body.

Bhagwan, Mahavir, the Jain prophet also attained "Nirvan" on this day.

Swami Ramtirth, the beloved "Ram Badshah" of millions of Indians was not only born on this day and took "Sanyas" but also took "Samadhi" on this day.

Swami Dayanand Saraswati, founder of Arya Samaj in 1875 in Mumbai, with his superb yogic powers greed his soul from his body and mingled with divinity on this auspicious day of Diwali.

We kindle innumerable lights on this day to immortalise the sacred memories of those great men who lived to brighten the lives of millions of their fellow beings.

One very interesting story about this Diwali day is from Kathopanishad of a small boy called Nichiketa who believed that Yam, the god of Death was as black as the dark night of amavasya. But when he met Yam in person he was puzzled seeing Yam's calm countenance and dignified stature. Yam explained to Nichiketa on this Diwali day of amavasya that by only passing through the darkness of death, man sees the light of highest wisdom and then only his soul can escape from the bondage of his mortal frame to mingle with the Supreme Power without whose will not an at ton moves in the world. And then Nichiketa realised the importance of worldly life and significance of death. Nichiketa's all doubts were set at rest and he wholeheartedly participated in Diwali celebrations.

The *Fourth day* is PADWA or VARSHAPRATIPADA which marks the coronation of King Vikramaditya and Vikaram-Samvat was started from this Padwa day.

Govardhan-Puja is also performed in the North on this day. As per Vishnu-Puran the people of Gokul used to celebrate a festival in honour of Lord Indira and worshipped him after the end of every monsoon season but one particular year the young Krishna stopped them from offering prayers to Lord Indra who in terrific anger sent a deluge to submerge Gokul. But Krishna saved his Gokul by lifting up the Govardhan mountain and holding it over the people as an umbrella.

Govardhan is a small hillock in Braj, near Mathura and on this day of Diwali people of Punjab, Haryana, Uttar Pradesh and Bihar build cowdung, hillocks, decorate them with flowers and then worship them.

This day is also observed as Annakoot meaning mountain of food. In temples specially in Mathura and Nathadwara, the deities are given milkbath, dressed in shining attires with ornaments of dazzling diamonds, pearls, rubies and other precious stones. After the prayers and traditional worship innumerable varieties of delicious sweets are ceremoniously raised in the form of a mountain before the deities as "Bhog" and then the devotees approach the Mountain of Food and take Prasad from it.

Goddess Lakshmi is worshipped in every Hindu household and her blessings sought for success and happiness. This day is looked upon as the most auspicious day to start any new venture. In many Hindu homes it is a custom for the wife to put the red tilak on the forehead of her husband, garland him and do his "Aarathi" with a prayer for his long life. In appreciation of all the tender care that the wife showers on him, the husband gives her a costly gift. This Gudi Padwa is symbolic of love and devotion between the wife and husband. On this day newly-married daughters with their husbands are invited for special meals and given presents. In olden days brothers went to fetch their sisters from their in-laws home for this important day.

The *Fifth and final day* of Diwali Festival is known by the name of “BHAYYA-DUJ” in the Hindi-speaking belt “BHAV-BIJ” in the Marathi-speaking communities and in Nepal by the name of “BHAI-TIKA”. As the legend goes Yamraj, the God of Death visited his sister Yami on this particular day. She put the auspicious tilak on his forehead, garlanded him and led him with special dishes and both of them together ate the sweets, talked and enjoyed themselves to their heart’s content, while parting Yamraj gave her a special gift as a token of his love and in return Yami also gave him a lovely gift which she had made with her own hands. That day Yamraj announced that anyone who receives tilak from his sister will never be thrown. That is why this day of Bhayyaduj is also known by the name of “YAMA-DWITIYA” Since then this day is being observed as a symbol of love between sisters and brothers. It became also imperative for the brother to go to his sister’s house to celebrate Bhayyaduj.

In today’s world when pressing everyday problems are teaming as under all the tender words of personal relationships, the celebrating of this day has its own importance in continuing to maintain the love between brothers and sisters for it is the day of food-sharing, gift-giving and reaching out to the inner most depths of the hearts. Diwali on the whole has always been the festival with more social than religious connotations. It is a personal, people-oriented festival when enmities are forgotten, families and friends meet, enjoy and establish a word of closeness.

As a festival of light and beauty it encourages artistic expressions through home-decorations stage-plays, elocution competitions singing and dancing programmes, making gift items and making delectable sweets thereby discovering new talents of younger people. As a result innumerable communities with varying cultures and customs mingle together to make Diwali celebrations a very happy occasion for all.

History of Diwali: India is a land of festivals. Diwali, the Festival of Lights, is celebrated with fervor and gaiety. The festival is celebrated by young and old, rich and poor, throughout the country to dispel darkness and light up their lives. The festival symbolizes unity in diversity as every state celebrates it in its own special way. The celebration of the four-day festival commences on Aswayuja Bahula Chaturdasi and concludes on Kartika Shudda Vijiya.

The first day of the festival Naraka Chaturdasi marks the vanquishing of the demon Naraka by Lord Krishna and his wife Satyabhama. 'Puranas' have it that Naraka, son of Bhudevi, acquired immense power from a blessing given by Lord Brahma after a severe penance. He soon unleashed a reign of terror in the kingdom of Kamarupa, harassing celestial beings with his invincible might. Unable to bear the tyranny of the demon, the celestial beings pleaded with Lord Krishna to save them from his torture.

But Naraka could not be easily killed as he had a boon that he would face death only at the hands of his mother Bhudevi. So, Krishna asks his wife Satyabhama, the reincarnation of Bhudevi, to be his charioteer in the battle with Naraka. When Krishna feigns unconsciousness after being hit by an arrow of Naraka, Satyabhama takes the bow and aims the arrow at Naraka, killing him instantly. Later Lord Krishna reminds her of the boon she had sought as Bhudevi.

The slaying of Naraka by Sathyabhama could also be taken to interpret that parents should not hesitate to punish their children when they stray on to the wrong path. The message of Naraka Chaturdasi is that the good of the society should always prevail over one's own personal bonds. The second day is Amavasya when Lakshmi puja is performed.

It is believed that on this day Goddess Lakshmi would be in her benevolent mood and fulfill the wishes of her devotees. One version says that it was on this day that Goddess Lakshmi emerged from Kshira Sagara (Ocean of Milk) when the Gods and demons were churning the sagara (ocean) for nectar (Amrit) The other version is that when Lord Vishnu in the guise of Vamana, sought three feet of land from the generous demon king Bali, the latter had to surrender his head as Vamana had conquered the earth and the sky in two strides. Lord Vishnu banishes Bali into the Pathala Loka (netherland) by keeping his third stride on Bali's head. Later, pleased by his generosity, Lord Vishnu grants him a boon and he in turn requests the Lord to guard his palace at Pathala Loka. Meanwhile, the Goddess is unable to bear the separation and her grief affects the functioning of the entire universe. Brahma and Lord Shiva offer themselves as guards and plead with Bali to relieve Vishnu. So, on the Amavasya day, Lord Vishnu returns to his abode and Goddess Lakshmi is delighted. It is believed that those who worship Goddess Lakshmi on this day would be bestowed with all the riches.

The third day is "Kartika Shudda Padyami." On this day Bali would come out of Pathala Loka and rule Bhuloka as per the boon given by Lord Vishnu. Hence, it is also known as "Bali Padyami". The fourth day is referred to as "Yama Dvitiya." On this day, sisters invite their brothers to their homes. However, in the northern part of India it is celebrated as the return of Ram along with Sita and Lakshman from his 14 years of exile after killing Ravana. To commemorate his return to Ayodhya, his subjects illuminated the kingdom and burst crackers. For the Gujaratis, Marwaris and other business community Diwali marks the worship of Goddess Lakshmi and also the beginning of the new financial year. For Bengalis, it is the time to worship Goddess Kali or Durga. The Goddess Durga continued her "Vilaya Tandava" even after killing demon Mahishasura.

Significance of Diwali: Deepavali is a festival where people from all age groups participate. They give expression to their happiness by lighting earthen 'diyas' (lamps), decorating the houses, bursting firecrackers and inviting near and dear ones to their households for partaking in a sumptuous feast. The lighting of lamps is a way of paying obeisance to god for attainment of health, wealth, knowledge, peace, valor and fame. It is one time in the whole year that children volunteer to leave their beds long before the day begins. In fact, the traditional oil bath at 3 a.m, is the only chore that stands between them and the pre-dawn adventures. They emerge, scrubbed clean to get into their festive attire, and light up little oil lamps, candles and scented sticks(agarbathis), the wherewithal for setting alight crackers and sparklers. Who shall set off the first chain of crackers that go boom, bang and vroom? and who is the owner of the 10-minute 'banger' that steals the thunder from your little chain of needle-sized crackers? Does the boy next door have more crackers than me? Competition is stiff, and even the little girl in silk frocks and their finery are watching out for the best sparklers and flowerpots, the rockets and Vishnuchakras, which light-up the night sky like a thousand stars. Grown-ups are the soul of generosity. Festive bonhomie abounds.

Diwali is the one Hindu festival that unites the whole of India. It is traditionally known as the "festival of lights", for the common practice is to light small oil lamps (called diyas) and place them around the home, in courtyards, gardens, verandahs, on the walls built around the home and also on the roof tops. In cities, especially, candles are substituted for diyas; and among the riches, candles are made to substitute for fashionable and classy neon lights. The celebration of the festival is customarily accompanied by the exchange of sweets and the explosion of fireworks. Diwali is an occasion for cheerfulness and togetherness.

This is an occasion for young and the old, men and women, rich and poor-for everyone to celebrate. Irrespective of their religious and economic background, the festival is celebrated throughout the country to ward off the darkness and welcome light into life as light is always associated with hope for the future Diwali is celebrated 20 days after Dussera, on Amavasya-the 15th day of the dark fortnight of the Hindu month of Ashwin (Aasho) (Oct/ Nov) every year. Diwali celebrates Rama's homecoming, that is his return to Ayodhya after the defeat of Ravana and his coronation as king The legend related to the festival is that King Dashratha had three wives namely Kaushalaya, Keykayee and Sumitra and four sons Rama, Bharat, Laxmana and Shatrughan.

Rama was the son of Queen Kaushalaya and Bharat was the son of Queen Keykayee. Keykayee wanted Bharat to be the next King of Ayodhya, while King Dasharatha wanted Rama, his eldest son to be the King. But Keykayee made full use of the two wishes King Dasharatha had promised. Keykayee asked for sending Rama to exile for the period of fourteen years and to crown Bharat as the king, though Bharat refused to accept the kingship. During that time Lord Rama fought and won fierce battle in the southern part of the Indian subcontinent, killing the king of Demons, Ravana who had forcibly taken away his wife Sita. Diwali marks his victorious return to his kingdom along with Hanuman, the Vanar who helped him in achieving success.

The legend states it took 20 days for Rama to return to his kingdom after defeating Ravana. As with other Indian festivals, Diwali signifies many different things to people across the country.

In north India, Diwali celebrates Rama's homecoming from fourteen years of exile that is his return to Ayodhya after defeating Ravana and his coronation as king; in Gujarat, the festival is celebrated to honour goddess Lakshmi, the goddess of wealth; and in Bengal, it is related with the goddess Kali. But everywhere, it is celebrated with the same sprit and signifies the renewal of life. Diwali is one of the most celebrated festivities in the Indian culture. Uniting all members of the community, young and old, rich or poor, the lighting of the lamps represents a way of paying obeisance to God for attainment of health, wealth, knowledge, peace and valoured fame People give expressions to their happiness by lighting earthen diyas and decorating the houses to welcome Lakshmi-the Goddess of wealth and prosperity, bursting fire crackers and inviting the near and dear ones to their households for partaking in the luxurious feast.

The lighting of lamps is a way of paying obeisance to God for attainment of health, wealth, knowledge, peace and fame and it also signifies goodness. It is also marked as the beginning of the Hindu New Year and as a brand new beginning for all. Diwali is celebrated for five days, each day having it's own significance, rituals and myths

The Jain communities of India celebrate Diwali as a New Year's Day. Lord Mahavira, the founder of Jainism, attained his Nirvana on the day of Diwali.

Sikhs celebrate Diwali to express joy at the return of the sixth Guru to Amritsar in 1620; Emperor Jahangir had imprisoned him along with 52 Hindu kings. The Guru was granted freedom but refused to leave until the kings were also released.

Diwali is by far the most enthusiastically enjoyed festival in India. People of different nationalities, races, religions and backgrounds come together to share their joys generating a feeling of universal brotherhood and inter-religious harmony.

Diwali, literally a garland of lamps, is an apt description of this festival of lights. Tradition maintains that lamps are lit to keep alive the memory of Prince *Rama's* return to Ayodhya after conquering the tyrant *Ravana*, the ruler of Lanka, who had abducted his consort *Sita*.

The heroic deeds of Rama are recounted in the Hindu epic *Ramayan* and Diwali symbolizes the victory of virtue over vice. Rama, we are told had gladly accepted an exile in the forest to keep his step-mother happy and save his father from embarassment. He is considered the epitome of a dutiful son and a responsible ruler. Another myth traces the origins of the festival to the annual 'inspection tours' of Lakshmi, the Hindu goddess of wealth and prosperity. The faithful believe that on this day Lakshmi goes around visiting her devotees and sets up residence in the house she finds best spruced up and most hospitable. Diwali is an occasion for spring cleaning, painting the walls, decorating the floor with attractive designs wrought in coloured powder or paste made with rice.

The ritual traditionally associated with Diwali is gambling. Friends get together to indulge in games of chance, dice or cards. The 'addicts' seek legitimacy for their unusual pastime by referring to the celestial game of dice played by the great lord *Shiva* with his companion *Parvati*-a scene superbly sculpted at *Kailash* temple, *Ellora*. Others rationalise that this is just to remind oneself of the fickleness of lady luck and to inculcate a sense of balance in our pursuit of material success.

The children can be seen bursting fire crackers and lighting candles or earthen lamps. This is a time of generously exchanging sweets with neighbours and friends. Puffed rice and sugar candy are the favourite fares.

Rangoli: Rangoli is one of the most popular art among Indian women, which is mainly painted on the ground in front of their houses using different colour powders. This art can be predominantly seen during the tamil month of MAARKAZHI in Tamil Nadu, India. The MAARKAZHI month falls between December 15th and January 15th in western calendar. According to Hindu mythology, during this month the Goddess ANDAL prayed to the Lord THIRUMAL to marry her.

It was said that her wish came true. So, this month is said to be so auspicious for unmarried girls to pray to god to have a spouse of their dreams. During this month unmarried girls arise before the Sun rise to paint beautiful rangolis to welcome the Lord THIRUMAL and they sing THIRUPPAVAI, praises of the Lord THIRUMAL which was said to be sung by the Goddess ANDAL.

3

Muslim Festivals

Muharram

Muharram is the first month of the Islamic calendar. It is one of the four sanctified months of the year. Fighting in this month is looked down upon and is often put to the side in respect for Islam. Since the Islamic calendar is lunar, Muharram moves from year to year when compared to the Gregorian calendar.

The first day of Muharram is the start of the Islamic New Year. The Festival of Muharram takes place during this month in which Shia Muslims especially commemorate the Battle of Karbala. The commemoration reaches its climax on the tenth day of Muharram, known as Ashurah.

This day is related to the time of Moses when he crossed the Red Sea escaping from the Pharaoh. Sunni Muslims often fast on this sacred day. Later, in the month of Ramadan it is recommended to fast so the day of Ashura is optional.

This month of Muharram also has traditions which have no support from Islamic teachings. For example, the celebration of the Muslim new year, and the partying and card giving, etc, associated with it is considered to be a bidah and even haraam to some.

Muharram is so called because it was unlawful to fight during this month; the word is derived from the word 'haram' meaning forbidden. It is held to be the most sacred of all the months. This months is most sacred to the Shi'a community and the fast on the first ten days of the month to commemorate the slaying of Hussain, a grandson of Muhammed, by the Sunnis. The tenth day is called Ashura, meaning, 'the tenth', and it is a day of voluntary fasting. The Sunnis also fast on the tenth day because they believe that Adam and Eve, heaven and hell, life and death, fate and the pen were created on this day. The Remembrance of Muharram is an important period of mourning in the Shiaite branch of Islam.

A banner (*aalam*) being carried in a procession during the Remembrance of Muharram in Bahrain. For the duration of the remembrance, it is customary for mosques to provide free meals (*nazar*) on certain nights of the month to all people.

These meals are viewed as being special and holy, as they have been consecrated in the name of Husayn, and thus partaking of them is considered an act of communion with God, Husayn, and humanity. In Trinidad and Tobago all ethnic and religious communities participate in the event, locally known as "Hosay".

Many of the events associated with the remembrance take place in congregation halls known as "Hussainia".

The Tenth of Muharram and Ashurah: The Islamic year begins with Muharram ul Haram, the first month of the Hijri Calendar. While followers of other religions spend their opening month in worthless merriment, the first month of Islam teaches us lessons of admonition, good counselling, knowledge of Allah Ta'ala, sacrifice, selflessness, patience and seeking the pleasure of Allah Ta'ala.

The tenth day of Muharram (Ashurah) has many distinctive qualities and features. Allah Ta'ala created the heavens and the earth on this blessed day. On this day He gave His infinite blessings and bounties to many of His Prophets and delivered them from the clutches of their enemies.

Allah Ta'ala created Hazrat Adam (Alaihis-Salam) in this month, pardoned him of his mistake, and Hazrat Noah's (Alaihis-Salam) Ark landed successfully on Mount Judi, and he saved Hazrat Ibrahim (Alaihis-Salam) from fire and rescued Hazrat Musa (Alaihis-Salam) from Pharaoh.

On the first of Muharram offer 2 rakats Nafil prayer. In each rakat after Surah Fateha recite Surah Ikhlas 3 times. After the Salam pray to Allah Ta'ala for all your needs and desires. From the blessing of this prayer, Allah Ta'ala will appoint an angel for such a person. The angel will guide him or her to do only good deeds and prevent them in engaging in sinful acts.

On the eve of "Ashurah" offer 100 rakats Nafl. In each rakat recite Surah Ikhlas 3 times after Surah Fateha. After Salam recite first 'Kalimah' 100 times. Allah Ta'ala will forgive all the sins of such a person.

Dua-e-Ashurah-An Insurance for a Year's Life: Hazrat Imam Zainul Abidain (Radi Allah Anhu) reports that who ever recites this dua on the tenth of Muharram, any time after sunrise and before sunset, or listens to its recitation from someone else, Allah Ta'ala will certainly make it an insurance for a years' life for him, by keeping death away from him. However, if one is to become the victim of death in that year, they will by some strange coincidence not remember to recite it.

Nafil Salat for the Eve of Ashurah: On the eve of Ashurah offer 4 rakats Nafil Salat as follows: In every rakat after Surah Fateha recite "Ayetul Kursi" once and Surah Ikhlas 3 times. After completing this Namaz recite Surah Ikhlas 100 times. Allah Ta'ala will purify such a person of all their sins and grant them endless bounties and blessings in paradise.

The Fast of Ashurah: On the 9th and 10th of Muharram, one should fast. If it is not possible to fast on both days, then every effort should be made to fast on the 10th day of Muharram, as there is great reward for this fast. (Muslim Shareef).

The following are some of the desirable acts one should do on the day of Ashurah:

1. To observe fast on this day.
2. To give as much charity as you can afford.
3. To perform Nafl Salat prayers.
4. To recite Surah Ikhlas 1000 times.

5. To visit and be in the company of pious Ulema.
6. To place a hand of affection on an orphan's head.
7. To give generously to one's relatives.
8. To put surma in one's eyes.
9. To take a bath.
10. To cut one's nails.
11. To visit the sick.
12. To establish friendly ties with one's enemies.
13. To recite Dua-e-Ashurah
14. To visit the shrines of Awliyas and the graves of Muslims.

Hazrat Abdullah bin Masood (Radi Allah Anhu), a Companion of the Holy Prophet Muhammad (Sall Allahu Alaihi wa Sallam) reports the following saying of the Messenger of Allah Ta'ala, "Whosoever prepares ample food and drink for his family on this sacred day and delights in feeding them generously, Allah Ta'ala will increase His provisions for that year and place much blessings and good therein."

Imam Hussain (Radi Allah Anhu) and his companions were martyred on the tenth of this month. Like any month in the Islamic Calendar there are in this first Islamic month, many anniversaries which are celebrated every where in the world.

Muharram festival commemorates the martyrdom of Hazrat Imam Hussain, the grandson of the Holy Prophet (peace be upon him). This festival starts at the 1st day of Muharram and lasts for 10 days until 10th of Muharram. Muharram is the first month of Islamic calendar.

During this month, while on a journey, Hazrat Imam Hussain, his family members and a number of his followers were surrounded by the forces of Yazid, the Muslim ruler of the time. During the siege, they were deprived of food and water and many of them were put to death. The incident happened at a place called Karbala in Iraq in 61st year after Hijra. This dispute was result of a disagreement among Muslims on the question of succession after the demise of Hazrat Ali, the fourth caliph.

Some sects of Muslims hold meetings where speeches are made on the happenings of Karbala and on the lives of martyrs. The Shias, however, observe this festival in a different fasion. As Muharram, the first month of the Muslim year, approaches, they put on black clothes, as black is regarded as a colour of mourning. Majalis (assemblies) are held every day during the first nine days where shia orators relate the incident of the martyrdom of Hazrat Imam Hussain and his party in a great detail.

On the 10th day of Muharram, large processions are formed and the devoted followers parade the streets holding banners and carrying models of the mausoleum of Hazrat Imam Hussain and his people, who fell at Karbala. They show their grief and sorrow by inflicting wounds on their own bodies with sharp metal tied to chain with which they scourge themselves. This is done in order to depict the sufferings of the martyrs. It is a sad occasion and everyone in the procession chants "Ya Hussain", with loud wails of lamentation. Generally a white horse beautifully decorated for the occasion, is also included in the procession, to mark the empty mount of Hazrat Imam Husain after his martyrdom.

During these first ten days of Muharram, drinking posts are also set up temporarily by the Shia community where water and juices are served to all, free of charge.

The 1st of Muharram is New Year's Day, and with it marks the beginning of the Islamic (Hijri) Calendar. Its real significance lies in the major turning point in the course of Islam. As told in the Noble Qur'an: "Verily the number of months with Allah is twelve months (in a year), so was it ordained by Allah on the Day when He created the heavens and the earth; of them four are Sacred. That is the right religion, so wrong not yourselves therein ...".

Today itself, as we usher in the new year, many of us take the time to at least briefly reflect on the major lessons in the past year and anticipate new experiences in the fresh year of 1422 Hijrah. This is also the day that we should be reminded of the Prophet's last pilgrimage and the message that he wants us to carry in our hearts.

The prophet offered the noon and afternoon prayers in Arafah along with 100,000 worshippers, and the victory of Islaam over blasphemy became decisive and final. Thereafter, the Prophet mounted his camel, and delivered the historical sermon. In it, he had said: "... All mankind is from Adam and Eve, an Arab has no superiority over a non-Arab nor a non-Arab has any superiority over an Arab, also a white has no superiority over black nor a black has any superiority over white except by piety and good action. Learn that every Muslim is a brother to every Muslim and that the Muslims constitute one brotherhood. Nothing shall be legitimate to a Muslim which belongs to a fellow Muslim unless it was given freely and willingly. Do not, therefore, do injustice to yourselves...".

The Period of mourning is observed in the first month of the Islamic calendar, and it commemorates the death of Hazrat Imam Hussain in the battle of Karbala. Muharram means 'respected'. It is the first month of the Islamic calendar.The first ten days of this month are observed as a period of mourning by Muslims, particularly by those belonging to the Shiah sect, in memory of the tragedy of 680 AD. Hazrat Imam Hussain, the grandson of Muhammad the Prophet was killed in the battle of Karbala. This event, called Muharram, is named after the month in which it took place. The tenth day, called Ashura, is observed as the day for a public expression of their grief and is the most important day of the month.

During the pre-Islamic period in the Arabian penninsula, fighting was prohibited in four months of the year.These months, of which Muharram was one, were considered sacred. This period of inactivity was a necessity in heavily decorated replicas of the tomb of the Imam and his family are made for Muharram the era of warring tribes. The tradition was maintained even after the advent of Islam, though provisions to accommodate and accept war in special situations, like a threat to the sovereignty of an empire, were introduced. The gory battle of Karbala was fought against this law and tradition of Islam. The inhabitants on the banks of rivers Euphrates and Tigris were traditional rivals. Their animosity was contained to some extent by Muhammad. But when his son-in-law Hazrat Ali was the

Caliph, the old enmity re-surfaced. Hazrat Ali had two descendants, Hazrat Imam Hussain and Hazrat Imam Hassan. Hussain was the ruler of the part of the empire known today as Iran.

The other part in modern Iraq was ruled by the Umayyads. Hussain was called upon by the Shiahs of Kufa, a small town in the Umayyad kingdom, to accept their allegiance and claim his place as the leader of the Islamic community. This was against the wishes of the ruler of Kufa, Yazid, who instructed his governor, Ibn-e-Ziad to take appropriate action. Meanwhile, in response to the call of the Shiahs, Hussain accompanied by his family members, headed for Kufa. When they reached Karbala, enroute to Kufa, the forces of the governor surrounded them and their 70 men. Hussain, his family and his troops were tortured and killed, and Hussain's head was severed and presented to the king. They received no help from the Shiahs of Kufa. This happened on the tenth day of Muharram and it was called Ashura.

To commemorate this tragedy, the 40 days starting from the first day of Muharram to Chehalum, are observedas a period of mourning by the Shiahs. During this period, women foresake alladornments, even their bangles. All kinds of celebration like marriage are disallowed during this period. Shiah Muslims are celibate for these 40 days. The first 10 days however, are the most important and are passionately observed asa period of mourning. During the first nine days of the month, majlish (enacted grief-stricken scenes from the battle of Karbala) are organised in Shiah mosques. Huge Shiah crowds wearing black assemble at imambaras, where plaintive verses in memory of Imam Hussain are recited.

These nine days are also spent in making Taziahs. On Ashura, the most important day, processions with Taziahs are taken out in commemoration of the sad event. The procession also includes a well-decorated horse, representing the horse of Imam Hussain. Emotional plays, enacting scenes from the battle of Karbala, are performed by bare-chested Shiah men. They strike their body with chains while some walk with bare feeton burning coals. Crying "hai Hussain hum na rahe", meaning 'Oh Hussain, we were not there', they express their anguish at their in ability to have prevented him from being tortured. By beating themselves, the Shiahs relive the pain Hussain suffered and thus express their sorrow.

They also distribute water, soft drinks and fruit juices to passers-by in an effort to quench the thirst of the six-month old son of Hazrat Imam Hussain and many others who are believed to have died asking for water. The Taziah processions from allover the town terminate at the Karbala of the city. Most old habitations with a Muslim tradition have a specially marked place to represent the original Karbala.

The Taziahs are buried there. Sometimes they are dismantled so that they can be used again. Often they are immersed in a river. According to a popular belief among the Shiahs, the mud on the grave of Hazrat Imam Hussain turns blood red on Ashura. Muharram is also a time for making vows. People pledge their promises to the Taziah of Hussain. They can do this in two ways.

The first is by sending milk,a soft drink, dates or refined sugar to the craftsman who is making the Taziahs. The craftsman recites the Al-Fatiha breaks a coconut and distributesits water with the soft drink or milk in small cups to those present. The second method of making a vow is by performing an act of penance or self-torture before the Taziah. This is generally practiced by woman who volunteer to stand and watch over the Taziahs for a night or more. They go to the place where it is built, and accompany it through its route to the Karbala. This commitment is performed on the ninth night of the month of Muharram.

Some people offer to roll on the ground for a certain distance in front of the Taziah as thanks giving for favours that have been granted or for wish fulfillment. Though the 10 days of Muharram are a period of mourning for the Sunni sect too, they do not indulge in passion plays and nor do they cry out Hussain Hussain because their tradition stipulates grieving in silence. They keep a two-day roja on the ninth and tenth of the month, wear only black clothes and read the Namaz and AlFatiha five times a day.

Contrary to popular belief, Muharram is not a particular day, but the name of a month that marks the beginning of the year according to the Islamic calendar. Muharram is one of four months that have been designated as holy according to the Islamic calendar, the other three being – Dhul-Qa'adah, Dhul-Hijjah and Rajab.

Fasting in the Month of Muharram : Fasting is advocated in the month of Muharram. The Prophet is believed to have said: "The best fasts after the fasts of Ramadan are those of the month of Muharram." Although the fasts of the month of Muharram are not obligatory, yet one who fasts in these days out of his own will is entitled to a great reward by Allah Almighty. Fasting on the tenth day of Muharram, called Ashura, is particularly important, as it supposed to lead to great rewards. A person does not have to fast for the whole month. On the contrary, each fast during this month has merit.

Muharram–an Auspicious Time: The month of Muharram is also associated with many auspicious events in Islamic history. Allah is supposed to have created the heavens and the earth on this blessed day. On this day He give His infinite blessings and bounties to many of His Prophets and delivered them from the clutches of their enemies.

Allah created Hazrat Adam in this month and pardoned him of his mistake. Hazrat Noah's Ark landed successfully on Mount Judi during this time centuries ago. God is also said to have saved Hazrat Ibrahim from fire and rescued Hazrat Musa from the Pharaoh during the month of Muharram.

You must be wondering what there is to mourn about then? The tenth day of Muharram or Ashura is of supreme importance for Shia Muslims as they celebrate the death anniversary of Hussain, the grandson of the Prophet Muhammad.

The Tragedy at Kerbala : In the month of Muharram many centuries ago, (approximately October 20th 680 A.D.), an event took place in Iraq at a place known as Kerbala on the bank of the river Euphrates.

A large army, which had been mobilised by the Umayyad regime, besieged a group of persons numbering less than a hundred and put them under pressure to pay allegiance to the Caliph of the time and submit to his authority. The Caliph was a man much taken with earthly pleasures that deviated from the Islamic way of life. The small group resisted and a severe battle took place in which they were all killed. The leader of the small band of men who were martyred in Kerbala was none other than Imam Husain, the grandson of the Holy Prophet.

Imam Husain's martyrdom at Kerbala represents a conscious confrontation with anti-Islamic forces and a courageous resistance for a sacred cause. The tragedy was that the one who stood up to defend Islam was cut down in so cruel a manner. It is for this reason that the death of Imam Husain is mourned annually in the Muslim world.

The Observances: "Among the Shias in India the following ceremonies are common, although considerable differences in detail may be observed according to regions. As soon as the new moon appears, people assemble in the imam bara (lit, enclosure of imam), a permanent meeting place built in stone or, as mostly in southern India, they assemble in the 'ashur khanah (lit, ten-day house), a temporary structure. There they recite thefatihah over some sherbat (sweetened, cool drink), rice or sugar in Husain's name. The cool drink is meant to remind the faithful of the terrible thirst Husain and his family and retinue had to suffer. Food and drink are later distributed to the public, especially to the poor. In some places a pit is dug in which a fire is lighted every evening of the festival, and young and old people fence across it with sticks or swords. Or they run around it calling out: Ya'Ali! Ya'Ali! Shah Hasan! Shah Husain! Dulha! Hae Dost! Rahiyo! Oh 'Ali! (Noble Hasan! Noble Husain! Bride-groom! Friend! Stay! Stay!)

"The'ashur khanah is usually draped with black cloth on which texts of the Quran are written. The imam bara, too, will be decorated. Inside are placed the tazian-s or tabuts, wooden structures covered with silver paper, coloured paper and tinsel fringes. They are made with imagination and artistic sense and are meant to represent Husain's mausoleum, erected on the plains of Karbala, or else the Prophet's tomb at Medina or even the Taj Mahal of Agra. Nearby are placed imitations of articles which Husain is supposed to have used at Karbala, *e.g.*, a turban of gold, a sword, a shield, a bow and arrow. There are also'alam-s or standards of different shapes, each one having its own special name and history. Often the 'a lam has the form of a human hand (panjab) fixed on top of the pole. This is the popular emblem representing the five members of the prophet's family: Muhammad, Fatima, 'Au, Hasan and Husain."

Processions and Other Ceremonies: "From the seventh to the tenth of Muharram processions are held to commemorate the martyrdom of Hasan's son, Qasim, who was slain shortly after his wedding, as well as the martyrdom of Husain. Along with the procession goes a white horse (duldul or dhu'l-janah) which represents the horse on which Husain rode, or it refers to the bridal horse of Qasim, who was married to Husain's favourite daughter Fatimat-us-sughra (as distinguished from Fatimah, the daughter of Muhammad), just before the battle of Karbala. With this in mind the people shout at intervals: Bride-groom! Bridegroom! On the eighth day a lance or spear is carried to represent Husain's head, which was carried on the point of a javelin by order of Yazid. In addition to these representations ta 'ziya h-s or tabut-s and standards of Hasan, Husain and Qasim are carried. All the time people beat their breasts, saying: Hasan, Husain! Sometimes the pro-cession halts, and then a group of men and boys, naked from the waist, beat themselves with a bundle of sharp blades so that the blood streams down their backs or, forming a large group, they beat their breasts in a uniform rhythm crying all together: Ya Hasan! Ya Husain! The tenth day is 'ashara 'ashurah. On this day the tabut-s or ta 'ziah-s are either stripped and thrown into the water, or they are taken to a ground set apart for this purpose (called Karbala) and literally buried in specially dug graves.

On the evening of the twelfth day people sit up all night, reading the Quran and reciting marsiyah-s and verses in honour of Husain. On the thirtieth day a quantity of food is cooked and, after saying the fatihah over it, it is given to the poor. With this act of charity the Muharram celebrations end."

The Memory of Karbala: Husain was the second son of Ali ibn Abu Talib and Fatimah bint Muhammad, the last

Prophet. He was born in the 4th year after the hijra. His older brother, Hasan was named as the successor to his father, after Ali was murdered in the mosque in Kufah, Iraq. After Ali's death, people pledged their allegiance to Hasan as the khalifa (successor). Soon after he took office, however, Mu'awiyah, who had fought with Ali over the caliphate, formed an army to attack Hasan. In the interests of peace and unity, Hasan handed over the position of khalifa to Mu'awiyah who ruled until his death and passing of the caliphate to his son, Yazid.

Mu'awiyah, who was the son of Abu Sufyan (the arch enemy of Islam until he accepted Islam after the Muslims returned to Makkah), was not well liked among the "religious" Muslims. They disliked his son, Yazid, even more. Yazid's open disregard for Islamic law (shariah) and practices made many Muslims cringe at the thought of him taking the caliphate. Mu'awiyah, however, who insisted on turning the caliphate into a monarchy, pushed people to pledge allegiance to his son. On his deathbed, Mu'awiyah told Yazid not to try to force Imam Husayn to give allegiance to him because this would cause too much trouble. Soon after, in 60 A.H., Mu'awiyah died.

Little time passed before Yazid made it clear to his governors in Madinah that they were to force Imam Husayn to pledge allegiance to him or send Imam Husayn's head to him in Damascus. Representatives of Yazid came to Husayn in Madinah and asked for his allegiance. Imam Husayn asked for some time before he made his decision. In the meantime, he was able to move his family to Makkah where they were protected by the Sacred Precincts, Masjid-al-Haraam. It is forbidden in Islam to harm anything within these precincts.

Many people in the Ummah at that time who were already dissatisfied with the caliphate began to send letters to Imam Husayn urging him to join them in the city of Kufah in Iraq. They swore to defend him to the death and gave their allegiance to him. To investigate the situation, Imam Husayn sent his cousin, Muslim ibn Aqil to Kufah. After discussing the situation with the people of Kufah, he was killed and beheaded by supporters of Yazid on Wednesday, 9th of Dhul-Hijja, the Day of Arafat, in the year 60 A.H. (680).

It was the time of pilgrimage in Makkah, and Imam Husayn had begun to perform the pilgrimage rites. When he learned that some of Yazid's men had come dressed as pilgrims to kill him in Makkah, he gathered his people together to leave for Iraq. He did not want his blood to be spilled within the sacred precincts and to have the sacred rite of Hajj dishonored by that violence. Thus, he, some members of his family, and a group of followers set out towards Kufah on 8th of Dhul-Hijjah.

As the Imam approached Iraq, he was informed that many of the people who had voiced their support for him had turned and now supported the reign of Yazid, possibly to save their own lives. It was then that many of his representatives, including Muslim Ibn Aqil were abused and killed. As he and his followers marched closer to Iraq, a person that he met along the way who learned where he was going urged and pleaded with him not to continue his journey towards Kufah, but the Imam replied:

"Servant of God," he answered, "wise decisions are not hidden from me. yet the commands of God, the Exalted, cannot be resisted. By God, (my enemies) will not leave me till they have torn the very heart from the depths of my guts. If they do that, God will cause them to be dominated and humiliated until they become the most humiliated of the factions among nations."

Before the Imam and his followers were able to reach Kufah, Yazid's army surrounded them about 44 miles outside of Kufah in a desert called Karbala. At this point, Yazid's army cut off Imam Husayn's water supply, and his followers began to suffer from extreme thirst. Among these people were members of the Prophet's family, companions, and some women and children.

As the days passed in the month of Muharram, the first month of the new year on the Islamic calendar, Yazid's army, numbering 30,000, closed the circle around Imam Husayn's followers who were suffering from dehydration.

On the tenth day of Muharram, called Ashura, Imam Husayn and his followers went out with less than 100 people to meet the army of 30,000.

Ali Zayn al Abidin, son of Imam Husayn, peace be upon them, reported:

When the cavalry began to approach al-Husayn, he raised his hands and said:

"O God, it is You in Whom I trust amid all grief. You are my hope amid all violence. You are my trust and provision in everything that happens to me, (no matter) how much the heart may seem to weaken in it, trickery may seem to diminish (my hope) in it, the friend may seem to desert (me) in it, and the enemy may seem to rejoice in it. It comes upon me through You and when I complain to You of it, it is because of my desire for You, You alone. You have comforted me in (everything) and have revealed its (significance to me). You are the Master of all grace, the Possessor of all goodness and the Ultimate Resort of all desire."

The Imam and his followers fought all day and fell to their deaths fighting in the cause of Allah. That day, all who fought were martyred. Among them were two children of Imam Hasan, and Imam Husayn's five year old child.

"When the Imam himself was ready to fight, he saw his six-month-old baby was dying from thirst. The Imam brought his infant near to the enemy and demanded some water for baby, saying: You want me but not this baby so take him and give him some water. The words of the Imam had not been finished that the thirst of the baby was quenched by a deadly poisoned arrow from the enemy which pinned the baby's neck to the arm of his father. The Imam threw some of his blood toward the sky saying: "O' Lord! Your Husayn has offered whatever You have given him. Bless me by acceptance of this sacrifice." Finally Imam came to the field and fought for a long time and was finally martyred. The army of Yazid having killed Imam Husayn, cut his head and raised it on a lance.

"The army of the enemy, after ending the war, burned the tents of the women and children accompanying the Imam and his companions, and plundered those helpless women. They decapitated the bodies of the martyrs, denuded them and threw them to the ground without burial. Then they moved women and children along with the heads of the martyrs to Kufah. They took with them the daughters and sisters of al-Husayn, peace be on him, together with 'Ali b. al-Husayn, peace be on him. The latter was still sick with a dysentery and was almost on the point of death. The bodies of the martyrs were under the sunshine for three days till a tribe passing that place found them and performed the burial.

"The event of Karbala, the capture of women and children of the Household of Prophet, their being taken as prisoners from town to town, and the speeches made by Zaynab, the daughter of Ali, who was one of the prisoners, became a scandal for the Umayyad Kingdom. Such abuse of the Household of Prophet nullified the propaganda which Muawiyah had built up for years. The scandal reached to the extent that Yazid denounced the actions of his agents in public. That was exactly what Imam Husain wanted to do, otherwise he would not bring women and children with him and sacrifice some, and let the rest to become captives. That was the only way to make a wave in order to awaken the Muslim nation.

"The event of Karbala was a major factor in the overthrow of Umayyad kingdom though its effect was delayed. Among its immediate results were the revolts and rebellions combined with bloody wars which continued for twelve years. During those riots none of the important elements in Karbala could escape revenge and punishment, including Yazid.

The Fast of Aashoorah The tenth day of this sacred month, Muharram is known as Aashoorah. It is one of the most important and blessed days of Allah in the Islaamic calendar. Some ulamaa (scholars) are of the opinion that before the fasts of Ramadhaan were made compulsory, the fast of the day of Aashoorah was compulsory upon the ummah. This is stated in a hadeeth reported by Aaishah radhiyallahu anha that the Holy Prophet sallallahu alayhi wasallam ordered the observance of the fast of Aashoorah. However, when the fast of Ramadhaan became compulsory, then whosoever wished, kept this fast and whosoever desired did not observe this fast. Bukhari Vol.1 Page 268 But, nevertheless the Prophet sallallahu alayhi wasallam continued to fast this day and encouraged his

Companions to do the same. Ibne Abbas radhiyallahu anhu says: I did not see Rasulullah sallallahu alayhi wasallam anxiously await the fast of any day, which he gave preference to over other days, but this day, the day of Aashoorah.

Bukhari Vol.1 Page 268 Humayd Ibne Abdur Rahamaan narrates that he heard Muaawiyah Ibne Abi Sufyaan radhiyallahu anhu on the day of 'Aashoorah, during the year he performed hajj, saying on the pulpit: "O the people of Madinah! Where are your ulamaa (scholars)? I heard Rasullullah sallallahu alayhi wasallam saying: This is the day of 'Aashoorah. Allah has not enjoined its fasting on you but I am fasting it. Whosoever wish, keep (this) fast and whosoever desires do not observe (this fast)." Bukhari Vol.1 Page 268. In another hadeeth, Ibne Abbas raahiyallahu anhu narrates that the Holy Prophet sallallaha alayhi wasallam came to Madinah and found the Jews fasting on the day of 'Aashoorah. Hence the Holy Prophet sallallahu alayhi wasallam inquired of them, "What is (the significance of) this day on which you fast?"

They replied, "This is a great day. On this day Allah saved Moosa and his people and drowned Fir'awn and his nation. Thus Moosa alayhis salaam fasted on this day as a token of thanksgiving, therefore we too fast on this day." The Messenger of Allah sallallahu alayhi wasallam said, "We are more worthy of Moosa and nearer to him than you." Thereafter, the Holy Prophet sallallahu alayhi wasallam fasted on this day and ordered (his Companions) that a fast be kept on this day. Muharram is observed by the Shia community of Muslims in commemoration of the martyrdom of Prophet Mohammed's grandson, Imam Hussain, who was killed in the Battle of Karbala in AD 680. The prophet's son-in-law Ali, and Ali's elder son Hassan, are also remembered during this period as having suffered and died for righteous causes.

The word muharram also means respect. The first ten days of the month are observed as a period of mourning. After the death of the Prophet Mohammed, the Quran was considered the final word. The Prophet had named no successor. One faction of his followers believed that succession should remain within Mohammed's family, while another disagreed. After a long dispute, Abu Bakr, a loyal follower of Mohammed, was elected his successor. His reign was peaceful, as was that of his successors.

However, during the reign of Ali, the Prophet's son-in-law, there was opposition from the masses. Ali was assassinated and his elder son Hassan was poisoned. His younger son Hussain, his family and his troops, were tortured and killed, and Hussain's head was severed and presented to the king.

The killing of Hussain happened on the tenth day of month of Muharram, and the event was called Ashura. It is now observed as a day for public expression of grief. These circumstances divided the Muslim community into the Shias and the Sunnis. The Shias consider Ali, Hassan and Hussain the rightful successors of Prophet Mohammed and mourn their death during Muharram. The Shias observe the entire month as a period of mass mourning. There is no celebration or expression of joy of any kind. Women are expected to forsake all adornments. Public enactments of grief, depicting scenes from the Battle of Karbala, are carried out in Shia mosques on the first ten days.

The Shias in India observe certain ceremonies in common, though the details differ considerably. As soon as the new moon appears, people clad in black assemble and recite plaintive verses over sweetened cold drink, in memory of Imam Hussain.

The cool drink is meant to remind people of the terrible thirst Hussain and his family had to suffer. Food and drink are later distributed to the public, especially to the poor. The first nine days are also spent in making bamboo and paper replicas of the martyr's tomb. On Ashura, the tenth day, decorated taziyas, or tombs embellished with precious metals, are carried through the city streets. A horse is led in procession in memory of Hussain's horse, Dul Dul.

Wrestlers and dancers enact scenes depicting the Battle of Karbala. Bare-chested Shia men strike their body with chains or walk barefoot over burning coal while uttering cries of anguish for the torture that Hussain suffered. Apart from reliving his suffering, it is also an expression of the people's inability to save Hussain from the brutalities.

Muharram or the 'sacred month' is the first month of the Islamic or Hegira calendar. The Hadith instructs to observe fasting on the 9th and 10th of this month. Fasting on *Ashura* (the 10th of Muharram) was a *faraz* (obligatory) until fasting in ramadan was made faraz. Both in pre-Islamic times as well as at the time of the Prophet *Muhammad* (Sm), it was *haram* (forbidden) to be in war in this month. Muslims of the Shiah group observe the first ten days of the month as a period of mourning for the death of Imam Husain (R), the grandson of Hazrat Muhammad (Sm).

The tenth day of Muharram is called Ashura. Imam Husain (R) was killed on this day at the hands of the troops of Yazid, the son of Muawiyah, the Umaiyya caliph. Shiahs take out processions with tazia, the replica of the tomb of Imam Husain (R) and they show their grief by clapping on their chests or flagellating themselves with knives or chains. The mourning continues for forty days till the first ten days of the next month Safar. Muharram had been observed since the 10th century. In Bengal also it has been observed for the last few centuries.

The centre of observances of Muharram in Dhaka is the *Husaini* dalan Imambara. As mark of mourning, Shiahs dress in black for at least ten days of Muharram. During this time, they refrain from merrymaking, listening to music, or seeing plays or movies. They also do not arrange weddings during this month. Keeping in mind that Imam Husain (R) and his followers suffered from unavailability of water, some Shiahs refrain from eating fish. During these first ten days of the month, *majlis* (mourning assemblies), are held at the imambaras, separately for men and women.

The story of the martyrdom of Hazrat Husain (R) is told and *marsiyas* (elegies) are sung or recited in the assemblies. At the end of the service, food is distributed to the people. On the seventh of Muharram, *shirni* (special offerings) are made and the people pray for Allah's blessings. Food and fruits in large quantities and varieties are distributed on the occasion. Those who pray for Allah's blessings, pick out a food item, and make a *manat*, or promise, not to eat that food for a year. In case the prayer is deemed accepted, they promise to offer shirni the next year. Along with the shirni, some also offer silver *panja*, the model of an open palm with five fingers that represent the five holy figures, the Prophet Muhammad (Sm), his daughter Fatima (R), his son-in-law Ali (R), and his two grandsons Hassan (R) and Husain (R).Muharram processions were common in Bengal in the 18th century. Horses and elephants were also used in the processions. Processions nowadays are much smaller. In Dhaka, the procession begins at Husaini Dalan and, after winding its way through the streets, terminates at a place designated Karbala on the banks of the Dhanmandi Lake.

The replica of *Duldul*, the horse of Imam Husain (R) and the flags in the procession show a symbolic presence of Imam Husain (R). Also latikhela (stick fights) are organised to remind of the battle between the troops of Imam Husain (R) and Yazid. As with other festivals in Bangladesh, Muharram has become an occasion for fairs at various places.

Id-ul-Zuha

Also called Bakrid, Id-ul-Zuha, is a festival of great rejoice. Special prayers and exchange of greetings and gifts marked the Id-ul-Zuha (Bakrid), the festival of sacrifice, celebrated with traditional fervour and gaiety in India. Id-ul-Zuha is a reminder of Prophet Ibrahim's readiness to sacrifice his son for God's sake. It also marks the completion of Haj (pilgrimage to Mecca). On this day, special 'Dua' is recited by thousands of muslims for peace and prosperity.

It is a commemoration of Hazrat Ibrahim's great test of obedience to Allah, who ordered him to sacrifice the person dearest to him. Ibrahim decided to sacrifice his son Ismail, at Mina, near Mecca. As the great religious leader was on the point of applying the sword to the throat of his dear son, it was revealed to him that the exercise was merely a test of his faith in Allah, and that he could sacrifice a ram instead. On Bakrid, the Muslims go to the mosques in the morning to offer prayers to Allah. and then sacrifice the animal at home. Bakr means 'sheep', and on Bakrid, the affluent sacrifice one animal per member of the family, and distribute two-thirds of the meat among the poor. A full-grown camel, cow, goat or sheep, free from any disease, is sacrificed. Bakrid is also a day for feasting and visiting friends to say Id Mubarak.

It is one of the grandest Muslim festivals, and is also known as *Bakrid*. It fails on the 10th day of the Muslim month Zil-Hijja. There is an interesting story about the celebration. Once Hazrat Ibrahim was ordered by Allah in a dream to sacrifice his dearest thing. To Ibrahim his son was the dearest, So, he decided to sacrifice his son on the altar of Allah. He sought the permission of the members of the family and blindfolded himself so that at the time of sacrifice his love for the son may not deter him from the act. He struck with his sword, but when he removed the fold from his eyes, to his great pleasure and surprise, he found that he had sacrificed a ram instead of his son. Since, then a ram, or goat or a camel is sacrificed and distributed among the neighbours and relatives.

The sacrifice of a ram or goat also symbolizes that man's position in the creation is far more high than any beast, and any sacrifice, however great, is a small thing for the sake of religion and Allah. The sacrificial ram or goat is reared with great care and is kept quite healthy and fat And the man who does the sacrifice must. be a man of a character and deeply religious. This Muslim festival of sacrifice, Id-ul-Zuha (Arabic) or Bakrid in India is celebrated all over the country. On this day Muslims sacrifice a goat or Bakr (Urdu) to commemorate the sacrifice of Prophet Ibrahim, who willingly agreed to kill his son at the behest of God.

According to Islamic belief, to test Ibrahim's faith, Allah commanded him to sacrifice his son Ismail. He agreed to do it but found his paternal feelings hard to suppress. So he blindfolded himself before putting Ismail on the altar at the mount of Mina near Mecca. When he removed his bandage after performing the act, he saw his son standing in front of him, alive. On the altar lay a slaughtered lamb. This festival coincides with the Haj pilgrimage in Mecca.

Prayers are offered in the mosques and the sacrificial meat is then distributed after the Id prayers. Special delicacies are prepared and served among family and friends on the occasion.

Bakr-Id: The feast of Bakr-Id is an occasion to give and to sacrifice. It is a day to thank the Almighty for one's good fortune and to share it with the less fortunate brethren.

Legend has it that Allah commanded Hazrat Ibrahim (Abraham) to sacrifice his son Ismail on Mount Mina near Mecca. Ibrahim, unable to see himself kill his son, blindfolded himself and carried out the pronouncement of God. When he took off the blindfold, a lamb lay slaughtered on the altar and his son stood there unharmed.

Ibrahim understood then that this willingness on Ibrahim's part to give up his only son was what God sought, and not the sacrifice of human flesh and blood. The legend ascertains that all God requires of man is a surrender of his will and self. Like Ibrahim, who willingly surrenders his beloved son to God, a true follower of Islam is expected to sacrifice something that is dear to him.

The animal sacrifices made during Bakr-Id are mainly to provide food to the poor and to commemorate the noble act of Ibrahim. This spirit of sacrifice is what truly underlines the spirit of Bakr-Id. Incidentally, the day also coincides with the day when the holy Quran was declared complete. Bakr-Id is celebrated from the tenth to the twelfth day in the Islamic month of Dhul Hijjah. Every year, while pilgrims to the Mount of Mina make animal sacrifices as part of the pilgrimage rituals, Muslims the world over celebrate Bakr-Id in a similar fashion.

Every true Muslim who possesses wealth equal to or more than 400 grams of gold or is capable of affording two square meals a day, is expected to sacrifice an animal. A goat (also called bakri, hence Bakr-Id), sheep, camel or any other four-legged animal is slaughtered during one of the three days of the festival, and the meat is distributed. The sacrificial offering is divided in three parts-one for the self, another for friends, and the third, most importantly, for the needy. The sacrifice can be offered at any time before the afternoon of the third day

Festivities mark the first day, when people wear new clothes offer prayers at the mosque, and greet friends and relatives Special prayers are offered on all three days. It is said that th celebrations are carried on over three days to ensure that the entire Muslim community partakes in the noble of act of giving and sharing.

Bakr-Id is celebrated all over India with much fervour, as it is in the rest of Islamic world. The name Bakr-Id, however, is most popular in India. In Arabic, the feast is usually referred to as Id-ul-Azha or Id-ul-Zuha.

Besides Hinduism, India is also the home of innumerable other faiths and the religious and cultural diversity of this nation is manifested in the large number of non-Hindu festivals.

The sizeable Muslim communities have their Ids in common with Muslims across the world. *Id-ul-Fitr, Id-ul-Zuha* and *Id-i-Milad* are the three festive occasions widely celebrated by Muslims in India.

Id is celebrated with great enthusiasm all over the country, and one can see Muslims of all age groups and from all stratas of society attired in new clothes, visiting mosques to offer *namaaz*.

The tombs of many Sufi saints attract devotees of all religious persuasions, especially during the urs or death anniversaries. The best known urs are centred at tombs in towns like Ajmer, Delhi, Manakpur, Nagore and Dongri.

The Id-ul-Azha commemorates the ordeal of Hazrat Ibrahim, who had been put to a terrible test by God when he was asked to sacrifice whatever was dearest to him and he decided to sacrifice the life of his son. As he was on the point of applying the sword to his son's throat, it was revealed to him that this was meant only to test his faith, and it was enough, if instead he sacrifices only a ram in the name of *Allah*. This is celebrated on the tenth day of *Zilhijja,* when the *Haj* celebrations at Mecca are rounded off by the sacrifice of goats or camels. In India, too, goats and sheep are sacrificed all over the country and prayers are offered.

Id-ul-Fitr (Ramzan Id)

Coming with the new moon, this festival marks the end of Ramzan, the ninth month of the Muslim year. It was during this month that the holy Koran was revealed. Muslims keep a fast every day during this month and on the completion of the period, which is decided by the appearance of the new moon, Id-ul-Fitr is celebrated with great eclat. Prayers are offered in mosques and *Idgahs* and elaborate festivities are held.

Id-i-Milad (Barah-wafat)

The Prophet was born on the twelfth day of *Rabi-ul-Awwal*, the third month of the Muslim year. His death anniversary also falls on the same day, the word *'barah'* standing for the twelve days of the Prophet's sickness. During these days, sermons are delivered in mosques by learned men, focusing on the life and noble deeds of the Prophet.

In some parts of the country, a ceremony known as *sandal* rite is performed over the symbolic footprints of the Prophet engraved in stone. A representation of *'buraq'*, a horse on which the Prophet is believed to have ascended to heaven, is kept near the footprints and anointed with sandal paste or scented powder, and the house and casket containing these are elaborately decorated. Elegies or *'marsiyas'* are sung in memory of the last days of the Prophet. The 12th day or the *Urs* proper is observed quietly, in prayers and alms giving.

Id-uz-Zuha or Id-ud-Dhua popularly caller Bakri Id or Id Ebaqr ia a day of thanksgiving to God by means of sacrificing some animal like a goat, sheep, camel or bull. This month of the year which is considered propitious for pilgrimage to Mecca.

Id-ul-Zuha or Id-ud-Duha are essential muslim festivals when thousands gather at mosques all over the country to offer prayers.

Id-ul-Fitr popularly known as Id is a festival celebrated on the first day of Shawwal, the tenth month of the Hijmi year since the time of Prophet Mohammed. Fitr means breaking the fast of refraining from fasting, while Id means happiness. The festical thus marks the end of the fast during the preceding month of Ramzan. Muslims regard this month as one of the great bounty from God.

Id-ul-Zuha, the festival of sacrifice popularly known as Bakr Id, is celebrated by Muslims in April/May. It marks the end of Ramzan, the month of fasting. Bakr Id celebrates the devotion of Prophet Abraham (Hazrat Ibrahim), who was willing to sacrifice his only son Ishmael at the behest of God. On this day Muslims sacrifice a goat (bakr in Urdu) to commemorate Hazrat Ibrahim's sacrifice. Two-thirds of the meat is kept by the family and one-third is distributed to the poor after Id prayers. The day is marked with family get-togethers, exchange of gifts and feasting on specially prepared delicacies like biryani, kebabs and kulfi. Id coincides with the Haj pilgrimage at Mecca.

Jamshed Navroz

Over 3000 years ago, Shah Jamshed of the Peshadian dynasty ascended the throne on the Spring Equinox. His descendants, the Parsi community, celebrate it as the New Year, the dawn of a new day (Navroz literally means "new day"). It is celebrated, even today, with prayers and feasting.

In homes, a special spread, Haft-Sinn-the seven S's-is prepared. Seven is considered to be a lucky number and the spread contains seven items that begin with "s" in farsi: sabzeh (home grown sprouts), samanou (wheat germ), sib (apples), sonbol (hyacinth), senjed (sorb tree berry), seer (garlic), somagh (sumac). The table also holds seven foods beginning with 'sh' in Persian, sharab (wine), shakkar (sugar), shir (milk), shirinberej (sweet meat), shirin (sweet), shira (syrup) and shahad (honey); a copy of the Gathas (scriptures); a lit lamp; a mirror; a bowl of water with live fish; a shallow earthenware plate with sprouted wheat or beans (for prosperity); flowers (for colour); a gold or silver coin (for wealth); painted eggs (for productivity); and sweets and rosewater in bowls (for sweetness and happiness). These are meant to symbolize creation and to welcome spring. Visitors to the house are first led to this table. They are asked to smile into the mirror, so that they may smile throughout the year. They are asked to look at the coin, so that they may have wealth the whole year round. They are sprinkled with rosewater so that they stay fragrant and healthy. After that, they are led to another table for a meal.

4

Sikh Festivals

Baisakhi

The Mughal Emperor, Aurangzeb, installed himself as the Emperor of India in 1657. To achieve his aim he had annihilated almost all his family opposition. Immediately after consolidating his power he embarked on a policy of religious persecution and set upon the process of Islamization of India.

The Brahmins were his primary target. He levied unethical religious taxes against Hindus, and shut their temples and places of learning. He had been convinced by his clerics that once the Brahmins accepted Islam the others would follow. The Brahmins, particularly the inhabitants of Kashmir, looked for some dynamic leadership to fight this subversion.

The Brahmins of Kashmir approached Guru Tegh Bahadur (1621-1675), the ninth in the line of Sikh Gurus, who was on the throne of the Sikh religion. They asked him for guidance on combatting the atrocities committed by the Mughal Emperor. At the time of their meeting, Guru Tegh Bahadur's nine year old son, Gobind Rai, was sitting beside him.

As Guru Tegh Bahadur went into a deep state of contemplation, his young son asked the reason of his repose. Guru Tegh Bahadur said that the matter was of vital importance; the world is aggrieved by oppression; and no brave man had yet come forward who was willing to sacrifice his life to free the earth from the burden of' Aurangzeb's persecution of Hindus. Young Gobind Rai replied: "For that purpose who is more worthy than thou who art at once generous and brave." So after entrusting the Guruship to Gobind Rai, Guru Tegh Bahadur proceeded towards Delhi, the seat of the Mughal Empire.

Upon reaching Delhi, the Guru and his loyal attendants were immediately imprisoned by Aurangzeb. While in prison, Guru Tegh Bahadur foresaw the beginning of his ecclesiastic journey. To test his son's courage and capability to carry on the Guru's mission, he wrote him saying, "My strength is exhausted, I am in chains and I can make not any efforts. Says Nanak, God alone is now my refuge. He will help me as He did his Saints." In reply young Guru Gobind Rai wrote: "I have regained my Power, my bonds are broken and all options are open unto me. Nanak, everything is in Thine hands. It is only Thou who can assist Thyself."

Guru Teg Bahadur offered his life for the freedom of conscience and conviction of anyone belonging to a faith other than his own. His spirit of sacrifice and courage was kindled into the heart of Gobind Rai.

Hundreds of people gathered around the place where Guru Tegh Bahadur was martyred in Delhi. The executioner abandoned the Guru's body in the open. No one came forward openly to claim the body to perform religious rites. Even ardent disciples withdrew unrecognized. Taking advantage of the stormy weather that followed the execution, two persons covertly took the body of Guru Tegh Bahadur for cremation. This cowardice fomented in Gobind Rai an urge to endow his Sikhs with a distinct identity.

With the criteria of courage and strength to sacrifice, Gobind Rai became the tenth Sikh Guru. He wanted to instill these principles in his downtrodden followers. He wanted to uplift their morale to combat the evil forces of injustice, tyranny, and oppression.

He was 33 years old when he had Divine inspiration to actuate his designs. Every year at the time of Baisakhi (springtime), thousands of devotees would come to Anandpur to pay their obeisance and seek the Guru's blessings. In early 1699, months before Baisakhi Day, Guru Gobind Rai sent special edicts to congregants far and wide that that year the Baisakhi was going to be a unique affair. He asked them not to cut any of their hair — to come with unshorn hair under their turbans and chunis, and for the men to come with full beards.

On Baisakhi Day, March 30, 1699, hundreds of thousands of people gathered around his divine temporal seat at Anandpur Sahib. The Guru addressed the congregants with a most stirring oration on his divine mission of restoring their faith and preserving the Sikh religion. After his inspirational discourse, he flashed his unsheathed sword and said that every great deed was preceded by equally great sacrifice: He demanded one head for oblation. After some trepidation one person offered himself. The Guru took him inside a tent. A little later he reappeared with his sword dripping with blood, and asked for another head. One by one four more earnest devotees offered their heads. Every time the Guru took a person inside the tent, he came out with a bloodied sword in his hand.

Thinking their Guru to have gone berserk, the congregants started to disperse. Then the Guru emerged with all five men dressed piously in white. He baptized the five in a new and unique ceremony called *pahul*, what Sikhs today know as the baptism ceremony called *Amrit*. Then the Guru asked those five baptized Sikhs to baptize him as well. He then proclaimed that the *Panj Pyare* — the Five Beloved Ones — would be the embodiment of the Guru himself: "Where there are Panj Pyare, there am I. When the Five meet, they are the holiest of the holy."

He said whenever and wherever five baptized (*Amritdhari*) Sikhs come together, the Guru would be present. All those who receive Amrit from five baptized Sikhs will be infused with the spirit of courage and strength to sacrifice. Thus with these principles he established *Panth Khalsa*, the Order of the Pure Ones.

At the same time the Guru gave his new Khalsa a unique, indisputable, and distinct identity. The Guru gave the gift of *bana*, the distinctive Sikh clothing and headwear. He also offered five emblems of purity and courage. These symbols, worn by all baptized Sikhs of both sexes, are popularly known today as Five Ks: *Kesh,* unshorn hair; *Kangha*, the wooden comb; *Karra,* the iron (or steel) bracelet; *Kirpan*, the sword; and *Kachera*, the underwear. By being identifiable, no Sikh could never hide behind cowardice again.

Political tyranny was not the only circumstance that was lowering peoples' morale. Discriminatory class distinctions (the Indian caste system) promoted by Brahmins and Mullahs were also responsible for the peoples' sense of degradation. The Guru wanted to eliminate the anomalies caused by the caste system. The constitution of the *Panj Pyare* was the living example of his dream: both the high and low castes were amalgamated into one. Among the original *Panj Pyare*, there was one *Khatri*, shopkeeper; one *Jat*, farmer; one *Chhimba*, washer-man; one *Ghumar*, water-carrier; and one *Nai*, a barber. The Guru gave the surname of *Singh* (Lion) to every Sikh and also took the name for himself. From Guru Gobind Rai he became Guru Gobind Singh. He also pronounced that all Sikh women embody royalty, and gave them the surname *Kaur* (Princess). With the distinct Khalsa identity and consciousness of purity Guru Gobind Singh gave all Sikhs the opporunity to live lives of courage, sacrifice, and equality.

The birth of the Khalsa is celebrated by Sikhs every Baisakhi Day on April 13. Baisakhi 1999 marks the 300th anniversary of Guru Gobind Singh's gift of Panth Khalsa to all Sikhs everywhere.

Vaisakhi (known as Baisakhi) marks the beginning of the new Spring year and the end of the harvest in India. Vaisakhi falls in the Nanakshahi calendar (neither in the Amantha-nor in the Purnimantha-calendar) on the first day of Vaisakh and marks the sun entering Mesha Rasi (this fact is called Mesha Sankranti). Vaisakhi is therefore determined by the sun and not the moon. It usually falls on April 13, falling on April 14 once every thirty-six years. It coincides with 'Rongali Bihu' in Assam, 'Naba Barsha' in Bengal, Puthandu in Tamil Nadu, 'Pooram Vishu' in Kerala, and the Sinhala/Tamil new year festival in Sri Lanka.

At the Vaisakhi festival of 1699, at Keshgarh Sahib near Anandpur, Guru Gobind Singh, the Tenth Guru of the Sikhs founded the Akal Khalsa (Community of the Pure). Guru Gobind Singh, had organised for followers from all over India to meet him at the Vasakhi Fair in Anandpur.

Guru Gobind Singh emerged from a tent with a sword, and asked for people to give their lives for their faith. A young Sikh volunteered, followed the Guru into a tent. Shortly after, the Guru reappeared alone with his sword covered with blood, and asked for a second volunteer. A second Sikh stepped forward and again the Guru took him into the tent, and re-appeared alone, his sword covered in more blood. This was repeated for a third, fourth and fifth volunteer.

The crowd became very unnerved, as many believed that the Güru had killed the five Sikhs. He soon came out of the tent again, this time followed by all five Sikhs who were alive and well and dressed in turbans and other symbols that have since become symbols of Sikh identity. He called the five Sikhs the Panj Pyare-the beloved five.

Then the Guru put water in a bowl for sprinkling over the five in a simple initiation ceremony. He said prayers as he stirred the water with a short steel sword; symbolising the need for strength. The Guru's wife, Mata Sundri, then came forward and placed some sugar crystals into the holy water or amrit as a reminder that strength must always be balanced by sweetness of temperament. After completing his prayers, the Guru then sprinkled the amrit over the five.

He declared them to be the first members of a new community of equals, to be called the Khalsa, meaning "pure". These "saint soldiers" were to dedicate their lives to the service of others and the pursuit of justice for people of all faiths. The Panj Pyare were asked to wear five distinctive symbols of their new identity, The Five Ks.

In a move to end social divisions the five dropped their surnames-then linked to caste or occupation-and took the common name *Singh*, meaning "lion", a reminder of the need for courage. At the same time, the Guru gave Sikh women the name or title *Kaur*, meaning "princess", to emphasise dignity and complete equality.

The Guru then knelt before the five and asked them to initiate him. Hence, the Khalsa became a community in which master and disciple were equal.

For Sikhs, this seasonal festival also has great importance as the founding of the (Soldiers of the Timeless One) at Anandpur Sahib, the famous Golden Temple of Amritsar, India. The Akal Khalsa played an important role in resistance against Mughal rule. This act of total surrender of one's life to the service of the AKAL (God), the Timeless One, and at the feet of Guru Gobind Singh created the Sikh religion. For many centuries after that, the first male child of many Hindu families in Punjab was ordained as a Sikh.

Vaisakhi used to fall on the 13th of April, but due to a change in the calendar it now falls on the 14th of April, once in 36 years.

Celebrations: To mark the celebrations, devotees, irrespective of their religion, throng gurdwaras-the Sikh place of worship-and temples in different parts of the area. The celebrations start early as devotees, with flowers and offerings in their hands, proceed towards the gurdwaras and temples before dawn. Processions through towns are also common.

Baisakhi is one of the major festivals of Sikhs and is celebrated with lot of enthusiasm and gaiety in the state of Punjab and all throughout the world where there is a significant Sikh population. For the large farming community of Punjab, Baisakhi Festival marks the time for harvest of rabi crops and they celebrate the day by performing joyful bhangra and gidda dance. For the Sikh community, Baisakhi Festival has tremendous religious significance as it was on a Baisakhi Day in 1699, that Guru Gobind Singh, the tenth Sikh Guru laid the foundation of Panth Khalsa-the Order of the Pure Ones.

Date of Baisakhi Festival falls on the first day of Vaisakh month (April-May) according to Nanakshahi or Sikh Calendar. For this reason, Baisakhi is also popularly known as Vaisakhi. According to English calendar, the date of Baisakhi corresponds to April 13 every year and April 14 once in every 36 years. This difference in Baisakhi dates is due to the fact that day of

Baisakhi is reckoned according to solar calendar and not the lunar calendar. The auspicious date of Baisakhi is celebrated all over India under different names and different set of rituals and celebrations. Baisakhi date coincides with 'Rongali Bihu' in Assam, 'Naba Barsha' in Bengal, Puthandu in Tamil Nadu and 'Pooram Vishu' in Kerala.Baisakhi CelebrationsPeople of Punjab celebrate the festival of Baisakhi with exuberance and devotion.

As the festival has tremendous importance in Sikh religion, major activities of the day are organized in Gurdwaras. People wake up early to prepare for the day. Many also take bath in the holy river to mark the auspicious occasion. After getting ready people pay a visit to their neighbourdood gurdwara and take part in the special prayer meeting organized for the day. At the end of the Baisakhi ardas, congregates receive specially prepared Kara prasad or sweetened semolina. This is followed by a guru ka langar or community lunch. Later, during the day people of Sikh faith take out a Baisakhi procession under the leadership of Panj piaras.

The procession moves through the major localities of the city amidst the rendition of devotional songs by the participating men, women and children. Mock duels, bhangra and gidda performances make the procession joyous and colourful. Celebrations by Farmers. For the large farming community of Punjab and Haryana, Baisakhi marks a New Year's time as it is time to harvest rabi crop. On Baisakhi, farmers thank god for the bountiful crop and pray for good times ahead. People buy new clothes and make merry by singing, dancing and enjoying the best of festive food. Cries of "Jatta aai Baisakhi", rent the skies as gaily men and women break into the bhangra and gidda dance to express their joy. Everyday farming scenes of sowing, harvesting, winnowing and gathering of crops are expressed through zestful movements of the body to the accompaniment of ballads and dhol music. In several villages of Punjab Baisakhi Fairs are organized where besides other recreational activities, wrestling bouts are also held.

Legends of Baisakhi: There are various legends associated with the colourful and vibrant festival of Baisakhi. A study of these interesting legends of Baisakhi reveal that the day of Baisakhi is significant not just for Sikhs but also for Hindus and Buddhists alike. Besides, it is joyous to note that as a harvest festival, people of all communities in Punjab celebrate Baisakhi in a harmonious manner.

Baisakhi Festival marks the time for the harvest of Rabi crops and is therefore celebrated with utmost joy and enthusiasm in the state of Punjab where agriculture is the predominant occupation of the people. To celebrate the occasion, people dress themselves gaily and perform the joyful bhangra and giddha dance on the tune of the dhol. Farmers in Punjab celebrate Baisakhi Festival to hilt by feasting and merrymaking before they hit on tiring but joyful task of harvesting from the next day. As a harvest festival, Baisakhi is also celebrated by different names and with different rituals in several regions of India. *Regional celebrations of Baisakhi* are marked as Rongali Bihu in Assam, Naba Barsha in Bengal, Puthandu in Tamil Nadu, Vishu in Kerala and Vaishakha in Bihar.

The day of Baisakhi marks the birth of Khalsa Panth and therefore holds tremendous significance for the Sikhs. It was on the *Baisakhi Day* meeting organized at Anandpur Sahib, in 1699, that the tenth Guru of Sikhs, Guru Gobind Sigh laid the foundation of Khalsa Panth and called on the Sikhs to sacrifice themselves for their community. Besides, it was on the Baisakhi Day that Guru Gobind Singh administered amrit (nectar) to his first batch of five disciples, the *Panj Piaras* making them Singhs, a martial community. After the Baisakhi Day in 1699 the tradition of gurus was discontinued, and the Granth Sahib-the Holy book of the Sikhs was declared the eternal guide of the Sikhs.

According to a popular legend in Sikhism, it was on the day of Baisakhi in 1567 that Guru Amar Das had first institutionalized Baisakhi as one of the special days when all Sikhs would gather to receive the guru's blessings at Goindwal. Martyrdom *of Guru Arjan Dev Yet* another legend related to Baisakhi, says that on the day of Baisakhi Guru Arjan Dev was martyred by the Muslim rulers. It is said that in an act of barbaric cruelty Muslim rulers threw the Guru alive into a cauldron of boiling oil. *Foundation of Arya Samaj* The day of Baisakhi Festival is also important for the Hindus as it on this day in 1875 that Swami Dayanand Saraswati founded the Arya Samaj-a reformed sect of Hindus who are devoted to the Vedas for spiritual guidance and have discarded idol worship. *Attainment of Nirvana by Gautam Buddha For* the Buddhist, the day of Baisakhi Festival is significant, as according to a popular legend it was on this auspicious day that Gautam Buddha attained enlightenment or Nirvana under the Mahabodhi tree in the town of Gaya. For this reason, the day of Baisakhi is celebrated as *Buddha Purnima* is several parts of the country.

Baisakhi Day or Vaisakhi Day of March 30th, 1699 is of significant importance for the Sikhs. It was on this day that Guru Gobind Singh-the Tenth Guru of the Sikhs founded the Akal Khalsa (Community of the Pure) at a ceremony organized at Keshgarh Sahib near Anandpur. The Akal Khalsa played a significant role in resistance against Mughal rule. Every year on April 13 Sikhs celebrate with pomp and gusto the birth of the Khalsa Panth. In the year 1667 Aurungzeb, the Mughal Emperor installed himself as the Emperor of India after annihilating almost all his family opposition. Immediately after gaining power, Aurungzeb embarked on a policy of religious persecution and started the process of Islamization of India. Brahmins became the prime targets of Aurungzeb in this regard as his clerics made him convinced that once the Brahmins accepted Islam the others would follow. Pursuing his agenda, Aurungzeb levied unethical religious taxes against Hindus and shut their temples and places of learning.

The Brahmins, particularly those of Kashmir, desperately felt the need for a dynamic leadership to fight this subversion by the Mughal Emperor. They approached Guru Tegh Bahadur (1621-1675), the ninth in the line of Sikh Gurus, who was on the throne of the Sikh religion and asked him for guidance on the issue. During this meeting, Guru Tegh Bahadur's nine-year-old son, Gobind Rai, was sitting beside him. Finding Guru Tegh Bahadur under deep contemplation, the young son asked the reason of his repose.

The Guru explained the situation to the child and said the world is aggrieved by oppression and no brave man had yet come forward to willingly sacrifice his life to free the earth from the burden of Aurangzeb's persecution of Hindus. To this young Gobind Rai replied, *"For that purpose who is more worthy than thou who art at once generous and brave."* Pleased with his son's reply, Guru Tegh Bahadur entrusted the Guruship to Gobind Rai and proceeded towards Delhi, the seat of the Mughal Empire.

Just as they reached Delhi, the mighty Aurangzeb imprisoned the Guru and his loyal attendants. Foreseeing his ecclesiastic journey during imprisonment, Guru Tegh Bahadur thought of testing his son's courage and capability to carry on the Guru's mission. In a letter to Gobind Rai, the Guru wrote, *"My strength is exhausted, I am in chains and I can make not any efforts. Says Nanak, God alone is now my refuge. He will help me as He did his Saints."* In his reply young Guru Gobind Rai wrote, *"I have regained my Power, my bonds are broken and all options are open unto me. Nanak, everything is in Thine hands. It is only Thou who can assist Thyself."* Later, Guru Tegh Bahadur was martyred in Delhi in the presence of hundreds of people. The executioner abandoned the Guru's body in the open. But no one dared to come forward to claim the body to perform religious rites. Even the ardent disciples withdrew unrecognized.

It was only when the stormy weather occurred, that two persons took advantage of the situation and covertly took the body of Guru Tegh Bahadur for cremation. This cowardice of Sikhs incited in Gobind Rai an urge to endow his Sikhs with a distinct identity. With the desire to instill courage and strength to sacrifice among his fellow men, Gobind Rai became the tenth Sikh Guru. At the age of 33, Guru Gobind had Divine inspiration to actuate his designs. The Guru found the occasion of Baisakhi could serve his purpose, as every year thousands of devotees would come to Anandpur at the time of Baisakhi (springtime) to pay their obeisance and seek the Guru's blessings. Early in the year 1699, months before Baisakhi Day, Guru Gobind Rai sent special edicts to congregates far and wide that that year

the Baisakhi was going to be a unique affair. He asked them not to cut any of their hair and to come with unshorn hair under their turbans and chunis. Besides, men were asked to come with full beards.

The Baisakhi Day of March 30, 1699 at the call of the Guru, thousands of people gathered at the Anandpur Sahib, the famous Golden Temple of Amritsar, India on the Vaisakhi Day, March 30, 1699. To instill courage in the fellow men, Guru Gobind made a powerful oration and revealed to them his divine mission of restoring amongst Sikhs and preserving the Sikh religion. At the end of his speech, the Guru flashed his unsheathed sword and said that every great deed was preceded by equally great sacrifice and demanded one head for oblation. To the Guru's call, Daya Ram, a Khatri of Lahore offered himself. The Guru took him inside a tent. A little later he reappeared with his sword dripping with blood, and asked for another head.

One by one four more earnest devotees-Daram Das-a Jat of Delhi, Mohkam Chand-a washerman of Dwarka (Gujarat), Himmat-a cook of Jagannath (Orissa) and Sahib Chand-a barber of Bidar (Karnataka) offered their heads. Every time the Guru took a person inside the tent, he came out with a bloodied sword in his hand. Astonished with their Guru's behaviour and believing him to have gone berserk, people started to disperse. Shortly after, Guru Gobind emerged with all five men dressed piously in white. He baptized the five in a new and unique ceremony called *'Khande di Pahul'* (the double-edged Sword Amrit), what Sikhs today call *Amrit.* After this, the Guru asked the five baptized Sikhs to baptize him as well.

They were then knighted as *Singhs,* as the Five beloved ones, the first members of the new community of equals, to be called the Khalsa, meaning "pure". Guru Gobind proclaimed that the *Panj Pyare or the Five Beloved Ones* would be the embodiment of the Guru himself, "Where there are Panj Pyare, there am I. When the Five meet, they are the holiest of the holy." These "saint soldiers" were to dedicate their lives to the service of others and the pursuit of justice for people of all faiths. The Guru also said whenever and wherever the five baptized or *Amritdhari Sikhs* comes together, the Guru would be present. All those who receive Amrit from five baptized Sikhs will be infused with the spirit of courage and strength to sacrifice. Thus with these principles, *Guru Gobind established Panth Khalsa, the Order of the Pure Ones.* The Guru also gave his new Khalsa a unique, indisputable, and distinct identity. The Guru gave the gift of *bana,* the distinctive Sikh clothing and headwear. He also offered five emblems of purity and courage.

Apart from fighting the political tyranny, Guru Gobind also sought to eliminate social discriminations in the name of caste with the establishment of Khalsa Panth. The Panj Piyaras set by the Guru amalgamated people of low and high caste into one as it consisted of people of different strata of the society. To further do away with the system of caste discrimination and to give to all Sikhs an opportunity to live lives of courage, sacrifice, and equality, the Guru gave the surname of Singh (Lion) to every Sikh and also took the name for himself. From Guru Gobind Rai, he became Guru Gobind Singh. He also pronounced that all Sikh women embody royalty, and gave them the surname *Kaur* (Princess).

Joyful festival of Baisakhi is celebrated with lot of charm and gusto in the vibrant state of Punjab. People perform set Baisakhi customs and traditions for the day with sincerity and devotion. Since Baisakhi is celebrated as the birth of Guru Gobind Singh-the Tenth Sikh Guru and the foundation day of Khalsa Panth, major activities for the festival are centred on gurdwaras-the Sikh place of worship. As a harvest festival Baisakhi is celebrated in open fields with energetic bhangra and gidda dance by gaily dressed men and women of Punjab. *Baisakhi Rituals at Gurudwaras* People following Sikh faith wake up early in the morning on a Baisakhi day and pay visit to gurdwaras to attend special prayer meetings.

While most Sikhs strive to visit the revered Golden Temple or Anandpur Sahib, where the Khalsa was pronounced, those who are unable to do so visit their neighborhood gurdwara.At a gurdwara, the Guru Granth Sahib, the holy book of Sikhs is ceremonially taken out and is given a symbolical bath with milk and water. After these simple rituals, Guru Granth Sahib is placed on its throne with care. The book is then read out to the followers gathered in the gurdwara.Just as on a *Baisakhi Day* ceremony held in 1699 under the guidance of Guru Gobind Singh where Panch Pyaras or the Five beloved ones chanted verses, five priests going by that name chant verses recited by the five originals.

Similarly, just as Guru Gobind Singh Ji had used amrita prepared in an iron vessel to bless the panch pyare, even to this date amrit or holy nectar is prepared in an iron vessel and is distributed amongst all gathered after the chanting of sacred verses. As a tradition, devotees sip amrita five times and take a vow to work for the brotherhood, the Khalsa Panth. Religious songs (kirtans) are sung after the amrit is drunk for the spiritual upliftment of those gathered. At noon, after the Baisakhi ardas, the Karah Prasad or sweetened semolina is offered to the guru for his blessings. It is then distributed to the congregation.

The ceremony culminates with a special guru-ka-langar or the community lunch. People sit in rows with their heads covered as volunteers serve them with vegetarian meal. Later, during the Baisakhi day, sacred Guru Granth Sahib is taken out in a procession. At the head of the procession are the Panj Piaras, symbolizing the journey made by the five fearless devotees from their homes to Anandpur, to be baptised by Guru Gobind Singh. *Baisakhi processions* are attended by men, women and children alike with faith and enthusiasm.

The procession moves through major localities of the city and is welcomed by citizens and members of social and cultural societies. Colourful bhangra and gidda dance apart from mock duels are performed during Baisakhi processions. Another fascinating part of Baisakhi celebrations is the accompaniment of drummers, bands playing religious times, devotees singing religious songs and men swinging swords. Loud Sikh chants of 'Bole so nihal', 'Deg teg fateh' and rhythmic chants of *'Sat nam'* and *'Wahe guru'* ring out from the middle of the singing and drumming. Some men may wear the headgear (bana) o Guru Nanak, others that of Guru Gobind Singh.In thei discourse at the end of the ceremony, Sikh religious leader strive to promote the feeling of charity amongst people, especiall children in honour of Guru Gobind Singh. In some places, especially Punjab, such processions are taken out even before Baisakhi. *Celebrations in the Fields.* Since Baisakhi is also celebrated as a harvest festival, farmers in Punjab celebrate Baisakhi with energetic performance of bhangra and gidda dance. Men and women clad themselves in their traditional Bhangra dress and dance to the beat of dhol in a joyful festive atmosphere.

Vibrant Festival of Baisakhi is considered to be an extremely important festival in India for number of reasons. Apart from being important for the farmers as a harvest festival, the festival is of prime importance in Sikhism as a foundation day of Khalsa Panth. Besides, auspicious Baisakhi day is of importance for astrological reasons too !! Astrological Significance of Baisakhi The festival of Baisakhi falls on April 13 every year and April 14 once in every 36 years. Change in date is because of the fact that date of Baisakhi is reckoned according to the solar calendar. Astrologically, the date of Baisakhi is significant as marks sun's entry into Mesh Rashi. For this very reason, many people also know Baisakhi as Mesha Sankranti.

The auspicious date of Baisakhi is celebrated all over India under different names and rituals. It is celebrated as 'Rongali Bihu' in Assam, 'Naba Barsha' in Bengal, 'Puthandu' in Tamil Nadu, 'Pooram Vishu' in Kerala and 'Vaishakha' in the state of Bihar. Significance of Baisakhi for Farmers For the agriculturally rich state of Punjab and Haryana, Baisakhi marks the time for harvest of Rabi (winter) crops and is therefore extremely significant for the farmers. Baisakhi Festival is also celebrated as a Thanksgiving Day festival in these states. After waking up early and dressing themselves in new clothes, farmers visit temples and gurdwaras to express gratitude to God for the good harvest and seek blessing for ensuing agriculture season. Farmers also celebrate Baisakhi by performing energetic bhangra and gidda dance and participating in Baisakhi Fairs. Significance of Baisakhi in SikhismBaisakhi is of major importance for the people following Sikh faith. As it was on a Baisakhi Day, in the year 1699 that the Tenth Guru of Sikhs,

Guru Gobind Singh founded Khalsa Panth or the Order of Pure Ones and gave a unique identity to Sikhs. On the same day the guru administered amrit (nectar) to his first batch of five disciples making them Singhs, a martial community.

By doing so, he eliminated the differences of high and low and established that all human beings were equal.Sikhs celebrate Baisakhi by participating in special prayer meetings organized at gurdwaras. They also carry out joyful Baisakhi processions to mark the day.Significance of Baisakhi in Other Religions The day of Baisakhi is of significance for the Hindus as it was on this day in 1875 that Swami Dayanand Saraswati founded the Arya Samaj-a reformed sect of Hindus who are devoted to the Vedas for spiritual guidance and have discarded idol worship. Besides, Baisakhi day is of relevance for the Buddhists as Gautama Buddha attained enlightenment and Nirvana on this auspicious day.

Baisakhi marks the arrival of the harvesting season. The festival always falls on April 14 and marks the beginning of the solar year. Just before the festival the farmer returns home with his bumper crop, the fruit of his whole year's hard labour.

This festival is in celebration to thank God for good harvest for the year and coming year also. Early morning of Baiskhai, people take dip in holy rivers. Cries of "Jatta aai Baisakhi" rent the skies as the people of Punjab attired in their best clothes break into the Bhangra dance to express their joy.

The dancers and drummers challenge each other to continue the dance. The scenes of sowing, harvesting, winnowing and gathering of crops are expressed through zestful movements of the body to the accompaniment of ballads. Both men and women, celebrate the day with Bhangra and Gidda.

Fairs are organized at various places in Punjab, where besides other recreational activities, wrestling bouts are also held. The occasion is celebrated with great gusto at Talwandi Sabo, where Guru Gobind Singh stayed for nine months and completed the recompilation of the Guru Granth Sahib. The Sikhs celebrate this day by visiting gurudwaras and distributing kada prasad. Processions led by the Panj Piaras or the five religious men are taken out. Kirtans and recital of passages from the Granth Sahib are also organized in gurdwaras, where people line up to receive the delicious prasad and perform kar sewa-that is, offering help in the daily chores of the gurdwara. The most sacred pilgrimage centres is Amritsar, where Golden Temple is situated. Relatives and friends are welcomed and offered lassi and sweets. This festival brings bright hopes for the future.

Baisakhi, also spelled Vaisakhi, is the festival which celebrates Sikh New Year and the founding of the Sikh community, known as the Khalsa.The story of the foundation of the Khalsa started with the martyrdom of Guru Teg Bahadur, the 9th Guru, who was publicly beheaded by Mughul rulers for protecting freedom of worship for both Sikhs and Hindus.The son of Guru Teg Bahadur, who was called Guru Gobind Singh, became the next Guru. He stated that Sikhs should always be prepared to stand up for their beliefs, whatever the cost. In 1699, Sikhs from all over the Punjab gathered together to celebrate the Hindu harvest festival of Baisakhi.

Guru Gobind Singh came out of a tent carrying a sword and requested that anyone prepared to give his life come forward. A young Sikh came forward and disappeared into the tent with the Guru. Then the Guru reappeared alone with his sword covered in blood and asked for another volunteer. This was repeated another four times until a total of five Sikhs had gone into the tent with him. Everyone present was very worried until eventually all five emerged from the tent alive, with Guru Gobind Singh, and wearing turbans. The five became known as the *Panj Piare*, or 'Beloved Five'. Guru Gobind Singh's wife mixed some amrit. The Guru said some prayers over the five and they were sprinkled with the amrit. This is how the Amrit ceremony came into being and these five Sikhs became the first members of the Khalsa.

India's rich and glorious civilization is mirrored in its innumerable festivals. These festivals mark the seasons which signal to man the time for work and the time for relaxation, the commencement of the agricultural cycle with sowing in spring, and its culmination with the harvesting of the golden grain. And then, of course, we have, in endless variations of legend and myth, the hallowed perceptions that there is an ever-renewed war of light and darkness, of the divine and the demoniac in the unceasing evolution of the world.

Generally, the sites of these festivities are on the banks of the rivers which have their sacred import with myths and legends woven around their origin and names.

Baisakhi, marks the beginning of New Year, particularly in the northern part of India. It is among the few Indian festivals that has a fixed date. Baisakhi is always on April 13th. In Kerala, Baisakhi is called as "*Vishu*" and in Tamil Nadu, it is celebrated as "*Puthandu*".

Considered a holy day, the devout celebrate the Baisakhi with a dip in the holy rivers just around the break of dawn. It is on this day that Sun enters Aries, the first sign of Zodiac. This signifies ushering of the new year.

In Punjab (the land of Green Revolution) particularly and in the northern belt of India in general, farmers perform their own prayers and rejoice. For on this day, they commence cutting their harvest. The fields can be seen full of nature's bounty. Dressed in their typical folk attire, both men and women, celebrate the day with Bhangra and Gidda. Sweets are distributed, old enmities are forgiven and life is full of joy, merriment and everyone seems to belong.

Baisakhi, however, has had a new dimension added to it by Guru Gobind Singh. For it was on the day of Baisakhi in 1669, that he established the Khalsa Panth and gave a final impetus to the course of the earlier nine Gurus of Sikhism.

People perform *Kar Sewa* (physical labour to help in the daily chores of the gurudwara as a symbol of humility) in gurudwaras and listen to recitations from Guru Granth Sahib. Colourful processions, led by the Panj Piaras, are taken out. Children and youth demonstrate their skills in martial arts to the accompaniment of musical bands. The Granth Sahib, which was designated the eternal guru of Sikhs by Guru Gobind Singh, is also taken out in procession.

Children are taught to perform acts of charity on this auspicious occasion and are expected to continue to do so all through the year. Many Sikhs choose to be baptized into the Khalsa brotherhood on this day. The wrappings of the Nishan Sahib flag post at most gurdwaras are changed on Baisakhi.

There is a mood of celebration in the air and what better way to express joy than to break into a dance! Men perform the vigorous Bhangra dance with energetic steps to the beat of *dholak* (traditional drum) while women perform Gidda dance wit h great fervour and rhythmic steps.

Though a community festival, Baisakhi is also celebrated in individual homes. Since it is a harvest festival, there is no fasting or special puja on this occasion. Houses are cleaned and freshly painted. Friends and relatives are invited for meals and a sumptuous feast is served. Meat and alcohol are part of the day's fare. Baskets of fruits and boxes of sweet are sent to the families of the married daughters. Guru Amar Das had first institutionalized Baisakhi in 1567 as one of the special days when all Sikhs would gather to receive the guru's blessings at Goindwal. It was on this day in 1699 that the tenth Guru of the Sikhs, Guru Gobind Singh, founded the Khalsa Panth.

He discontinued the tradition of Gurus in Sikhism by declaring the Granth Sahib to be the eternal Guru of all Sikhs. He asked his followers to be ready to lay down their lives to save others. Five volunteers of five different castes were made the Panj Piaras, who would lead the rest. They came from different places like Punjab, Uttar Pradesh, Andhra Pradesh and Bihar. The first lesson on how to be a true Sikh was imparted to these people by Guru Gobind Singh, who asked them not to cut their hair or beard (*kesh*), to always carry a comb (*kangha*), a sword (*kirpan*) so that they would be always ready for battle, to wear an underwear (*kachcha*) and an iron bangle (*kada*). These are known as the five Ks and are mandatory for every Sikh.

The Panj Piaras in turn baptized Guru Gobind Singh into the Khalsa brotherhood. On this day, Guru Arjan Dev was martyred by the then Muslim rulers. Again, on this day in

1875, Swami Dayanand Saraswati founded the Arya Samaj-a reformed sect of Hindus who are devoted to the Vedas for spiritual guidance and have discarded idol worship.

Fairs: A number of cattle fairs are organised at this time of the year. The villages wear a festive look and vendors selling ice cream, flossy sugar lollipops and chaat make a brisk business. Toys, handicrafts and mundane household goods are sold at these places.

On this memorable Baisakhi day (March 30 of A.D. 1699), Guru Gobind Singh Sahib called a big meeting at Kesgarh Sahib near the City of Anandpur Sahib. Between fifty to eighty thousand Sikhs attended this meeting. When all were expecting to hear words of comfort and consolation from the lips of their Guru, they were perturbed to see him with a drawn sword in his hand and cried ' Is there anyone here who would lay down his life for Dharam?' There was a big silence, but the Guru went on repeating his demand. At the third call Daya Ram, a Khatri of Lahore, rose from his seat and offered himself. The Guru took him into an adjoining enclosure....(and soon after) came out with the (blood) dripping....(sword in hand) and flourshing it before the gathering, asked again, 'Is there any other Sikh here who will offer himself as a sacrifice (for the cause of dharma)? At this Daram Das, a Jat of Delhi (Haryana side) came forward and was taken into the enclosure....(The Guru again came out with the blood-stained sword, and made his previous demand). In the same way three other men stood up, one after another, and offered themselves for the sacrifice. One was Mohkam Chand, a washerman of Dwarka (Gujarat State); another was Himmat, a cook of Jagannath (Orissa State); and the third was Sahib Chand, a barber of Bidar (Karnataka State). The Guru, after dressing the five in handsome clothes, brought them from the assembly.

These five were then administered 'Khande di Pahul' (the double-edged Sword Amrit). They were then knighted as Singhs, as the Five beloved ones, the first members of the Order of the Khalsa. The Guru then asked them to administer the Pahul to him in the same manner in which he had given the Pahul to them, and it was done so.

With the creation of Khalsa, the Khalsa created history and since the birth of Khalsa, the history of Punjab has been the history of Sikhs. Baisakhi played a significant role in this regard. In 1762, Ahmed Shah Abdali, with the sole purpose to destroy the entire Sikh nation, declared 'Jehad'(holy-war) against the Sikhs and all the Muslims of the Punjab rallied under this slogan. The Sikhs were surrounded near the village Kup in Ludhiana District. Chronicles mention that about twenty thousand Sikhs were martyred in a single day.

This event is known in the history of the Sikhs as "Ghallughara" (Bloody Carnage). After this, Ahmed Shah Abdali thought that he had crushed the entire Sikh nation, but was greatly disillusioned when after a few months heard that the Sikhs in large number are celebrating Baisakhi at Amritsar. In due course of time Baisakhi reminds every Sikh of his cultural and religious heritage. On Baisakhi day all the Sikhs used to assemble at Amritsar and decide their problems relating to politics and religion. This convention still goes on.

The celebrations of Baisakhi are similar to the three-day schedule of the the celebrations of other Gurpurabs. It is generally celebrated on 13th April every year.

This also marks the beginning of a month long *Vaisakha* bathing. The pilgrimage to the holy shrine of Badrinath, in the Himalayas, also commences from this day. The charities done during Vaisakha month are believed to earn great religious merits and so people generously give money, grains and other things to the poor and needy and the *Brahmins*, and observe fast, chant the glories of the lord and practice such other pious activities.

The holy book of the Sikhs, 'Granth Sahib' is taken in a procession, led by the 'Panj Pyaras' (five senior Sikhs) who are symbolic of the original leaders. It was on this day that Guru Gobind Singh organised his first batch of five disciples making them Singhs, a martial community. Kirtans and recital of passages from the 'Granth Sahib' are also organized in gurdwaras, where people line up to receive the delicious Kada prasad (sweetened semolina) and perform kar sewa-that is, offering help in the daily chores of the gurdwara. The occasion is celebrated with great gusto at Talwandi Sabo, where Guru Gobind Singh stayed for nine months and completed the recompilation of the Guru Granth Sahib and in the Golden temple in Amritsar. On Baisakhi day, water is drawn from all the sacred rivers of India and poured in to the huge tank surrounding.

Guru Govind Singh Jayanti

Punjab, rightly claimed as the traditional sword-arm of Bharatvarsha, has valiantly borne the first brunt of all the pre-European aggressors on her. And one of the most luminous stars which rose in that north-western horizon and shed its lustre over the entire length and breadth of the country is undoubtedly Guru Govind Singh the tenth and the final Guru in the holy tradition initiated by that great saint Guru Nanak.Richly had Guru Govind Singh inherited the legacy of the fearless martyrdom of his father-Guru Tegh Bahadur.

Guru Tegh Bahadur, with a view to instilling courage and confidence among the Kashmiri Hindus to withstand Aurangzeb's fanatical tyranny and threats to Islamize them, challenged the Moghal emperor to convert him first. And the great Guru preferred to have his head roll down in Chandni Chowk of Delhi rather than sacrifice his faith, Govind Singh was just a boy of nine years at that time. On coming to know of his father's terrible end he exclaimed: "He saved with his blood the honour of Hindu Dharma. Oh, what a remarkable act in this Kaliyuga! He preferred to give up his life, but not his faith!"

An overview of Guru Gobind Singh's life: Guru Gobind Singh (1666-1708 C.E.) lived during an extremely dangerous time. His father, Guru Tegh Bahadur, had sacrificed his life to protect the freedom of worship by Hindus, who were being threatened with conversion or death by zealous Muslim rulers. Abduction of women and pillage of goods were rampant, but the people were too timid and terrorized to resist. In the midst of this political situation, Guru Gobind Singh gained great stature as both Saint and soldier a leader of firm spiritual principles and intense devotion to God, and at the same time, fearless dedication to protecting all people from oppression and injustice through the practice of Kshatradharma.In 1699, He dramatically initiated five men from the lower castes as His Five Beloveds, blessing them with great courage as well as nearness to God. They became models for the Khalsa, the Order of the Pure, which Guru Gobind Singh created to stand on the front line against injustice.

The Khalsa were held to a very strict moral and spiritual discipline and under Guru Gobind Singh's courageous inspiration, helped to turn the tide against Mughal oppression in India.In addition to his spiritual and military leadership, Guru Gobind Singh was a gifted intellectual and had many poets in his court. He was inspired to write many powerful spiritual compositions that infused a martial spirit in the people.This included the Jaap Sahib, but He did not include them in the Sikh scripture, the Guru Granth Sahib. His writings have instead been collected in a separate volume, called the Dasam Granth. Upon His passing away, He instructed his Sikhs to regard the Guru Granth Sahib as their teacher. 'Granth' literally means 'volume' (especially, a Holy volume). 'Sahib' is a term of reverence used for anything sacred. The Guru Granth Sahib is the perpetual guru of the Sikhs today.The prasad of Ugadi/Gudi Padwa is the bitter leaves of the neem tree with jaggery. There are special foods prepared for this festival. In the southern states, puligore-a sour tamarind rice dish, bobbatlu, holige-sweet stuffed bread and Ugadi Pachadi made of jagerry, raw mango pieces, neem flowers and tamarind is prepared. In Maharastra, shrikhand-a fragrant yogurt dessert, with poori-a fried puffy bread is prepared.

The celebration is generally similar for all Gurpurabs; only the hymns are different. The birthday celebration usually lasts three days. Generally two days before the birthday, *Akhand Path* (a forty-eight-hour non-stop reading of the *Guru Granth Sahib*, the holy book of the Sikhs) is held in the *Gurdwaras*.

The day prior to the birthday, a procession is organised which is led by the *Panj Pyaras* (Five Beloved Ones). They head the procession carrying the Sikh flag, known as the *Nishan Sahib* and the *Palki* (Palanquin) of Siri Guru Granth Sahib.

They are followed by teams of singers singing hymns, brass bands playing different tunes, 'Gatka' teams (Martial Arts) display their swordmanship, and devotees sing the chorus. The procession pours into the streets of the town which are covered with buntings and decorated gates for this special occasion. The leaders also spread the message of Guru Nanak.

On the day of the Gurpurab, the day begins early in the morning with the singing of *Asa-di-Var* (morning hymns) and hymns from the Sikh scriptures followed by *Katha* (exposition of the scripture) together with lectures and recitation of poems in the praise of the Guru. Following that is the *Langar* or special community lunch, which is arranged at the *Gurudwaras* by volunteers. The idea behind the free communal lunch is that people should be offered food in the spirit of *seva* (service) and *bhakti* (devotion). Guru Nanak Jayanti is celebrated by the Sikh community all over the world and is one of the most important festivals in the Sikh calendar. The celebrations are especially colourful in Punjab and Haryana.

Gurupurb

Gurupurb is not a single festival or occasion. These are holy days and are associated with anniversaries of the many of the Sikh Guru's birth or death, martyrdom day and anniversary of the installation of the Adi Granth Sahib. People from Sikh religion celebrate Gurupurbs.

Some Gurupurbs are local events celebrated only where the original event took place. Some are celebrated universally.

Some of the important Gurpurab's are the birth anniversaries of Guru Nanak, the founder of Sikhism (Oct.-Nov.) and of Guru Gobind Singh, the last Guru (Dec.-Jan.).

Celebrations are done by reading of the holy verses in the Guru Granth Sahib and by holding processions where the 'Guru Granth Sahib' is carried in procession through the town. The holy book is placed on a van strewn with flowers and has a troop of five armed guards around it.

The Sadh Sangat of Sikh Dharma held its first celebration of Baisakhi in Los Angeles in April, 1970. In December of 1970,

84 Western Sikhs traveled on a yatra to India with Yogi Harbhajan Singh (later to have the titles of Siri Singh Sahib and Bhai Sahib bestowed on him at Akal Takhat Sahib), and in Amritsar, those 'new' Sikhs received Amrit from the Panj Piare at Akal Takhat Sahib.

These were American youth in their early twenties, inspired to live as Khalsa as a result of their deep respect for and aspiration to live to the example of Siri Singh Sahib Bhai Sahib Harbhajan Singh Khalsa Yogiji, who had embarked upon his service of inspiring the youth of the West to the Khalsa life-style, as a step in the fulfillment of Guru Gobind Singh's prophesy that 960,000,000 we shall be. He was most humble in his approach to his service of Guru, as exemplified by his action at that moment when these 84 students came to cross the threshold of Akal Takhat Sahib to receive Amrit. He would not cross the threshold with them; "I have brought you this far. Now you go the remainder of the distance without me, as this is a relationship between you and Guru."

In June of 1973, the Siri Singh Sahib appointed Singh Sahib Dayal Singh as Head Granthee for Sikh Dharma and bestowed upon him the title of Bhai Sahib. Bhai Sahib Dayal Singh was only 17 years old at the time but he had a fervent love for the Guru and Gurbani. He was a constant sevadar, mowing lawns, cooking langar, sweeping the Gurdwara steps, placing fresh cut flowers in front of the Guru. Always full of love, smiles, and constant encouragement for everyone. With his incredible devotion he was one of the first persons to teach many Western Sikhs how to read Gurmukhi, how to recite their Banis, and how to do Prakash and Sukhasn seva and conduct a kirtan programme. On Baisakhi Day, April 13, 1974 Sant Mihen Singh and his followers, while visiting Los Angeles, distributed Amrit to Western born Sikhs at Guru Ram Das Ashram and Bhai Sahib Dayal Singh served as one of the Panj Piare on that day, thus becoming the first Western born Sikh ever to administer Amrit. An Amrit Sanchar was held every year thereafter on Baisakhi in Los Angeles.

It was a great loss to the Panth Khalsa when Bhai Sahib Dayal Singh left for the heavenly abode resulting from a fatal car accident on September 22nd, 1975, just short of his 21st birthday, en route to New York, where he was to depart for India and a visit to the Golden Temple.

Council of the Western Hemisphere began to hold its annual spring meetings the week of Baisakhi in Los Angeles. The Sadh Sangat would come to Los Angeles from all parts of the world where Sikh Centers were being established: Central and South America, Canada, Europe, Africa, and Asia. Under the direction and inspiration of Siri Singh Sahib Bhai Sahib Harbhajan Singh Khalsa Yogiji, and with Guru as their constant guide, the Khalsa spirit among these new Sikhs grew and flourished.

The Sadh Sangat continued to grow and by the early 1980s attendance at the Baisakhi kirtan programme was large enough to require a bigger venue to accommodate the hundreds of people attending the Baisakhi Kirtan programme. The Siri Singh Sahib Ji inspired the sangat members of Sikh Dharma to invite all of the Gurdwaras of California to participate and join the celebration. He had a deep desire to see the Sikh community unified and working closely together. He inspired the sadh sangat of Guru Ram Das Ashram to extend invitations to all the Gurdwaras of California to participate in the Baisakhi celebration.

Similarly, he encouraged everyone to participate in programmes held by other Gurdwaras, not only here in Los Angeles, but throughout California and the world. In his wisdom, he deeply understood the cultural challenges, including acceptance of Westerners into the Punjabi culture and vice versa. One of his messages to Western Sikhs everywhere was that we should be grateful for the great devotion of all those Sikhs who have carried the Guru for 400 years and made huge sacrifices through the centuries, so that we can all enjoy the darshan of Siri Guru Granth Sahib today. He also had a vision of Sikh Dharma being a Dharma beyond borders and nationality, which he referred to as "sarab dharma," a dharma that includes people of all races and cultures.

Since the late 1980s, the Sikh Dharma Baisakhi Celebration has been held at the vast Los Angeles Convention Center, in collaboration with a network of Southern California Gurdwaras.

The Baisakhi Gurupurb has been attended throughout the years by many dignitaries from India, including Gurcharan Singh Tohra, S. Tarlochan Singh, Jethadars of Akal Takhat, S.S. Professor Darshan Singh, S.S. Professor Manjit Singh, and many members of SGPC.

The programmes have also been graced by some of the most well known Ragi Jethas, Bhai Harjinder Singh, Sant Anoop Singh, Master Darshan Singh, Bhai Hari Singh, Bhai Nirmal Singh, and many, many others. Each year the programme has been attended by prominent Los Angeles, state of California and U.S. political dignitaries, including Lt. Governor Cruz Bustamante, Congressman Howard Berman, Congresswoman Diane Watson, many L.A. county supervisors and council members and, most recently, then Los Angeles Mayor elect Antonio Villaraigosa (who donned a full turban for the occasion).

The idea of adding a Nagar Kirtan (Parade) to the Baisakhi Celebration had been percolating among the Guru Ram Das Ashram organizing committee for several years prior to 1997. This year celebrates the ninth year the Nagar Kirtan has been a joyful part of the Baisakhi Celebration and, thanks to the seva of many devoted Sikhs, it is one of the most inspiring traditions that we continue to cherish during Baisakhi. A lot of acknowledgement goes to all sangat members who make financial contributions to both the Kirtan Darbar and Nagar Kirtan.

Teachings of Guru Nanak: He was not only the founder of the Sikh religion, he was a great poet, philosopher, humanist and a powerful social reformer, a teacher of mankind. Nanak said that one need not become a sanyasi sacrificing one's family, to please God. Those who practice devotion, whose mind is pure and who have sympathy, patience and honesty, are in no way inferior to a sanyasi. He considered that all human beings were highborn; no one was low.He stressed, "Do not ask someone's caste; those whose devotion is accepted by God are good people. God appreciates those who have conquered the 'I' and 'greed'. Nanak washes the feet of those who concentrate their minds on God, the source of truth".

Celebrations: The akhand path or the continuous reading of Granth Saheb, the sacred book of the Sikhs, begins three days before Guru Nanak Jayanti. The sacred scripture is read non-stop from beginning to end. The Akhand Path culminates on the day of the Guru Purab and the holy book is then taken out in a procession. It is beautifully decorated with flowers and carried on a float. Children participate in the procession and march to the tune of local band playing religious hymns. Five armed guards who are called the panj pyare lead the procession. At the head of the procession is the Nishan Saheb or the Sikh flag.

A few days before Guru Purab, people take out Prabhat Pheris or the early morning processions from the Gurdwaras. They go around their locality singing shabd or the religious hymns.

Langar: Later in the day, special kirtans are arranged in the Gurdwaras. The devotees attend langar or the common meals where everyone eats the same food irrespective of caste, class, or creed. Devotees offer their services for cooking food, cleaning the Gurdwara or carrying out other chores. This is called the Kar Seva. In the evening, the Gurdwaras are illuminated and people visit them in large numbers. People also illuminate their homes with candles and earthen lamps.

The 7th Day of bright half of MaargashiraPunjab, rightly claimed as the traditional sword-arm of Bharatvarsha, has valiantly borne the first brunt of all the pre-European aggressors on her. And one of the most luminous stars which rose in that north-western horizon and shed its lustre over the entire length and breadth of the country is undoubtedly Guru Govind Singh the tenth and the final Guru in the holy tradition initiated by that great saint Guru Nanak.Richly had Guru Govind Singh inherited the legacy of the fearless martyrdom of his father-Guru Tegh Bahadur. Guru Tegh Bahadur, with a view to instilling courage and confidence among the Kashmiri Hindus to withstand Aurangzeb's fanatical tyranny and threats to Islamize them, challenged the Mughal emperor to convert him first. And the great Guru preferred to have his head roll down in Chandni Chowk of Delhi rather than sacrifice his faith,

Govind Singh was just a boy of nine years at that time. On coming to know of his father's terrible end he exclaimed: "He saved with his blood the honour of Hindu Dharma. Oh, what a remarkable act in this Kaliyuga! He preferred to give up his life, but not his faith!"It is with such a fiery note of idealism that the young Govind Singh embarked upon his life-mission even from his infancy.

As a child he had drunk deep at the fount of *Raamaayana*, *Mahaabhaarata* and *Puraanas*. He was inspired with the heroic examples of Sri Rama, Sri Krishna, Bheema and Arjuna. He felt convinced that he too like those great forbears was born to vanquish the wicked and protect *Dharma*. He began preparing himself in a thorough-going fashion to play that historic role. He assimilated the spiritual truths enshrined in the *Vedas*, *Upanishads* and the *Bhagavad Geeta*. He became adept in Persian, Arabic and Punjabi languages just as in Samskrit and Hindi, and was a peerless poet as well.

As an archer he was unequalled in the whole of Hindusthan. No wonder, equipped as he was with such a rare combination of *brahmateja* and *kshaatrateja*, he wrote in his autobiographical poem *Vichitranaatak* that he was commanded by God to take birth to uphold the true path of *Dharma*.No catastrophe to his personal self or to his family members, however tragic, could shake his rock-like resolve to pursue his chosen mission. When his two elderly sons, Ajit and Jujhar whom he had sent to lead the battle laid down their lives before his very eyes thus did the Guru offer prayers to God: "O Lord, I have surrendered to Thee what belonged to Thee." Later, when his two younger kids Jorawar and Phatte were bricked alive by the Moghals for refusing to succumb to Islam, and the heart-rending news reached the Guru, he simply lifted his hands in prayer and uttered the words: "These two, Thy trust, I have rendered unto Thee."

The Guru's mother, Gujjari Devi, from whom the two kids had been snatched away, broke her heart and died.The tone of the historic epistle which the Guru wrote some time later to Aurangzeb is evidence of the majestic equanimity and the supremely high moral posture he maintained even in the wake of such dire calamities: "I know you believe neither in God nor in your prophet, nor do you know the worth of an oath on Koran. Did your God ask you to tyrannise over others? Fie on your sovereignty and on your regard for God and religion! Fear God, who is the Master of earth and heaven and Whose vengeance is terrible. What if you have killed my four sons? By putting out a few sparks, you cannot quench the blazing fire.

My protection is God than Whom there is no one higher."The Guru bore all the cruel blows of Fate with an invincible will and fortitude and pressed forward in rousing and organizing his countrymen in the cause of *Swadesh* and *Swadharma*. He moved from the north to the southern parts of the country contacting and trying to string together the various patriotic forces. Finally, in the south he found a great warrior turned into a yogi, Maadhav Daas by name, and charged him with the task of proceeding to Punjab to lead the struggle there. Maadhav Daas, known in history as Bandaa Bairaagi, abided by the Guru's command and carried out the war of liberation with such remarkable ability and was crowned with such rare success-finally falling a martyr to the cause in the true tradition of the Gurus-that even to this day he stands as a glowing testimony to the magic touch of Guru Govind Singh.Finally the Guru himself, while in the south at Nanded, fell a martyr to the treacherous designs of the Moghals and embraced *Mahaasamaadhi* in the true tradition of *yogis*.Could such a string of stirring martyrdoms of all his four sons, his father, his mother and finally he, the great Guru himself, followed by that of his successor, ever go in vain?

The flames of those sacrificial offerings soon spread and inflamed millions of hearts. By the turn of the century, the vast areas of the strategic north-western region of Bharat right up to the Khybar Pass were freed from the foreign Islamic yoke and the tide of one thousand-year old invasions from that quarter turned back once and for all.The spirit of oneness and harmony which the Guru infused in the society has also made him a social reformer of the highest order. His vision encompassed the whole of Bharat, and his love embraced within itself the lowliest in the society. The *Panch Pyaare*, the five self-sacrificing heroes of the *Khaalsa* whom he chose through a fiery ordeal on a a*Vaishaakha Pratipada*, were those drawn from distant parts of the country, right from Bidar in Karnataka, Jagannaath Puri in Orissa, Dwaraka in Gujarat to Delhi and Lahore.

And three of them belonged to the so-called lower castes.The Guru's breadth of national vision could not brook any idea or gesture which would even remotely suggest an exclusive or a warped mind. The *Khaalsa*, the Pure, were to be the devotees of *Akaal*-The Timeless Reality-in the true tradition of the Hindu *tapaswis*. The Guru had founded the creed for the achievement of all-round glory of Hindu society and Hindu Dharma.

He thundered: *Sakala jagat me Khaalsa panth gajei* (may the creed of the pure and the dedicated flourish the world over) and *Jagai dharma Hindu sakala bandha bhajai*. (may the wickedness vanish and the Hindu dharma live for ever.)The five signs the Guru prescribed for the *Khaalsas* signified the highest virtues of heroic Hindu manhood; unshorn hair like that of the ancient sages and *kshatriyas* as a pledge of dedication, a comb to keep it clean, a steel bracelet indicating the universality of the Almighty, an underwear to denote chastity, and a steel dagger to remind him of his role as the defender of Faith.The Guru knew the potency of ancient Hindu epics and *Puraanas* and had organized a Poets' Council to translate the *Puraanas* into Hindi. His own poetry composed in Hindi, in its Braj form, overflowed with the essence of *Raamaayana*, *Mahaabhaarata* and all the *Puraanic* legends and their Gods and Goddesses and radiated the lofty spiritual message of *Upanishads* and *Bhagavadgeeta*. *Sarvakaal* was to him the father and *Devi Mahaa Kaali* the mother.

The *Guru Granthsaheb* which he re-edited contained the hymns and couplets of saints of various regions. Neither the Sikhs nor the rest of Hindus ever considered themselves distinct or separate from each other. Right up to the recent times, every Hindu family used to nominate one of its boys as a Sikh. Blood relationship between the *Keshadhaaris* and non-*Keshadhaaris* continues undisturbed even to this day. Brother belonging to both sections living under a common paternal roof is not an uncommon sight even today.Rarely do we come across in the annals of human history a life of such all-round greatness as that of *Guru Govind Singh*-a *yogi* and a warrior-martyr, a poet and a social reformer, a national emancipator and a *dhaarmic* rejuvenator-all rolled into one supremely majestic personality commanding the reverence of his countrymen and even of his enemies.No better appreciation could be there of the inspiring legacy left behind to the entire nation by that great Guru than what Swami Vivekananda has observed: "Mark me, every one of you will have to be a Govind Singh, if you want to do good to your country.

You may see thousands of defects in your countrymen, but mark their Hindu blood. They are the first gods you will have to worship, even if they do everything to hurt you; even if every one of them sends out a curse to you, you send out to them words of love. If they drive you out, retire to die in silence like that mighty lion, Govind Singh. Such a man is worthy of the name of Hindu; such an idea ought to be before us always."

5

Christian Festivals

Christmas

Jesus "Christ" is known as the founder or central figure of "Christianity." Christmas is a Christian holiday on December 25 that commemorates the birth of Jesus. Ancient Romans also commemorated Jesus' birth by marking a division of the calendar still in use today. The years before Jesus' birth are marked as B.C. (Before Christ), and the years after Jesus' birth are marked A.D. (Anno Domini, which means, in thè year of our Lord).

Christmas literally means the Mass (celebration) of Christ. "Christ" is a Greek word and title, meaning "anointed" or one set apart by God for a special purpose. "Christ" is equivalent to the Hebrew word "Messiah." Based on the words of ancient prophets, the first century Jewish people expected the arrival of the Messiah promised by God as a great deliver of the people.

Luke's biography records how Mary and her husband Joseph left their home in Nazareth to travel to Joseph's ancestral home, Bethlehem, to enroll in the census ordered by the Roman emperor, Augustus. Finding no room in inns in the town, they set up primitive lodgings in a stable. There Mary gave birth to Jesus in a manger or stall. Jesus' birth in Bethlehem, the home of the house of King David from which Joseph was descended, fulfilled the prophecy of Isaiah. This is confirmed to Mary by a visit from angels and shepherds.

Matthew's biography begins by recounting the genealogy and virgin birth of Jesus, and then moves to the coming of the Wise Men from the Orient (likely China) to where Jesus was staying after his birth in Bethlehem. The wise men, or Magi, first arrived in Jerusalem and reported to the king of Judea, Herod the Great, that they had seen a star heralding the birth of a king. Further inquiry led them to Bethlehem of Judea and the location of Mary and Joseph. They presented Jesus with treasures of "gold, frankincense, and myrrh."

In Jesus' adult years, Jesus claimed to be this King, the Jewish Messiah Ultimately, Jesus' claim to be Christ caused controversy and the religious trial leading to his execution. Christians commemorate Jesus' execution and believed return from the dead (resurrection) during "Easter."

Jesus also described His birth on earth as the most important "Good News," signifying that God Himself chose to come from heaven to earth to help make earth more like heaven Many people throughout the world have been prompted to ask questions about the life, death, and message of Jesus. Here's some of what you can investigate further at Jesus Institute, an educational resource about the person of Jesus: Christmas is a Christian holiday held on December 25 which celebrates the birth of Jesus. Eastern Orthodox Churches, which use the Julian Calendar to determine feast days, celebrate on January 7 by the Gregorian Calendar. Both dates are merely traditional and neither is thought to be the actual birthdate of Jesus. Christ's birth, or nativity, is said to fulfill Old Testament prophecies concerning the coming of a messiah, or savior.

The word *Christmas* is derived from Middle English *Christemasse* and from Old English *Cristes masse.* It is a contraction meaning "Christ's mass". The name of the holiday is often shortened to Xmas because Roman letter "X" resembles the Greek letter *x* (chi), an abbreviation for Christ.

In Western countries, Christmas has become the most economically significant holiday of the year. The popularity of Christmas can be traced in part to its status as a winter festival. Many cultures have their most important holiday in winter because there is less agricultural work to do at this time. Examples of winter festivals that are believed by some to have influenced Christmas include the pre-Christian festivals of Yule and Saturnalia.

In Western culture, the holiday is characterized by the exchange of gifts among friends and family members, some of the gifts being attributed to Santa Claus (also known as Father Christmas, Saint Nicholas, and Father Frost). However, various local and regional Christmas traditions are still practiced, despite the widespread influence of American, British and Australian Christmas motifs disseminated by film, popular literature, television, and the nativity narratives in the Gospel of Luke and the Gospel of Matthew focus on different aspects of the event. The Gospel of Mark, considered the earliest and most historical gospel according to the doctrine of Markan priority, does not include a nativity narrative.

In Luke, Mary learns from an angel that the Holy Spirit has caused her to be with child. Mary points out that she is a virgin and the angel responds that "with God nothing shall be impossible." Shortly thereafter, she and her husband Joseph leave their home in Nazareth to travel about 150 kilometres (90 miles) to Joseph's ancestral home, Bethlehem, in order to register for a census ordered by Emperor Augustus. Finding no room at the inns, they lodge in a stable. There Mary gives birth to Jesus. An angel of the lord goes to the fields and tells the shepherds the "tidings of joy." A heavenly host proclaims, "Glory to God in the highest, and on earth peace to men on whom his favour rests." The shepherds come to the manger to adore the infant Jesus (Luke 1:5-2:20).

In Matthew, magi arrive at the court of King Herod in Jerusalem and ask, "Where is the child who has been born king of the Jews? We have observed the rising of his star, and we have come to pay him homage." (Compare to Numbers 24:17.) The word *magi* is traditionally translated as "wise men." The word connects them to the magi of Babylon who select Daniel their chief in the Book of Daniel. Daniel's magi interpret dreams and other portents. The book was well-known in ancient times for its prophecy concerning the messiah (Daniel 9:24-27), a man who will be sent by God to lead the Jewish people.

Neither the names of the magi nor their number are specified in the Bible, but tradition tells us there were three: Balthassar, Melchior, and Caspar. Balthassar is a Greek version of the

Babylonian name Belshazzar. This is the name of a king in Daniel. Melchior means "The king is my light" in Aramaic. Caspar is a Latinized version of Gondophares, a Parthian (*i.e.* Persian) name. The magi are sometimes called kings because of prophecies that kings will do homage to the messiah (Isaiah 60:3, Psalms 72:11).

Herod is disturbed by the magi's words and questions them closely, attempting to determine when the star first appeared and when the child was born. The king asks his advisors where the messiah will be born. They answer Bethlehem, birthplace of King David, and quote Micah 5:2-4. "When you have found him, bring me word so that I may also go and pay him homage," a deceitful Herod tells the magi.

As they travel to Bethleham, the magi follow a star that leads them to a house where they find Jesus. Jesus is no longer in the manger described by Luke. He is a child (*paidion*), not an infant (*brephos*). The magi present Jesus with gold, frankincense, and myrrh. (If these gifts were chosen in view of Isaiah 60:1-7, it may explain the magi's earlier trip to Jerusalem.) In a dream, the magi received a divine warning of Herod's intent to kill the child, who he sees as a rival. Consequently, they return to their own country without telling Herod the result of their mission. An angel tells Joseph to flee with his family to Egypt. Meanwhile, Herod orders that all male children of Bethlehem under the age of 2 be killed. After Herod's death, the family settles in Nazareth (Matthew 2:1-23).

Date of Feast Selected: Although no one knows what date Jesus was born on, there were several reasons for early Christians to favour December 25. The date is nine months after the Festival of Annunciation (March 25), and hence the Incarnation. It is also the date on which the Romans marked the winter solstice.

Around 220, the theologian Tertullian declared that Jesus died on March 25, AD 29. Although this is not a plausible date for the crucifixion, it does suggest that March 25 had significance for church even before it was used as a basis to calculate Christmas. Modern scholars favour a crucifixion date of April 3, AD 33 (also the date of a partial lunar eclipse).

By 240, a list of significant events was being assigned to March 25, partly because it was believed to be the date of the vernal equinox. These events include creation, the fall of Adam, and, most relevantly, the Incarnation. The view that the Incarnation occurred on the same date as crucifixion is consistent with a Jewish belief that prophets died at an "integral age," either an anniversary of their birth or of their conception.

Aside from being nine months later than Annunciation, December 25 is also the date the Romans marked the winter solstice, which they referred to as *bruma*. For this reason, some have suggested the opposite of the theory outlined above, *i.e.* that the date of Christmas was chosen to be the same as that of the solstice and that the date of Annunciation was calculated on this basis. (The Julian calendar was originally only one day off, with the solstice falling on December 24 in 45 BC. Due to calendar slippage, the date of the astronomical solstice has moved back so that it now falls on either December 21 or December 22).

The idea that December 25 is Christ's birthday was popularized by Sextus Julius Africanus in *Chronographiai* (AD 221), an early reference book for Christians. This identification did not at first inspire feasting or celebration. In 245, the theologian Origen denounced the idea of celebrating the birthday of Jesus "as if he were a king pharaoh." Only sinners, not saints, celebrate their birthdays, Origin contended.

In 274, Emperor Aurelian designated December 25 as the festival of Sol Invictus (the "unconquered sun"). Aurelian may have chosen this date because the solstice was considered the birthday of Mithras, a syncretic god of Persian origin. Mithras is often identified with Sol Invictus, although Sol was originally a separate Syrian god.

Christmas soon outgrew the Christological controversy that created it and came to dominate the medieval calendar. The forty days before Christmas became the "forty days of St. Martin," now Advent. The fortieth day after Christmas was Candlemas. The Egyptian Christmas celebration on January 6 was adopted as Epiphany, one of the most prominent holidays of the year during Early Middle Ages. Christmas Day itself was a relatively minor holiday, although its prominence gradually increased after Charlemagne was crowned on Christmas Day, 800.

Although the nativity narrative is among the most compelling stories in the Bible, other Christian holidays such as Easter are more significant from a strictly religious point of view. The popularity of Christmas can be better understood if it is viewed as a form of winter celebration. Agricultural societies typically hold their most important festival in winter since there is less need of farm work at this time.

The Romans had a winter celebration known as Saturnalia. This festival was originally held on December 17 and honored Saturn, a god of agriculture. It recalled the "golden age" when Saturn ruled. In imperial times, Saturnalia was extended to seven days (December 17-23). Combined with festivals both before and after, the result was an extended winter holiday season. Business was postponed and even slaves feasted. There was drinking, gambling and singing naked. It was the "best of days," according to the poet Catallus. With the coming of Christianity, Italy's Saturnalian traditions were attached to Advent (the forty days before Christmas). Around the 12th century, these traditions transferred again to the "twelve days of Christmas" (*i.e.* Christmas to Epiphany).

Northern Europe was the last part to Christianize, and its pagan celebrations had a major influence on Christmas. Scandinavians still call Christmas *Jul* (Yule), originally the name of a twelve-day pre-Christian winter festival. Logs were lit to honour Thor, the god of thunder, hence the "Yule log." In Germany, the equivalent holiday is called *Mitwinternacht* (mid-winter night). There are also twelve *Rauhnächte* (harsh or wild nights).

The Reformation and Modern Times: Santa Claus hands out gifts to Union soldiers during the US Civil War in Thomas Nast's first Santa Claus cartoon, *Harper's Weekly*, 1863.

During the Reformation, Protestants condemned Christmas celebration as "trappings of popery" and the "rags of the Beast".

The Catholic Church responded by promoting the festival in a more religiously oriented form. When a Puritan parliament triumphed over the King Charles I of England, Christmas was officially banned (1647). Pro-Christmas rioting broke out in several cities. For several weeks, Canterbury was controlled by the rioters, who decorated doorways with holly and shouted royalist slogans. The Restoration (1660) ended the ban, but Christmas celebration was still disapproved of by the Anglican clergy (and, therefore, more thoroughly enjoyed by Catholics and Dissenters).

The phrase "Christmas tree" is first recorded in 1835 and represents the importation of a tradition from Germany, where such trees became popular in the late 18th century. Queen Victoria and her German-born husband Prince Albert enthusiastically promoted Christmas trees, as well as the idea of placing gifts under them. The royal family's tree of 1848 was widely publicized and imitated. Christmas cards were first designed in 1843 and became popular in the 1860s. The commercial calendar, created to answer children's questions concerning when Christmas would come, dates from 1851.

The Puritans of New England disapproved of Christmas and celebration was outlawed in Boston (1659-81). Virginia and New York, meanwhile, celebrated freely. Christmas fell out of favour after the American Revolution, when it was considered an "English custom". Interest was revived by Washington Irving's stories, by German immigrants, and by the homecomings of the Civil War years. It was declared a federal holiday in 1870.

Santa Claus is derived from Saint Nicholas, or *Sinterklaas,* who gave candy to the Dutch children on December 6. Dutch settlers in New York brought this tradition with them. Irving writes of Saint Nicholas "riding over the tops of the trees, in that selfsame wagon wherein he brings his yearly presents to children." The connection between Santa Claus and Christmas was popularized by the poem "A Visit from Saint Nicholas" (1822) by Clement Clarke Moore, which depicts Santa driving a sleigh pulled by reindeer and distributing gifts to children. His image was created by German-American cartoonist Thomas Nast

(1840-1902), who drew a new image annually beginning in 1863. By the 1880s, Nast's Santa had evolved into the form we now recognize. The image was standardized by advertisers in the 1920s.[14] Father Christmas is first recorded in the 15th century, but was associated with holiday merrymaking and drunkenness until Victorian Britain remade his image to match that of Santa.

In the midst of World War I, there was a Christmas truce between German and British troops in France (1914). Soldiers on both sides spontaneously began to sing Christmas carols and stopped fighting. The truce began on Christmas Day and continued for some time afterward. There was even a soccer game between the trench lines in which Germany's 133rd Royal Saxon Regiment is said to have bested Britain's Seaforth Highlanders 3-2.

Other Dates of Celebration: Although Christmas may be celebrated on December 25 in historically Catholic and Protestant nations, in eastern Europe it is often celebrated on January 7. This is because the Orthodox church continues to use the Julian calendar for determining feast days.

The Orthodox churches fast during the forty days before Christmas. Christmas is dubbed the "Feast of the Nativity of our Lord, God, and Saviour Jesus Christ." Armenian Christians celebrate Christmas on January 6.

Dates for the secular aspects of the Christmas celebration also vary. In the United Kingdom, the Christmas season traditionally runs for twelve days beginning on Christmas Day. These twelve days of Christmas, a period of feasting and merrymaking, end on Twelfth Night, the eve of the Feast of the Epiphany. In medieval times, Swedish law provided for a Christmas peace (*julefrid*) of twenty days during which fines for robbery and manslaughter were doubled. On Knut's Day, the twentieth day after Christmas (January 13), Swedish children celebrate and throw out the family Christmas tree (*julgransplundring*).

The Christmas festive period has grown longer in some countries. In the U.S., the pre-Christmas shopping season begins on the day after Thanksgiving. In the Philippines, radio stations usually start playing Christmas music during what is called the "-ber months" (September, October, etc.).

Countries that celebrate Christmas on December 25 recognize the previous day as Christmas Eve and have various names for the day after Christmas. In the Netherlands, Germany, Scandinavia, Lithuania and Poland, Christmas Day and the following day are called First and Second Christmas Day. In many European and Commonwealth countries, December 26 is referred to as Boxing Day. In Finland, Ireland, Italy, Romania, Austria, and Catalonia (Spain), the day is known as St. Stephen's Day. In Quebec, the December 26 holiday is referred to as *Lendemain de Noël* ("the day after Christmas").

Santa Claus and Other Bringers of Gifts: Gift-giving is a near-universal part of Christmas celebrations. The concept of a mythical figure who brings gifts to children derives from Saint Nicholas, a bishop of Myra in fourth century Lycia, Asia Minor. He made a pilgrimage to Egypt and Palestine in his youth and soon thereafter became Bishop of Myra. He was imprisoned during the persecution of Diocletian and released after the accession of Constantine. He may have been present at the Council of Nicaea, though there is no record of his attendance. He died on December 6 in 345 or 352. In 1087, Italian merchants stole his body at Myra and brought it to Bari in Italy. His relics are preserved in the church of San Nicola in Bari. An oily substance known as Manna di S. Nicola, which is highly valued for its medicinal powers, is said to flow from his relics.

The Dutch recogized a Saint Nicholas, or Sinterklaas, who gave gifts on the eve of his feast day of December 6. He became associated with Christmas in 19th century America and was renamed Santa Claus or Saint Nick. In the Anglo-American tradition, this jovial fellow arrives on Christmas Eve on a sleigh pulled by reindeer, and lands on the roofs of houses. He then climbs down the chimney, leaves gifts for the children, and eats the food they leave for him. He spends the rest of the year making toys and keeping lists on the behaviour of the children.

Saint Nicholas: One belief in the United Kingdom, United States, and other countries passed down through the generations is the idea of lists of good children and bad children. Throughout the year, Santa supposedly adds names of children to either the good or bad list depending on their behaviour. When it gets closer to Christmas time, parents use the belief to encourage children to behave well. Those who are on the bad list receive a booby prize, such as a piece of coal or a switch with which their parents beat them, rather than presents.

The French equivalent of Santa, Père Noël, evolved along similar lines, eventually adopting the Santa image. In some cultures Santa Claus is accompanied by Knecht Ruprecht, or Black Peter. In other versions, elves make the holiday toys. His wife is referred to as Mrs. Claus. Many shopping malls in North America, the United Kingdom, and Australia have a Santa Claus children can visit to ask for presents.

In many countries, children leave empty containers for Santa to fill with small gifts such as toys, candy, or fruit. In the United Kingdom, the United States, and Canada children hang a Christmas stocking by the fireplace on Christmas Eve because Santa is said to come down the chimney the night before Christmas to fill them. In other countries, children put their empty shoes out for Santa to fill on the night before Christmas, or for Saint Nicholas to fill on December 5, the eve of his saint's day. Family members and friends also bestow gifts on each other.

Timing of Gifts: In the Netherlands, Saint Nicholas's Day remains the principal day for gift giving while Christmas Day is a more religious holiday. In much of Germany, children put shoes out on window sills on the night of December 5, and find them filled with candy and small gifts the next morning. The main day for gift giving in Germany is December 24, when gifts are brought by Santa Claus or are placed under the Christmas tree. It is the same in Hungary, except that the Christmas gifts are usually brought by Jesus, not by Santa Claus. In Spain, gifts are brought by the magi on Epiphany (January 6). In Poland, Santa Claus gives gifts on two occasions: on the night of December 5 (so that children find them on the morning of

December 6) and on Christmas Eve, December 24, (so that children find gifts that same day). In Finland, *Joulupukki* personally meets children and gives gifts on December 24. In Russia, *Grandfather Frost* brings presents on New Year's Eve, and these are opened on the same night.

The song "Twelve Days of Christmas", celebrates an old British tradition of gifts each day from Christmas to Epiphany. In most of the world, Christmas gifts are given at night on Christmas Eve or in the morning of Christmas Day. Until recently, the British gave gifts to non-family members on Boxing Day.

Declaration of Christmas Peace: The Declaration of Christmas Peace has been a tradition in Finland from the Middle Ages every year, except in 1939 due to the war. The declaration takes place on the Old Great Square of Turku, Finland's official Christmas City and former capital, at noon on Christmas Eve. It is broadcast on Finnish radio and television.

Decorations: In the United States and Europe, rolls of paper with secular or religious Christmas motifs are manufactured for the purpose of wrapping gifts. Common motifs include Christmas trees, wreaths, Santa Claus, the Nativity, angels, Christmas tree ornaments, candies, stars, snowflakes, snowmen, and penguins.

Christmas trees may be decorated with lights and ornaments. The interior of a home may be decorated with garlands and evergreen foliage, particularly holly and mistletoe. In Australia, North and South America and to a lesser extent Europe, it is traditional to decorate the outside of houses with lights and sometimes with illuminated sleighs, snowmen, and other Christmas figures.

Since the 19th century, the poinsettia has been associated with Christmas. Other popular holiday plants include holly, mistletoe, red amaryllis, and Christmas cactus.

Municipalities often sponsor decorations as well. Christmas banner may be hung from street lights and Christmas trees placed in the town square. In the U.S., decorations once commonly included religious themes. This practice has led to many lawsuits, as some say it amounts to the government endorsing a religion. In 1984, the US Supreme Court ruled that a city-owned Christmas display, even one with a Nativity scene, does not violate the First Amendment.

Although Christmas decorations, such as a tree, are considered secular in many parts of the world, the Kingdom of Saudi Arabia bans such displays as symbols of Christianity.

Social Aspects and Entertainment: In many countries, businesses, schools, and communities have Christmas parties and dances in the weeks before Christmas. Christmas pageants may include a retelling of the story of the birth of Christ. Groups may visit neighborhood homes to sing Christmas carols. Others do volunteer work or hold fund-raising drives for charities.

On Christmas Day or Christmas Eve, a special meal of Christmas dishes is usually served. In some regions, particularly in Eastern Europe, these family feasts are preceded by a period of fasting. Candy and treats are also part of Christmas celebration in many countries.

Many people also send Christmas cards to their friends and family members. Many cards are also produced with messages such as "season's greetings" or "happy holidays", so as to including senders and recipients who may not celebrate Christmas.

Because of the focus on celebration, friends, and family, people who are without these, or who have recently suffered losses, are more likely to suffer from depression during Christmas. This increases the demand for counseling services. It is widely believed that suicides and murders spike during the holiday season. However, the peak months for suicide are May and June. Because of holiday celebrations involving alcohol, drunk driving-related fatalities increase.

Christmas in the Arts and Media: Many fictional Christmas stories capture the spirit of Christmas in a modern-day fairy tale, often with heart-touching stories of a Christmas miracle. Several have become part of the Christmas tradition in their countries of origin.

Among the most popular are Tchaikovsky's ballet *The Nutcracker* and Charles Dickens's novel *A Christmas Carol. The Nutcracker* tells of a nutcracker that comes to life in a young German girl's dream. Charles Dickens' *A Christmas Carol* is the tale of curmudgeonly miser Ebenezer Scourge. Scourge rejects compassion, philanthropy, and Christmas until he is visited by the ghosts of Christmas Past, Present and Future, who show him the consequences of his ways.

Some Scandinavian Christmas stories are less cheery than Dickens's. In H. C. Andersen's *The Little Match Girl,* a destitute little slum girl walks barefoot through snow-covered streets on Christmas Eve, trying in vain to sell her matches, and peeking in at the celebrations in the homes of the more fortunate. She dares not go home because her father is drunk. Unlike the principals of Anglophone Christmas lore, she meets a tragic end.

In 1881, the Swedish magazine *Ny Illustrerad Tidning* published Viktor Rydberg's poem *Tomten* featuring the first painting by Jenny Nyström of the traditional Swedish mythical character *tomte,* which she turned into the friendly white-bearded figure and associated with Christmas.

Economics of Christmas: Christmas is typically the largest annual stimulus for many nations. Sales increase dramatically in almost all retail areas and shops introduce new products as people purchase gifts, decorations, and supplies. In the U.S., the Christmas shopping season now begins on Black Friday, the day after Thanksgiving. The economic impact of Christmas continues after the holiday. During Christmas sales and New Year's sales, stores sell off excess inventories.

More businesses and stores close on Christmas Day than any other day of the year. In the United Kingdom, the Christmas Day (Trading) Act 2004 prevents all large shops from trading on Christmas Day.

Many religious Christians, as well as anti-consumerists, decry the commercialization of Christmas. They accuse the Christmas season of being dominated by money and greed at the expense of the holiday's more important values. Frustrations over these issues and others can lead to a rise in Christmas time social problems.

Most economists agree, however, that Christmas produces a deadweight loss under orthodox macroeconomic theory, due to the surge in gift-giving. This loss is calculated as the difference between what the gift giver spent on the item and what the gift receiver would have paid for the item. It is estimated that in 2001 Christmas resulted in a $4 billion deadweight loss in the U.S. alone. Because of complicating factors, this analysis is sometimes used to discuss possible flaws in current macroeconomic theory.

In North America, film studios release many high-budget movies in the holiday season, including Christmas films, fantasy movies or high-tone dramas with rich production values. This helps the studio capture holiday crowds and position themselves for the Academy Awards. Christmas is the most lucrative season for the industry aside from summer. Christmas-specific movies generally open in late November or early December as their themes and images are not nearly as popular once the season is over. Home video release is often delayed until the following Christmas season.

Christmas was not among the earliest festivals of the Church. Irenaeus and Tertullian omit it from their lists of feasts; Origin, glancing perhaps at the discreditable imperial *Natalitia*, asserts that in the Scriptures sinners alone, not saints, celebrate their birthday; Arnobius can still ridicule the "birthdays" of the gods.

Alexandria: The first evidence of the feast is from Egypt. About A.D. 200, Clement of Alexandria (Strom., I, xxi in P.G., VIII, 888) says that certain Egyptian theologians "over curiously" assign, not the year alone, but the day of Christ's birth, placing it on 25 Pachon (20 May) in the twenty-eighth year of Augustus. [Ideler (Chron., II, 397, n.) thought they did this believing that the ninth month, in which Christ was born, was the ninth of their own calendar.] Others reached the date of 24 or 25 Pharmuthi (19 or 20 April). With Clement's evidence may be mentioned the "De paschs computus", written in 243 and falsely ascribed to Cyprian (P.L., IV, 963 sqq.), which places Christ's birth on 28 March, because on that day the material sun was created. But Lupi has shown (Zaccaria, Dissertazioni ecc. del p. A.M. Lupi, Faenza, 1785, p. 219) that there is no month in the year to which respectable authorities have not assigned Christ's birth. Clement, however, also tells us that the Basilidians celebrated the Epiphany, and with it, probably, the Nativity, on 15 or 11 Tybi (10 or 6 January). At any rate this double commemoration became popular, partly because the apparition to the shepherds was considered as one manifestation of Christ's glory, and was added to the greater manifestations celebrated on 6 January; partly because at the baptism-manifestation many codices (*e.g.* Codex Bez) wrongly give the Divine words as *sou ei ho houios mou ho agapetos, ego semeron gegenneka se* (Thou art my beloved Son, this day have I begotten thee) in lieu of *en soi eudokesa* (in thee I am well pleased), read in Luke 3:22. Abraham Ecchelensis (Labbe, II, 402) quotes the Constitutions of the Alexandrian Church for a *dies Nativitatis et Epiphania* in Nicaan times; Epiphanius (Har., li, ed. Dindorf, 1860, II, 483) quotes an extraordinary semi-Gnostic ceremony at Alexandria in which, on the night of 5-6 January, a cross-stamped Korê was carried in procession round a crypt, to the chant, "Today at this hour Korê gave birth to the Eternal"; John Cassian records in his "Collations" (X, 2 in P.L., XLIX, 820), written 418-427, that the Egyptian monasteries still observe the "ancient custom"; but on 29 Choiak (25 December) and 1 January, 433, Paul of Emesa preached before Cyril of Alexandria, and his sermons (see Mansi, IV, 293; appendix to Act. Conc. Eph.) show that the December celebration was then firmly established there, and calendars prove its permanence. The December feast therefore reached Egypt between 427 and 433.

Cyprus, Mesopotamia, Armenia, Asia Minor: In Cyprus, at the end of the fourth century, Epiphanius asserts against the Alogi (Hær., li, 16, 24 in P. G., XLI, 919, 931) that Christ was born on 6 January and baptized on 8 November. Ephraem Syrus (whose hymns belong to Epiphany, not to Christmas) proves that Mesopotamia still put the birth feast thirteen days after the winter solstice; *i.e.* 6 January; Armenia likewise ignored, and still ignores, the December festival. (Cf. Euthymius, "Pan. Dogm.", 23 in P.G., CXXX, 1175; Niceph., "Hist. Eccl,", XVIII, 53 in P.G., CXLVII, 440; Isaac, Catholicos of Armenia in eleventh or twelfth century, "Adv. Armenos", I, xii, 5 in P.G., CXXII, 1193; Neale, "Holy Eastern Church", Introd., p. 796). In Cappadocia, Gregory of Nyssa's sermons on St. Basil (who died before 1 January, 379) and the two following, preached on St. Stephen's feast (P.G., XLVI, 788; cf, 701, 721), prove that in 380 the 25th December was already celebrated there, unless, following Usener's too ingenious arguments (Religionsgeschichtliche Untersuchungen, Bonn, 1889, 247-250), one were to place those sermons in 383. Also, Asterius of Amaseia (fifth century) and Amphilochius of Iconium (contemporary of Basil and Gregory) show that in their dioceses both the feasts of Epiphany and Nativity were separate.

Jerusalem: In 385, Silvia of Bordeaux (or Etheria, as it seems clear she should be called) was profoundly impressed by the splendid Childhood feasts at Jerusalem. They had a definitely "Nativity" colouring; the bishop proceeded nightly to Bethlehem, returning to Jerusalem for the day celebrations. The Presentation was celebrated forty days after. But this calculation starts from 6 January, and the feast lasted during the octave of that date. (Peregr. Sylv., ed. Geyer, pp. 75 sq.) Again (p. 101) she mentions as high festivals Easter and Epiphany alone. In 385, therefore, 25 December was not observed at Jerusalem. This checks the so-called correspondence between Cyril of Jerusalem (348-386) and Pope Julius I (337-352), quoted by John of Nikiu (c. 900) to convert Armenia to 25 December (see P.L., VIII, 964 sqq.).

Cyril declares that his clergy cannot, on the single feast of Birth and Baptism, make a double procession to Bethlehem and Jordan. (This later practice is here an anachronism.) He asks Julius to assign the true date of the nativity "from census documents brought by Titus to Rome"; Julius assigns 25 December. Another document (Cotelier, Patr. Apost., I, 316, ed. 1724) makes Julius write thus to Juvenal of Jerusalem (c. 425-458), adding that Gregory Nazianzen at Constantinople was being criticized for "halving" the festival. But Julius died in 352, and by 385 Cyril had made no change; indeed, Jerome, writing about 411 (in Ezech., P.L., XXV, 18), reproves Palestine for keeping Christ's birthday (when He hid Himself) on the Manifestation feast. Cosmas Indicopleustes suggests (P.G., LXXXVIII, 197) that even in the middle of the sixth century Jerusalem was peculiar in combining the two commemorations, arguing from Luke 3:23 that Christ's baptism day was the anniversary of His birthday.

The commemoration, however, of David and James the Apostle on 25 December at Jerusalem accounts for the deferred feast. Usener, arguing from the "Laudatio S. Stephani" of Basil of Seleucia (c. 430. — P.G., LXXXV, 469), thinks that Juvenal tried at least to introduce this feast, but that Cyril's greater name attracted that event to his own period.

Antioch: In Antioch, on the feast of St. Philogonius, Chrysostom preached an important sermon. The year was almost certainly 386, though Clinton gives 387, and Usener, by a long rearrangement of the saint's sermons, 388 (Religionsgeschichtl. Untersuch., pp. 227-240). But between February, 386, when Flavian ordained Chrysostom priest, and December is ample time for the preaching of all the sermons under discussion. (See Kellner, Heortologie, Freiburg, 1906, p. 97, n. 3). In view of a reaction to certain Jewish rites and feasts, Chrysostom tries to unite Antioch in celebrating Christ's birth on 25 December, part of the community having already kept it on that day for at least ten years.

In the West, he says, the feast was thus kept, *anothen*; its introduction into Antioch he had always sought, conservatives always resisted. This time he was successful; in a crowded church he defended the new custom. It was no novelty; from Thrace to Cadiz this feast was observed — rightly, since its miraculously rapid diffusion proved its genuineness. Besides, Zachary, who, as high-priest, entered the Temple on the Day of Atonement, received therefore announcement of John's conception in September; six months later Christ was conceived, *i.e.* in March, and born accordingly in December.

Finally, though never at Rome, on authority he knows that the census papers of the Holy Family are still there. [This appeal to Roman archives is as old as Justin Martyr (Apol., I, 34, 35) and Tertullian (Adv. Marc., IV, 7, 19). Julius, in the Cyriline forgeries, is said to have calculated the date from Josephus, on the same unwarranted assumptions about Zachary as did Chrysostom.] Rome, therefore, has observed 25 December long enough to allow of Chrysostom speaking at least in 388 as above (P.G., XLVIII, 752, XLIX, 351).

Rome: At Rome the earliest evidence is in the Philocalian Calendar (P. L., XIII, 675; it can be seen as a whole in J. Strzygowski, Kalenderbilder des Chron. von Jahre 354, Berlin, 1888), compiled in 354, which contains three important entries. In the civil calendar 25 December is marked "Natalis Invicti". In the "Depositio Martyrum" a list of Roman or early and universally venerated martyrs, under 25 December is found "VIII kal. ian. natus Christus in Betleem Iudes". On "VIII kal. mart." (22 February) is also mentioned St. Peter's Chair. In the list of consuls are four anomalous ecclesiastical entries: the birth and death days of Christ, the entry into Rome, and martyrdom of Saints Peter and Paul. The significant entry is "Chr. Cæsare et Paulo sat. XIII. hoc. cons. Dns. ihs. XPC natus est VIII Kal. ian. d. ven. luna XV," *i.e.* during the consulship of (Augustus) Csar and Paulus Our Lord Jesus Christ was born on the eighth before the calends of January (25 December), a Friday, the fourteenth day of the moon.

The details clash with tradition and possibility. The epact, here XIII, is normally XI; the year is A.U.C. 754, a date first suggested two centuries later; in no year between 751 and 754 could 25 December fall on a Friday; tradition is constant in placing Christ's birth on Wednesday. Moreover the date given for Christ's death (*duobus Geminis coss.*, *i.e.* A.D. 29) leaves Him only twenty eight, and one-quarter years of life. Apart from this, these entries in a consul list are manifest interpolations. But are not the two entries in the "Depositio Martyrum" also such? Were the day of Christ's birth in the flesh alone there found, it might stand as heading the year of martyrs' spiritual *natales*; but 22 February is there wholly out of place. Here, as in the consular *fasti*, popular feasts were later inserted for convenience' sake. The civil calendar alone was not added to, as it was useless after the abandonment of pagan festivals. So, even if the "Depositio Martyrum" dates, as is probable, from 336, it is not clear that the calendar contains evidence earlier than Philocalus himself, *i.e.* 354, unless indeed pre-existing popular celebration must be assumed to render possible this official recognition.

Were the Chalki manuscript of Hippolytus genuine, evidence for the December feast would exist as early as c. 205. The relevant passage [which exists in the Chigi manuscript Without the bracketed words and is always so quoted before George Syncellus (c. 1000)] runs:

> *He gar prote parousia tou kyriou hemon he ensarkos [en he gegennetai] en Bethleem, egeneto [pro okto kalandon ianouarion hemera tetradi] Basileuontos Augoustou [tessarakoston kai deuteron etos, apo de Adam] pentakischiliosto kai pentakosiosto etei epathen de triakosto trito [pro okto kalandon aprilion, hemera paraskeun, oktokaidekato etei Tiberiou Kaisaros, hypateuontos Hrouphou kai Hroubellionos. — (Comm. In Dan., iv, 23; Brotke; 19)*

"For the first coming of Our Lord in the flesh [in which He has been begotten], in Bethlehem, took place [25 December, the fourth day] in the reign of Augustus [the forty-second year, and] in the year 5500 [from Adam]. And He suffered in His thirty-third year [25 March, the parasceve, in the eighteenth year of Tiberius Csar, during the consulate of Rufus and Rubellio]."

Interpolation is certain, and admitted by Funk, Bonwetsch, etc. The names of the consuls [which should be Fufius and Rubellius] are wrong; Christ lives thirty-three years; in the genuine Hippolytus, thirty-one; minute data are irrelevant in this discussion with Severian millenniarists; it is incredible that Hippolytus should have known these details when his contemporaries (Clement, Tertullian, etc.) are, when dealing with the matter, ignorant or silent; or should, having published them, have remained unquoted (Kellner, op. cit., p. 104, has an excursus on this passage.)

St. Ambrose (de virg., iii, 1 in P. L., XVI, 219) preserves the sermon preached by Pope Liberius I at St. Peter's, when, on *Natalis Christi*, Ambrose' sister, Marcellina, took the veil. This pope reigned from May, 352 until 366, except during his years of exile, 355-357. If Marcellina became a nun only after the canonical age of twenty-five, and if Ambrose was born only in 340, it is perhaps likelier that the event occurred after 357. Though the sermon abounds in references appropriate to the Epiphany (the marriage at Cana, the multiplication of loaves, etc.), these seem due (Kellner, op. cit., p. 109) to sequence of thought, and do not fix the sermon to 6 January, a feast unknown in Rome till much later. Usener, indeed, argues (p. 272) that Liberius preached it on that day in 353, instituting the Nativity feast in the December of the same year; but Philocalus warrants our supposing that if preceded his pontificate by some time, though Duchesne's relegation of it to 243 (Bull. crit., 1890, 3, pp. 41 sqq.) may not commend itself to many.

In the West the Council of Saragossa (380) still ignores 25 December (see can. xxi, 2). Pope Siricius, writing in 385 (P. L., XII, 1134) to Himerius in Spain, distinguishes the feasts of the Nativity and Apparition; but whether he refers to Roman or to Spanish use is not clear. Ammianus Marcellinus (XXI, ii) and Zonaras (Ann., XIII, 11) date a visit of Julian the Apostate to a church at Vienne in Gaul on Epiphany and Nativity respectively. Unless there were two visits, Vienne in A.D. 361 combined the feasts, though on what day is still doubtful. By the time of Jerome and Augustine, the December feast is established, though the latter (Epp., II, liv, 12, in P.L., XXXIII, 200) omits it from a list of first-class festivals. From the fourth century every Western calendar assigns it to 25 December. At Rome, then, the Nativity was celebrated on 25 December before 354; in the East, at Constantinople, not before 379, unless with Erbes, and against Gregory, we recognize it there in 330. Hence, almost universally has it been concluded that the new date reached the East from Rome by way of the Bosphorus during the great anti-Arian revival, and by means of the orthodox champions. De Santi (L'Orig. delle Fest. Nat., in Civiltæ Cattolica, 1907), following Erbes, argues that Rome took over the Eastern Epiphany, now with a definite Nativity colouring, and, with as increasing number of Eastern Churches, placed it on 25 December; later, both East and West divided their feast, leaving Ephiphany on 6 January, and Nativity on 25 December, respectively, and placing Christmas on 25 December and Epiphany on 6 January. The earlier hypothesis still seems preferable.

The Christmas Tree: While Santa Claus became increasingly familiar to Americans, the German Christmas tree also acquired popularity in North America. As early as the 17th century, Germans had transformed this pagan symbol of fertility into a Christian symbol of rebirth. According to legend, the Christmas tree tradition began with the founder of German Protestantism, Martin Luther. While walking through the forest on Christmas Eve, Luther was so moved by the beauty of the starlit fir trees that he brought one indoors and decorated it with candles to remind his children of God's creation. In 1841 Prince Albert of Germany gave his wife, Queen Victoria of England, a gift of a Christmas tree. This was reputedly the first Christmas tree in England, but the custom spread quickly. German immigrants took the Christmas tree to other parts of Europe and to the United States and Canada, where it soon became a popular tradition. Blown-glass ornaments, tin angels, paper chains, candles, cornucopias filled with sugarplums, and other decorations made the simple evergreen tree into a beautiful parlor centerpiece at Christmas time.

Christmas Cards: The practice of exchanging Christmas cards also became a widespread custom in the 19th century. Europeans had distributed wood prints of religious themes for Christmas during the Middle Ages (5th century to 15th century). In 1843 English illustrator John Callcott Horsley created the first modern Christmas card. The card depicted a family celebration and its caption read, "A Merry Christmas and a Happy New Year to You." In the United States, German-born printer Louis Prang made advances in colour lithography that enabled him to mass-produce a colorful Christmas card in 1875. The card sold extremely well, and soon the custom of exchanging Christmas cards spread throughout the country.

The inhabitants of the United States have emigrated from all over the world. As a result, many traditions have mingled to form modern American Christmas celebrations and folklore. Some Swedish American communities hold Santa Lucia festivals to honour a young girl who was killed in the 4th century for her Christian beliefs. German Americans in Pennsylvania create elaborate landscapes, called putzes, beneath their Christmas trees. These displays—made of moss, pine branches, stones, and logs—depict the birth of Christ. Christmas Eve bonfires illuminate the banks of the Mississippi River in Louisiana so that *Papa Noël* (French for "Father Christmas") will be able to find his way to the homes of the local Cajun children. In the southwestern United States, Mexican Americans hold festivals called *posadas* that recreate Mary and Joseph's search for a place to stay where Mary could give birth to Jesus (*see* Virgin Mary and Joseph). In addition to these Christian celebrations, the eight-day Jewish festival of Hanukkah and the seven-day African American festival of Kwanzaa are popular celebrations that coincide with the Christmas season.

Despite this variety of people and faiths, there is a striking unity to Christmas celebrations in the United States. For many people, the holiday season begins with the arrival of Santa Claus in the annual Thanksgiving Day parade in New York City sponsored by Macy's department store. Television advertisements heralding the beginning of the Christmas shopping season can begin even earlier in autumn. Many Americans participate in a communal sense of holiday spirit: Cities decorate their streets with Christmas lights; stores fill their shelves with extra merchandise; friends and relatives exchange holiday cards; communities decorate public Christmas trees; and volunteers from the Salvation Army ring bells on city streets to solicit charity donations.

6

Jain Festivals

Mahavir Jayanti

According to the *Digambara* school of Jainism, Lord Mahavira was born in the year 615 BC, but the *Swetambaras* believe that he was born in 599 BC. Both sects however agree that he was the son of Siddhartha and Trisala. Legend has it that he was conceived by Devananda, wife of a Brahmin named Rishabhdeva. It is believed that the gods, ingeniously, transferred the embryo to the womb of Trisala. It is said that the expectant mother had sixteen auspicious dreams before the child was born (only 14 according to the Swetambaras). Astrologers intepreting these dreams, stated that the child would be either an emperor or a *Teerthankara*.

This religious event is largely observed by the Jains by visiting sacred sites and worshipping the *Teerthankara*. The event holds special significance in Gujarat and Rajasthan due to the ancient shrines at Girnar and Palitana in Gujarat. Mahavir Jayanti is also celebrated at Parasnath Temple in Kolkata and at Pawapuri in Bihar.

Mahavira, also known as Vardhamana, is the last one in the galaxy of Twenty-four Teerthankaras (Jain Prophets). He was born in the year 599 B.C. and has been acclaimed as one of the greatest prophets of peace and social reformation that Bharat has ever produced. He was born to a pious couple, Siddhartha and Priyakarani or popularly Trishala Devi-who were deeply permeated with the philosophy of jainism preached by Parswanatha, the 23rd Teerthankara. Siddhartha was the king of Kaundinyapura on the outskirts of Vaishali (near Patna in Bihar).

Even as a boy, Mahavira came to be associated with many episodes of absolute fearlessness which earned him the name 'Mahavira'. He grew up as a prince, excelling in physical prowess as well as intellectual acumen. However, he renounced the pleasures and luxuries of the place, as also the power and prestige of kingship, and undertook a life of intense penance for more than twelve years. He calmly bore not only the rigors of nature but the torments from the ignorant and mischievous among his own countrymen also. He finally became self-illumined. But not content with his own personal salvation, he chose to become a great human redeemer.

He looked around and found the society corrupted by the distortions of the true concept of Dharma. Violence in the form of animal sacrifice had overshadowed the true spirit of yajna and yaga. Spiritual values had been supplanted by superstitions and lifeless rituals and dogmas. Propitiating various Gods and Goddesses was considered as a means of acquiring religious merit-Punya-to the exclusion of the true spiritual significance of these Vedic practices. Mahavira, with his penetrating insight born out of self-realization, struck mercilessly at these perversions. He simplified the religious procedures and concentrated on righteous conduct.

Mahavira's simple and convincing method of appealing to the highest and noblest impulses in the living breast soon won him a large following. He would, for example, pose the following question in order to bring home the grand message of non-injury to every living being: "Can you hold a red-hot iron rod in your hand merely because some one wants you to do so?" The listeners would instantly reply, "No, never". Then Mahavira would ask them, "Then, will it be right on your part to ask others to do the same thing just to satisfy your desire? If you cannot tolerate infliction of pain on your body or mind by others' words and actions, what right have you to do the same to others through your words and deeds?" Mahavira would then sum up his message: "Do unto others as you would like to be done by. Injury or violence done by your to any life in any form, animal or human, is as harmful as it would be if caused to your own self."

Mahavira's emphasis on this 'Unity of Life' forms one of the highest saving principles of human life. The modern civilization, which seeks to exploit and destroy every other kind of living species in order to satiate the never ending cravings of man, is landing the entire human species itself in a deadly peril.

As one deeply conversant with the needs, capacities and aptitudes of human being, Mahavira initiated a simple five-fold path for the householders: Ahimsa (Non-injury-physical or mental-to others), Asteya (non-stealing), Brahmacharya (temperance in sexual pleasures) and Aparigraha (non-acquisition of property).

Mahavira's injunctions for the monks and nuns were however very exacting. Abstinence from every kind of physical comfort and material possession and absolute dedication to the highest ethical and spiritual discipline were enforced. Even to this day, 2500 years after the passing away of that great master, this pure and upright tradition of the monks has been maintained. Thousands of white clad Sanyasins and Sanyasinis and also nude monks move on foot from village to village and town to town, throughout the length and breadth of the country, carrying Mahavira's gospel of peace, non-injury and brotherhood among people.

Mahavira left his mortal coils at the age of 71 on the Deepavali day. But the lamp of peace which he lit continues to glow through the myriad lights of that Festival of Lights.

A Grand Celebration: On this auspicious day, grand chariot processions with the images of Mahavira are taken out, rich ceremonies are held in the temples, fasts and charities are observed, Jain scriptures are read, and at some places grand fairs are set up.

Mahavira, the great teacher and the twenty-fourth Tirthankara of Jainism was a contemporary of Lord Buddha. His mother Trisala or Priyakarini had a series of miraculous dreams heralding the birth of Mahavira. Vardhaman achieved enlightenment under an Ashoka tree after two and a half days fasting and meditation. Then he stripped himself of all his clothes and wore none there after, but Shvetambars believe that Indra then presented him a white robe.

After his enlightenment he gave away all his wealth and possessions and owned nothing. Mahavira underlined the importance of austerity and complete non-violence as the essential means of spiritual evolution and salvation.

Mahavir Jayanti is celebrated as the anniversary of Vardhman Mahavir, the founder of Jain religion. Commemorating his birthday on this day, Mahavir was the most revered religious leader in this century and was perceived as a reformer who vehemently opposed the ritualism and false beliefs. The twenty-fourth and last Jain Tirthankara, Mahavir was born in 599 BC and lived for 72 years. He was born of Sidhartha, the Raja of Kundalpura, and Queen Trishala, who was also known by the name Priyakarni.

His Divine Life: Prince Vardhamana became extremely penitent and resolved to give up everything worldly. He gave up attachment to his parents, friends and relatives. Distributing all his wealth among the poor, he went to the forest and became a monk. Mahavir practised rigorous austerities, including fasts that lasted many days. He meditated on the pure nature of the Soul. Mahavir lived a life of absolute truthfulness, a life of perfect honesty and a life of absolute chastity.

His Teachings: Mahavira taught that people can save their souls from the contamination of matter by living a life of extreme asceticism and by practising non-violence towards all living creatures. This advocacy of non-violence encouraged his followers-monastic and lay-to become strong advocates of vegetarianism. Mahavira's followers were aided in their quest for salvation by the five mahavatars. Attributed to Mahavira, these great vows were the renunciation of killing, of speaking untruths, of greed, of sexual pleasure, and of all attachments to living beings and non-living things.

Sects: The main sects now are the Digambaras and Shvetambaras, with the latter again divided into Deravasis and Sthanakvasis. While the Deravasis visit the temples and worship the statue of Mahavir, the Sthanakvasis emphasise the internalisation of the faith. Mahavir himself was against idol worship.

On the day of Mahavir Jayanthi (Birth anniversary), many members of the community make offerings of milk, rice, fruit, incense, lamps and water to the tirthankar. Some sections of the community even participate in a grand procession.

Mahavira is the last and the greatest Tirthankar of the Jain religion, and Mahavir Jayanti is the birth anniversary of Lord Mahavira, the 24th Tirthankara. Mahavir Jayanti is celebrated in the first day of Bhadrapad, when there is a grand cradle procession, and a general celebration of the auspicious day.

The two sects of Jainism, Svetambaras and Digambaras, however, do not come to a concencous on the date of His birth.. According to the Digambara sect, his birth took place in 615 BC, whereas the Svetembaras claim that it occurred in 599 BC.

About Mahavira, His Birth and Enlightenment: According to the Jain mythology, Mahavir had acquired all the necessery qualities to become a Tirthankara in His pervous life. Six months prior to his birth, the supreme powers created an atmoshphere congenial and condusive to Mahavira's birth, who was a great being. Gods and Goddesses came down to bestow their blessings on the Tirthankara's expecting mother, and to cater to her needs. Wealth was showered from the heavens, relieving everyone from poverty and extending the superior ambience.

Just before Mahavira was born, His mother had sixteen dreams. Mahavira was born at four in the morning, which is considered very auspicious in Jainism and Hinduism.

Her sixteen dreams were:

- A white elephant
- A lion
- Goddess Lakshmi with two elephants at her side showering flowers
- The moon lighting the universe with silvery beams

- A pair of jumping fish
- The radiant sun, a golden pitcher
- A lake full of lotus flowers
- A calm ocean of milk
- A celestial palace
- A throne of rubies and diamonds
- A celestial king ruling the earth
- A garland
- A white bull
- A fragrant Mandara flowers
- and a vase as tall as Mount Meru, filled with gems.
- And immediately after this, she felt a white elephant enter her through her mouth. She also didn't feel any pain associated with childbirth.

It is believed that at the exact moment of his birth, the life forms in all the three worlds were cheerful and content. Several gods and goddesses descended from the heavens to pay homage to the tirthankara. They bathed him ceremonially and named him Vardhaman, Vir, Mahavira, Ativira and Samvati. The child was of exceptional beauty and developed great physical and spiritual strength. At the age of thirty, Mahavira renounced the material world, and sat for meditation. After 12 years of meditation under an Ashoke tree, also called Jonesia Ashoka, he attained the ultimate enlightenment. The divine Gods witnessed this great event, and carried him in a pamaquin to a park where he was put on a five-tiered throne and acknowledged as Mahavira. Here he stripped himself of all his clothes. Instead of shaving his head, he tore his hair out from the roots, for he was above pain. According to the Digambaras, Mahavira wore no clothes thereafter, but the Svetambaras believe that Indra presented him with a white robe.

Mahavira preached non-violence and prohibited any kind of killing. He also believed that the most virtuous life is spent sitting still and fasting, as then a man does not run the risk of injuring life even involuntarily, by swallowing or treading upon insects. On his birth anniversary, every Jain resolves to follow his teachings

Many feel that Jainism is actually an ancient atheist religion. Lord Mahavira preached that no single superior being could either produce or maintain the world.

Those people who follow Jainism believe that the world does not start or end, as is suggested by many other religions.

Mahavira was a believer in simplicity and as such suggested followers of Jainism should follow very simple rules:

- *Aparigraha:* No greed (taking more than you deserve or need)
- *Astyea:* No theft
- *Brahmacharya:* Control of sexual pleasure
- *Ahimsa:* No hurting others either emotionally or physically.

Jainism aims to achieve pure and perfect autonomy. Based almost entirely on celestial principles, Jainism believes in eternity.

Mahavir Jayanti is celebrated widely throughout the Jain community. Due to the high numbers of Jains in Rajasthan and Gujarat, most celebrations are seen in these states.

However, those that follow Jainism travel to recognized Jain shrines to celebrate Mahavir Jayanti. In Gujarat, the shrines are located at Girnar and Palitana. Others flock to Mahavirji in Rajasthan.

Lord Mahavira was born in Vaishali, which also hosts a majestic celebration.

Mahavir Jayanti Celebration

- Temples that host Mahavir Jayanti festivals are decorated with flags to mark the birthday of Lord Mahavira.
- Each locality holds a traditional bath (*abhishek*) for a deity of Lord Mahavira.
- Following the bath, the deity is carried in a parade throughout the region.
- Each parade varies but generally includes drummers horses, elephants, singers and lamps.

- Depending on the region, the parade ends at a temple, shrine or large communal area where people may pray and meditate.

Donations made during Mahavir Jayanti are made in the form of food, medicines or knowledge.

The birthday of Lord Mahaveer is called "Mahaveer Janma Kalyanak" and also popularly known as Mahaveer Jayanti.

Five hundred and forty-three years before Vikrama Era (in 599 B.C.) Bhagwan Mahaveer, the twenty-fourth and the last Tirthankar was born at midnight on the thirteenth day of the bright half of the month Chaitra. He was in the womb of Devananda for 82 days and in the womb of Trishala for a period of 195 days and a half (in all nine months and seven and a half days).

The birth of this great saviour spread divine light in the whole universe. All beings were steeped in divine bliss. In accordance with the established convention, the thrones of the fifty-six goddesses presiding over all the directions, started receiving tremors and realising that it was the signal of the great event of the birth of the saviour,they all flew towards Bhagwan Mahaveer and his blessed mother. They bowed down to them, bathed them, applied scented pastes, dressed and decked them artistically. With their mission fulfilled, they returned to their respective abodes.

In West India: The festival is celebrated on a large scale in Gujarat and Rajasthan where many people practice Jainism. Festivities can be witnessed at Jain shrines in Girnar and Palitana in Gujarat, at Pawanpuri in Bihar and at Parasnath temple in Calcutta.

Lord Mahavir was conceived by Devananda, the wife of a Brahmin called Rishabhdeva. However, the Gods transferred the embryo to Trisala's womb. When astrologers were asked to interpret the dreams of the expectant mother, they predicted that the child would be either an emperor or a Teerthankar. Vardhaman Mahavir went on to become the 24th Tirthankara of the Jain religion. Rishabhadeva, the first Tirthankara, is believed to have founded Jainism. At the age of 30, Mahavir became a wandering ascetic and attained enlightenment after 13 years of meditation.

As the emphasis is on renunciation, liberation of man from the material world, there is no exhibition of pomp and gaiety on Jain festivals. Rather, devotees spend their time in quiet introspection. Mahavir Jayanti is largely spent in prayer. In some places, peaceful processions are taken out. Children enact scenes depicting different phases of Mahavir's life. It is considered an auspicious day to embark on new ventures or for social activities. Jain devotees visit sacred places and worship the Teerthankaras or the religious gurus.

"There is no doubt that Jainism prevailed even before Vardhaman or Parshvanath." In the 12th century A.D. King Kumarapala was won over to Jainism and made Gujarat a model Jam state. Today the followers of the lain religion form a community of more than one million and a half living in India.

Mahavir is the "Jina" or "Conqueror", under whose guidance his devotees are encouraged to conquer the karma-rebirth cycle, this being the goal of the lain religion. Mahavir was a kshatriya prince (warrior caste) of North Bihar in Northern India. At the age of 30 he became a wandering ascetic. Thirteen years later he reached illumination. His followers form four orders: monks (muni or sadhu), nuns (sadhvi), laymen (shravaka) and laywomen (shravika).

Digambaras and Shvetambaras: Around the year 80 A.D. the Jains split into two sects: Digambaras (space clothed) and Shvetambaras (clothed in white). Digambaras hold that sadhus must be naked as a sign of total renunciation. Other doctrines held by the Digambaras but rejected by the Shvetambaras are 1. Only men can obtain final liberation (moksha), women must be reborn as men. 2. The images of the Tirthankars must be represented with downcast eyes, nude and unadorned. 3. Mahavir never married. 4. Once the highest stage of knowledge is reached, a saint can sustain life without eating, and 5. By the 2nd century AD the entire canon of sacred books was lost.

Dash Laxanparva: The holiest feast of the Jains is Dashlaxanparva, which is celebrated by the Digambaras from the 5th to the 14th of the bright half of Bhadrapad. During these days there is an atmosphere of joy in every lain temple. Every day in the morning after taking bath all men and women go to worship in the temple.

Then each day there is a lecture on each of the ten chapters of the holy book "Shritatvarth Sutra". These ten chapters dwell on the following ten duties (dharma): 1. Kshama (forgiveness), 2. Mardava (humility), 3. Arjava (simplicity and frankness). 4. Shaucha (cleanliness), 5. Satya (truthfulness), 6. Samyama (self-control), 7. Tap (austerity), 8. Tyag (renunciation). 9. Akimchanya (detachment), and 10. Bramhacharya (celibacy). On the day dedicated to "tyag" gifts are offered to social service institutions, and on the first day of the dark half of Ashvin, at the end of the celebration, all the men come together and embracing each other they ask pardon for the of-fences committed during the past year.

The 14th day of the bright half of Bhadrapad is known as Anant Chaturdashi (endless fourteenth). This is a very important day for the Jains, this being the last day of the Dashlaxanparva. According to Jam scriptures one can gain much merit by observing a vow on this day. The Jaiṇs of the Shvetambara sect celebrate the Paryushan Feast, from the 12th of the dark half of Bhadrapad to the 4th of the bright half of Ashvin.

Legend of Mahaveera: According to Swetambar sect of Jains, in 599 B.C. on Chaitra Shukla Trayodsahi *i.e.* the thirteenth day of the bright half of Chaitra (March-April), a child was born to King Siddhartha and queen Priyakarani or popularly known as Trishala Devi. Siddhartha was the king of Kaundinyapura near Patna in Bihar.

The child who was named Mahaveera and also Vardhamana (which means ever advancing) and Sanmati, was destined to become one of the greatest prophets of Jainism. He was the last 24th Teerthankara (Jain prophets) of the Jains. Vardhamana from his childhood was brave and fearless which earned him the name of 'Mahaveera', 'Maha' means great and 'Veera' means a hero. He grew up as a prince excelling in all arts of prowess and intellectual sphere. His parents being the followers of

Jainsim preached by Parswanatha, the 23rd Teerthankara, Mahaveera was much influenced by its philosophy. It is seems 'Tirtha' literally means a ford, a means of crossing over. Metaphorically, it denotes a philosophy or a spiritual guide who helps to cross over the ocean of recurring births in this world. 'Kara' means one who makes. Mahaveera was very obedient to his parents. It is said at the age of eight to observed the twelve vows of Ahims etc. He also grew up to be a great statesman but he did not marry. He lived a life of truthfulness, honesty and chastity. He realised the transitory pleasures of the world and engrossed himself in Self-contemplation. He renounced the pleasures and luxurious of the palace and its kingship. He gave up attachment to his parents, relatives and friends and undertook a life of intense penance for more than twelve years. He knew that renunciation was the only means of attaining eternal bliss.

During his long penance, he went through a rigorous life of austerities, fasted and meditated on the pure nature of the Soul. He was unmoved by the beautiful damsel whom God sent to test him. Again, he not only bore the inclements of Nature but the torments of his jealous opponents, his own countrymen but finally attain self-enlightenment. Mahaveera was not content with his own salvation. He wanted to become a true human redeemer. He found that the real concept of Dharma was mis interpreted and there was much corruption in the religious sphere also. In the name of religion animal sacrifices took place during Yagnas etc. He did not believe in rituals and spirituals that were distorted and were filled with more superstitions than reality. He remarked, worshipping Gods and Goddesses were more for attaining Punya or religious merit for oneself than practising goodness and understanding the true significance of the Vedic scriptures. He ruthlessly condemned the existing ill practices of the religious priests.

Instead, he introduced simple codes of righteous conduct which appealed to all and he won a large number of followers. Mahaveera preached non-injury to other creatures and beings. He would ask "Can you hold a red-hot iron rod in your hand merely because some one wants you to do so?" The listeners would ofcourse answer "No never". Then, Mahaveera would ask them, "Then, will it be right on your part to ask others to do the same thing just to satisfy your desires? If you cannot tolerate infliction of pain on your body or mind by others' words and actions, what right have you to do the same to others through your words and deeds" His sermon was "Do unto others as you would like to be done by.

Injury or violence done by you to any life in any form, animal or human, is as harmful as it would be if caused to your own self. "His message and emphasis was on 'Unity of Life' and Brotherhood. Before renunciation Mahaveera had distributed all his wealth to the poor with his own hands. When he went to the forest it seems he took off even the piece of cloth which he was wearing. Before he became a meak, he rooted out with his hands five tufts of hair from his head and turning to the North said, "Salutations to the Siddhas! "Mahaveera, the greatest Teerthankara spread his teachings to Magadha, Mithila and other distant places, and even many kings became his disciples.

Even today, we find Jain whiteclad monks and Sanyasins spreading Mahaveera's teachings of Peace, non-injury and Brotherhood throughout the length and breadth of the country. Mahaveera lived for 72 years and entered into Nirvana in 527 B.C. on the Deepavali day but the lamp of Peace which he lit still continues to glow.

Look at traditional Mahavir Jayanti celebrations where the emphasis is on piety, self-control and a willingness to help the less fortunate.

Mahavir Jayanthi usually begins with the idol of Lord Mahavir being given a ceremonial bath. This is followed by various offerings to the idol in the form of fruit, rice and milk. Incense sticks and lamps are lit in the temple which is also decorated with red and saffron flags on the occasion.

After the ceremonial bath called the abhishek, the idol is taken around the neighborhood by a large procession of devotees. Celebrations are particularly high profile in the ancient Jain shrines at Girnar and Palitana in Gujarat where thousands of pilgrims congregate.

Paryushana

The Paryushana is the most important festival among the Jain festivals and it is observed during every Chaturmas commencing on the twelfth day of the shukla phase of Bhadrapad month and ending on the fourth day of Krishna Phase of Bhadrapad. This is in August-September, and peak monsoon time (this year it starts from 15th August 2001 and ends on 22nd Aug'01). For the Swetambara sect of Jains, Paryushana is an eight-day event, while for the Digambaras it stretches over ten days.Its origin is related to the staying of the monks in one place in Chaturmas (4 months of monsoon).

As during this time the monks have settled in the town for a longer duration, it is time for the householders to have an annual renewal of the faith by listening to the statement of the Dharma and by meditation and vratas (self-control). And for the monks, almost as importantly, staying in one place during the monsoon reduces the risk of causing accidental death to numerous insects and smaller forms of life that thrive during the rains. Paryushana is a time of reflection on actions and meditation on the past year. Paryushana is marked by strict observance of the ten cardinal virtues: forgiveness, charity, simplicity, contentment, truthfulness, self-restraint, fasting, detachment, humility and continence.

During the eight-day Paryushana festival, the Swetambaras recite the religious text, the Kalpa Sutra (including a section on the birth of Lord Mahavira), on the fifth day.The Digambara sect recites the Tatvartha-sutra of Umaswati.During this festival, Jains of all ages visit the divine temples or Upashrayas to listen to the discourses and readings of Kalpa Sutra. In the evenings, Jains perform a kriya called Pratikraman, a form of meditation to reflect on spiritual journey. Most Jains fast in some form of the other in these days.

It is not and uncommon sight to see 8 day fasters, who do not consume anything in these eight days. Even water must be boiled and can be drunk only between 10 a.m. and 5 p.m. (approx.) Every now and then one does come across a faster who has not eaten for a whole month too!!! Penance and fasting are the key words in these days. Many jains abstain from onions,garlic,potatoes, root vegetables and green vegetables.In the Digambaras,

The Paryushana is the most important festival among the Jain festivals and it is observed during every Chaturmas commencing on the twelfth day of the shukla phase of Bhadrapad month and ending on the fourth day of Krishna Phase of Bhadrapad. This is in August-September, and peak monsoon time (this year it starts from 15th August 2001 and ends on 22nd Aug'01). For the Swetambara sect of Jains, Paryushana is an eight-day event, while for the Digambaras it stretches over ten days.

Its origin is related to the staying of the monks in one place in Chaturmas (4 months of monsoon). As during this time the monks have settled in the town for a longer duration, it is time for the householders to have an annual renewal of the faith by listening to the statement of the Dharma and by meditation and vratas (self-control). And for the monks, almost as importantly, staying in one place during the monsoon reduces the risk of causing accidental death to numerous insects and smaller forms of life that thrive during the rains.

Paryushana is a time of reflection on actions and meditation on the past year. Paryushana is marked by strict observance of the ten cardinal virtues: forgiveness, charity, simplicity, contentment, truthfulness, self-restraint, fasting, detachment, humility and continence. During the eight-day Paryushana festival, the Swetambaras recite the religious text, the Kalpa Sutra (including a section on the birth of Lord Mahavira), on the fifth day.The Digambara sect recites the Tatvartha-sutra of Umaswati.

During this festival, Jains of all ages visit the divine temples or Upashrayas to listen to the discourses and readings of Kalpa Sutra. In the evenings, Jains perform a kriya called Pratikraman, a form of meditation to reflect on spiritual journey.

Most Jains fast in some form of the other in these days. It is not and uncommon sight to see 8 day fasters, who do not consume anything in these eight days. Even water must be boiled and can be drunk only between 10 a.m. and 5 p.m. (approx.) Every now and then one does come across a faster who has not eaten for a whole month too!!! Penance and fasting are the key words in these days. Many jains abstain from onions,garlic,potatoes, root vegetables and green vegetables.

In the Digambaras, the 10-day period of Paryushana starts from Bhadrapada Shukla panchami during which the dashalakshana vrata is undertaken. Paryushan for Digambars ends on Chaturdashi of Bhadrapada. In the Swetambaras an 8-day festival is celebrated that ends with Bhadrapada Shukla panchami. The last day is called Samvatsari, short for Samvatsari Pratikramana. Seven days are days of attainment and the eighth day is one of fulfillment or achievement. In this manner,the Samvatsari Mahaparva the annual festival is celebrated.

It is at this time that Jains embark on their respective annual pratikramana-a reflection on their spiritual journey for the past year. On this day they also observe a unique custom, where they ask every individual they may have offended during the year for forgiveness. Old quarrels are forgotten and friendships and relationships renewed, as they fold their hands and ask for "Micchamidukadam" or forgiveness.

Michchhami means to be fruitless (forgiven) and Dukkadam (Dushkrut) means bad deeds. Therefore the meaning of Michchhami Dukkadam is my bad deeds (with you) be fruitless. So concept behind saying or writing someone "Michchhami Dukkadam" is that if I have done any harm to you then those bad deeds to be forgiven (be fruitless).

The following is the prayer we say while doing Pratikraman:

"KHAMEMI SAVVE JIVE,

SAVVE JIVA KHAMANTU ME

METTI ME SAVVE BHUYESU,

VERAM MAJAHAM N KENAI"

It means:

"I forgive (from the bottom of my heart without any reservation) all living beings (who may have caused me any pain and suffering either in this life or previous lives), and I beg (again from the bottom of my heart without any reservation) for the forgiveness from all living beings (no matter how small or big to whom I may have caused pain and suffering in this life or previous lives, knowingly or unknowingly, mentally, verbally or physically, or if I have asked or encouraged someone else to carry out such activities). (Let all creatures know that) I have a friendship with everybody and I have no revenge (animosity or enmity) toward anybody."

Pratikramana includes:

- Samayika: to stay in equanimity by withdrawing to the self.
- Prayers to the Five Supremes, 24 Jinas and the 4 mangalas, including the Dharma as presented by the ancient Masters.
- Prayer to the Master(Guru) or the Deity.
- Reflections on vratas and past transgressions.
- Kayotsarga: detachment from the body by controlling it.
- Pratyakhyan: making resolutions for the next period (next year for Samvatsari Pratikramana).

Dasha-Lakshana Vrata

This is a vrata that celebrates components of the dharma: Noble kshama (forbearance), mardava (gentleness), arjava (uprightness), shaucha (purity), satya (truth), sanyam (restraint), tapa (austerity), tyaga (renunciation), akinchanya (lack of possession) and brahmcharya (chastity), as described by Umaswati.

In the full form, it is a 10 day vrata that spans 10 years. It may be undertaken during Shukla Panchami to Chaturdashi of Bhadrapada, Magh or Chaitra. However it it common to do it during Bhadrapada, in which case it starts with Paryushana.

Origin of Paryushan: Its origin is related to the staying of the monks in one place for the rainy season. "Paryushanaa" is staying of the monks in one place. In popular terminology this stay is termed "chaturmasa" because the rainy season is regarded to be about four months. However the minimum duration of Paryushanaa is regarded to be 70 days. For this minimum duration, Paryushanaa must be initiated by panchami (fifth day) of the shukla phase of the Bhadrapada month. In the scriptures it is described that Lord Mahavira used to start Paryushanaa on Bhadrapada Shukla panchami.

The date for the Paryushana festival is thus Bhadrapada Shukla panchami for both major sects. Because of computational and other differences there can be some minor differences among various subsects. Recently there has been an attempt to get everyone to agree to use the same date.

Because at this time the monks have settled in the town for a longer duration, it is time for the householders to have an annual renewal of the faith by listening to the statement of the Dharma and by meditation and vratas (self-control). In the Digambaras, it is done by starting a 10-day period from Paryushana (Bhadrapada Shukla panchami) during which the dashalakshana vrata is undertaken.

In the Shvetambaras an 8-day festival is celebrated that ends with Bhadrapada Shukla panchami. The last day is called Samvatsari, short for Samvatsari Pratikramana, as described below.

During the 8-day festival, the Kalpa Sutra is recited in the Swetmbara sect, that includes a recitation of the section on birth of Lord Mahavira on the fifth day. In the Digambara sect the Tatvartha-sutra of Umaswati is recited. On the dashami, the sugandha-dashami vrata occurs. The Digambaras celebrate Ananta-chaturdashi on the chaturdashi, special worship is done on this day. Many towns have a procession leading to the amin temple.

The original Prakrit(ardhamagadhi) term for Paryushana is "Pajjo-savana". Remember that in case of Jain terms, the Prakrit forms of the words are the original.

Dasha-Lakshana Vrata: This is a vrata that celebrates 10 components of the dharma: Noble kshama (forbearance), mardava (gentleness), arjava (uprightness), shaucha (purity), satya (truth), sanyam (restraint), tapa (austerity), tyaga (renunciation), akinchanya (lack of possession) and brahmcharya (chastity), as described by Umaswati.

In the full form, it is a 10 day vrata that spans 10 years. It may be undertaken during Shukla Panchami to Chaturdashi of Bhadrapada, Magh or Chaitra. However it it common to do it during Bhadrapada, in which case it starts with Paryushana.

Requesting Forgiveness: At the conclusion of the festival, the Sravakas request each other for forgiveness for all offenses committed during the last year. This occurs on the the Paryusha day for the Swetambara and on Pratipada (first) of Ashwin Krashna for the Digambara.

7

Baudh Festivals

Buddha Purnima

Buddha Poornima, which falls on the full moon night in the month of Vaisakha (either in April or May), commemorates the birth anniversary of Lord Buddha, founder of Buddhism, one of the oldest religions in the world. Notwithstanding the summer heat (the temperature routinely touches 45 degrees C), pilgrims come from all over the world to Bodh Gaya to attend the Buddha Poornima celebrations.

The day is marked with prayer meets, sermons on the life of Gautam Buddha, religious discourses, continuous recitation of Buddhist scriptures, group meditation, processions, worship of the statue of Buddha and symposia. The Mahabodhi Temple wears a festive look and is decorated with colourful flags and flowers. The Chinese scholar, Fa-Hien, has recorded celebration of this festival.

It is an important to give a summarized description on the Buddhist festivals in India, especially in the main places of worship. The principal annual ceremony for all the Buddhist is the Vaisaka Purnima known in Sri Lanka as Wesak festival and in India as Buddha Jayanti. Vaisaka Purnima day is fixed by the full-moon day of the month Vaisaka, which falls in May. Like all other Buddhist festivals it falls according to the Lunar year. It was of this day of the year, according to the year. He attained Supreme Enlighten, or Buddha hood, beneath the Bodhi-tree at Boddha Gaya. Forty-five years later at the age of eighty, he finally passed away in Parinivana on the same day of the year at Kushinagar. Vaisaka Purnima is celebrated especially in Boddha Gaya, Lumbini and in Kushinara as they are the holy places that were connected with the blessed ones birth, enlighten and the Parinirvana. Buddhists in Sri Lanka, Burma, Thailand, Tibet, China, Korea, Laos, Vietnam, Mongolia, Bhutan, Cambodia, Nepal, Japan and quite a number of western Buddhists participate Vaisaka Purnima Day religious activities in a festive mood. Sarnath the capital of Buddhism too celebrates Vaisaka Purnima day in a grand way. The great Buddhist festival, Vaisaka, although is an occasion for rejoicing doesn't encourage hectic gaiety and abandon. The happiness that the Buddhists feel, when they are celebrating it is a tranquil, peaceful joy. The festival has its gay side as well. In most of the Buddhist countries the villages, roads, streets, temples and houses are brightly illuminated with colour Lanterns, electric lights and colorful, tasteful decorations.

The decision to agree to celebrate Vesak as the Buddha's birthday was formalized at the first Conference of the World Fellowship of Buddhists (W.F.B.) held in Sri Lanka in 1950, although festivals at this time in the Buddhist world are a centuries-old tradition. The Resolution that was adopted at the World Conference reads as follows, "That this Conference of the World Fellowship of Buddhists, while recording its appreciation of the gracious act of His Majesty, the Maharaja of Nepal in making the full-moon day of Vesak a Public Holiday in Nepal, earnestly requests the Heads of Governments of all countries in which large or small number of Buddhists are to be found, to take steps to make the full-moon day in the month of May a Public Holiday in honour of the Buddha, who is universally acclaimed as one of the greatest benefactors of Humanity."

Hence on Vesak Day, Buddhists all over the world commemorate three great events: The birth, enlightenment and the passing away of Gautama Buddha. As Buddhism spread from India to all parts of the world, the teachings were readily assimilated with the cultures of the people who accepted the teachings. As a result, Buddhist art and culture took on a rich variety of forms with profound gentleness and kindness as the Buddha expressly forbade the use of force. The practice of

Buddhism was adapted in many ways to suit the nature of the various cultures that accepted it. As a result of this, Vesak is celebrated in many different ways all over the world. But in essence many practices have become universal. This sacred day is purely a religious festival, and not a festive occasion. On this day all Buddhists are expected to reaffirm their faith in the Buddha Dhamma and to lead a noble religious life. It is a day for meditation and for radiating Loving-Kindness.

Considered to be the ninth avatar of Vishnu. Buddha Jayanti or Buddha Purnima is marked as the most important day, commomerating the three most significant events in the life of Gautama Buddha that occurred on the same day. His birth, enlightenment and death (nirvana), all happened in the month of Vaishak, on a full moon night in April/May. Thus, this makes the day-called Buddha Purnima Festival or Buddha Jayanti Festival-all the more sacred for Buddhists.

Festival Of Peace The Bodhi tree in Bodhgaya has stood for centuries as a reminder of the Buddha's attainment of enlightenment. Gaya is a sacred place of pilgrimage for Buddhists. Each year, the tree is venerated and the viharas nearby resound to the chants of Buddhist monks. The great celebration of the month of Vaishakh falls on the full moon day on which Gautama, the Buddha, was born. To Buddhists the world over, all full moon days are festive and important. However, the full moon of Vaishakh is the most auspicious of all. Gautama, the Buddha was born in 544 BC in Lumbini, Nepal. Unlike most other religious teachers, he was born into a roval family and surrounded by wealth and material ease.

According to Buddhist lore, Mahamaya his mother, often dreamt of white elephants at the time of her pregnancy and thus knew that a divine child of miraculous charisma and destiny would Then as a young adult Siddharth, the prince born to King Suddhadhana and Queen Mahamaya, undertook a short journey in the course of which he observed the futility of human life. He saw the way a man grew into adulthood passed into old age and then became helpless, sick and feeble before death. Saddened by the realization that life was a meaningless and hollow passage from one state of being to the next, the prince went into deep meditation under a Bodhi tree near Gaya, until he finally attained enlightenment, once again on the full moon day of Vaishakh. He was then 35 years of age and thereafter became known as Gautama, the Buddha. He gave his first sermon in Sarnath, near the holy city of Varanasi, to his followers who formed a Sangha, also on the Vaishakh Purnima. A tableux shows the Buddha delivering his first sermon at the deer park in Sarnath, near the holy city of Varanasi. A golden idol of the Buddha seated in repose, at Bodhgaya.

The surrounding images are of odhisatvas. Vesakha or Buddha Purnima, is a festival of lights in many Buddhist countries. In Sri Lanka it is particularly beautiful and picturesque. The Buddha, who is considered the ninth avatar of Vishnu, reached Nirvana or the extinction of self and freedom from the cycle of rebirth, also on the full moon day of Vaishakh. Therefore Buddha Purnima marks the three major events in the life of this great apostle of peace. Buddhist countries like Japan, Burma and Sri Lanka celebrate this festival with special fervour. In Sri Lanka it is celebrated like Diwaliwith paper and bamboo stick lanterns twinkling under the night sky. Kheeris shared by families and distributed to the poor. Buddhists free birds from their cages and refrain from eating meat on this day.

Buddha was a real historical character at the same time he was a mythical man of legend. Buddhist mythology is replete with legends relating to his birth. It is believed that Buddha had come into being after through a series of birth and death. In some he was reborn as human and in some, as an animal. And that Buddha is the final phase in which he achieved the ultimate Nirvana, the parinirvana. According to a Tibetan belief, that he would be reborn, had been prophesied many years before Gautam Buddha was born.

He was born in 544 B.C. in a garden at Lumbini, of Northern India, now Nepal. He was the son of Suddhadhan, the king of Lumbini, and was an heir to the throne.

Like all prophets his birth was legendary. According to one story, Queen Mayadevi was strolling in the garden at Lumbini. Feeling tired, she sat under a tree and fell asleep. She dreamt that a six-tusked white elephant had entered her body. Following this the queen gave birth to a child through the right side of her ribcage. After the birth of the child, named Siddhartha, his horoscope was made.

The horoscope predicted that he would become either a world monarch or a great ascetic.Since Suddodhana did not want his son to become a hermit, he raised him in great luxury. Nothing sad or painful was allowed to touchthe life of Siddhartha.Shielding him from the harsh realities of life, the King created a paradise on earth for his beloved son.

So, Siddhartha lived his early life as a prince.And the prince was a man of exceptional physical appearance. In fact, there are numerous references to the perfection of his physical body.And the charming young Prince was married to Princess Yashodhara at a tender age. So as to get him more involved in worldly affair. Soon Siddhartha became father. But things soon turned out to be altogether different.

Legend says, it was a matter of four passing sights that brought in to light the ascetic in him and drove him out in quest of Truth. This is how the Prince saw them.

While the prince was traveling in his royal chariot, he chanced upon an old man, a sick person, a dead body and an ascetic. This was the first time he was exposed to the sufferings in the world. The decrepit old man made him aware of the old age, the final phase of life cycle. The sick man made him aware of the pangs of an ailing uncared man. The corpse made him aware of the Death, that terminates human life. He was deeply distressed.

Now restless and dissatisfied with his opulent lifestyle, Siddhartha decided to renounce his kingdom, even his wife and son. He was just 29 then. And he longed for finding out some answers to the questions of life. The quest for eternal truth.

Siddhartha renounced his kingdom in search of 'truth'. But 'truth' was not easy to be found. He took to the life of an ascetic, like the one he saw as the last of the Four Passing Sights. The ascetic, with a peaceful face, inspired him most.

During his search, he traveled to distant lands. And for six years he lived as a solitary forest-dweller, at first as the disciple of two renowned Hindu masters. Then, after deciding he had learned all that they could teach him-which he felt was not enough-he joined a band of ascetics and with them he practiced such extreme austerities and ate so little that he was about to die.

Study with the Hindus had not brought him the enlightenment he was seeking, nor had his experiment with asceticism. Rejecting self-indulgence as well as self-mortification, he determined to follow what he called the Middle Path and to devote himself to a course of mental cultivation and mystical concentration.

In the town of Bodhgaya in Northeast India, Siddhartha sat down beneath a tree to embark on an extended period of meditation. And he determined not to rise until he had found the truth. For 49 days he meditated, formulating a body of wisdom which was to bring mankind a new religion.When he arose he was enlightened, he was the Buddha, ready to go forth and teach others how to become enlightened.

The tree under which he meditated came to be known as the 'Bodhi Tree', the tree of wisdom.

And the place where this happened is still known as Bodh Gaya, now in north eastern part of India. It is believed that he attained nirvana on the day of the full moon in the month of Vaishakha, or Vesakha. It became a great Holy Day for the Buddhists. It was also on this day Buddha gave his first sermon at Sarnath, also in the North Eastern India.

This is why the Buddhists rotate the prayer wheels in the belief the prayers written on the wheels get dispersed on this day. The day when Prince Siddhartha became Gautam Buddha and again the day when he gave his first sermon at Sarnath.

Soon after his enlightenment the Buddha preached to a small group of the curious and those who heard his words became his disciples. From then on the Buddha devoted the rest of his life to teaching those who sought his advice, his compassion, his wisdom. The growth in the number of his disciples led to his establishment of the Sangha, the Buddhist monastic order. It was his disciples who passed along his teachings, by word of mouth, from generation to generation. Not until some considerable time after his death, were the words of the Buddha recorded in written form.

Finally Buddha liberated himself from the cycle of rebirth and achieved mahaparinirvana, also on the auspices of Vesak.

His Teachings: Buddhism is one of the most ancient and highly philosophical Indian tradition. "Buddha" means "Awakened One", someone who has awakened from the sleep of ignorance and sees things as they actually are. Buddhism, is Buddha's teachings and the inner experiences or realizations of these teachings. Buddha have eighty-four thousand teachings. All these teachings and the inner realizations of them constitute Buddhism.

Rituals: The day falls in the Vaishaka month of the Indian calendar. Prayers, sermons and non-stop recitations of Buddhist scriptures resonate in monasteries, religious halls and homes. In monasteries in Sikkim, monks hold day-long readings of the scriptures before the Buddha's statue. The lay people listen to these recitals, and also give gifts to the monks and the statue.

The statue of Buddha, in fact, receives special attention everywhere, with people offering it incense, flowers, candles and fruits. The Banyan tree-called the Bodhi tree for its part in Buddha's enlightenment-also receives a fair share of garlands and coloured flags adorn it. People also sprinkle milk and scented waters on its roots and light rows of lamps around it.

On Vesak day, devout Buddhists are expected to assemble in various temples before dawn for the ceremonial hoisting of the Buddhist flag and the singing of hymns in praise of the holy triple gem: The Buddha, The Dharma (his teachings), and The Sangha (his disciples). Devotees may bring simple offerings of flowers, candles and joss-sticks to lay at the feet of their teacher. These symbolic offerings are to remind followers that just as the beautiful flowers would wither away after a short while and the candles and joss-sticks would soon burn out, so too is life subject to decay and destruction. Devotees are enjoined to make a special effort to refrain from killing of any kind. They are encouraged to partake of vegetarian food for the day.

In some countries, notably Sri Lanka, two days are set aside for the celebration of Vesak and all liquor shops and slaughter houses are closed by government decree during the two days. Birds and animals are also released by the thousands in a symbolic act to liberation, of giving freedom to those who are in captivity. However, it is not recommended that birds be released in the heart of crowded cities, because by doing so we may cause harm to the poor bewildered birds which are unable to fly far after a long period of captivity.

Unscrupulous bird dealers would recapture such birds for resale to well meaning devotees. If birds are to be released it is recommended that this be done in rural areas where the birds can achieve real freedom. Some devout Buddhists will wear a simple white dress and spend the whole day in temples with renewed determination to observe the observance of the Eight Precepts.

Devout Buddhists understand how to lead a noble life according to the teaching by making a daily affirmation to observe the eight Precepts. However, on special days, notably new moon and full moon days, they observe additional disciplines to train themselves to practice morality, simplicity and humility.

The Eight Precepts are:

1. Not to kill
2. Not to steal
3. Not to engage in improper sexual activity
4. Not to indulge in wrong speech
5. Not to take intoxicating drinks and drugs
6. To abstain from taking food at unreasonable time
7. To refrain from sensual pleasures such as dancing, singing and self-adornment
8. To refrain from using high and luxurious seats in order to practice humility.

Devotees are expected to listen to talks given by monks. On this day monks will recite verses uttered by the Buddha twenty-five centuries ago, to invoke peace and happiness for the Government and the people. Buddhists are reminded to live in harmony with people of other faiths and to respect the beliefs of other people as the Buddha had taught.

Bringing Happiness to Others: Celebrating Vesak also means making special efforts to bring happiness to the unfortunate like the aged, the handicapped and the sick. To this end, Buddhists will distribute gifts in cash and kind to various charitable homes throughout the country. Vesak is also a time for great joy and happiness. But this joy is expressed not by pandering to one's appetites but by concentrating on useful activities such as decorating and illuminating temples, painting and creating exquisite scenes from the life of the Buddha for public dissemination. Devout Buddhists also vie with one another to provide refreshments and vegetarian food to devotees who visit the temple to pay homage to the Blessed One.

Paying Homage to the Buddha: The Buddha himself has given invaluable advice on how to pay homage to him. Just before he died, he saw his faithful attendant Ananda, weeping. The Buddha advised him not to weep, but to understand the universal law that all compounded things (including even his own body) must disintegrate. He advised everyone not to cry over the disintegration of the physical body but to regard his teachings (The Dhamma) as their teacher from then on, because only the Dhamma truth is eternal and not subject to the law of change. He also stressed that the way to pay homage to him was not merely by offering flowers, incense, and lights, but by truly and sincerely striving to follow his teachings.

This is how devotees are expected to celebrated Vesak: to use the opportunity to reiterate their determination to lead noble lives, to develop their minds, to practise loving-kindness and to bring peace and harmony to humanity.

Bibliography

Agrawala, S. V. : *The Glorification of the Great Goddess*, All-India Kashray Trust, Varanasi, 1963.

Ainslee T. Embree : *Imagining India: Essays on Indian History*, Oxford Univ. Press, Delhi, 1989.

Ali, Tariq : *An Indian Dynasty: The Story of the Nehru-Gandhi Family*, Putnam, New York, 1985.

Alston, A. J. : *The Devotional Poems of Mirabai*, Motilal Banarsidass, Delhi, 1980.

Annemarie Schimmel : *Mystical Dimensions of Islam,* University of North Carolina Press, Carolina, 1975.

Arthur Green : *Jewish Spirituality I: From the Bible through the Middle Ages*, Crossroad, New York, 1986.

Baker, Christopher J.: *An Indian Rural Economy: The Tamiland Countryside*, Clarendon Press, Oxford, 1984.

Barter, James: *The Ganges,* Lucent Books, San Diego, 2003.

Bernard McGinn: *Classics of Western Spirituality,* Paulist Press, New York, 1978.

Bhardwaj, Surinder Mohan: *Hindu Places of Pilgrimage in India: A Study in Cultural Geography*, University of California Press, Berkeley, 1973.

Bhattacharya, Deben: *Love Songs of Vidyapati*, Motilal Banarsidass, Delhi, 1987.

Boas, Franz: *Indian Myths and Legends from the North Pacific Coast of America,* Talonbooks, Vancouver, 2002.

Bowes, Pratima: *Hindu Intellectual Tradition,* Allied Publishers, New Delhi, 1977.

Boxberger, Daniel: *To Fish in Common: The Ethnohistory of Lummi Indian Salmon Fishing,* University of Nebraska Press, Lincoln, 1989.

Brown, Judith M.: *Modern India: The Origins of an Asian Democracy,* Oxford University Press, New York, 1994.

Burke, Mary Louise: *Swami Vivekananda in America: New Discoveries,* Advaita Ashrama, Calcutta, 1966.

Cauquelin, J.: *Asian Values. Encounters with Diversity*, Surrey, Richmond, 2000.

Chakravarti, C.: *The Tantras: Studies on their Religion and Literature*, Punthi Pustak, Calcutta, 1963.

Chand, Tara: *History of the Freedom Movement in India*, Kali Ram Press, Calcutta, 1961.

Chaturvedi, M.D.,: *Hinduism, The Eternal Religion,* Bharatiya Vidya Bhavan, Bombay, 1992.

Cunningham, Joseph Davey: *History of the Sikhs, From the Origins of the Nation to the Battles of the Sutlej*, Sultan Chand, Delhi, 1955.

Das, Veena: *Mirrors of Violence: Communities, Riots, and Survivors in South Asia*, Oxford University Press, New Delhi, 1992.

Dasgupta, Chidananda: *The Painted Face: Studies in India's Popular Cinema*, Roli Books, New Delhi, 1992.

Datta, V.N.: *Sati: Widow Burning in India*, Manohar, New Delhi, 1990.

De Bary: *Self and Society in Ming Thought*, Columbia University Press, New York, 1970.

Desai, Jigna: *Beyond Bollywood: The Cultural Politics of South Asian Diasporic Film*, Routledge, London, 2003.

Dissanayake, Wimal and M. Sahai: *Sholay: A Cultural Reading*, Wiley Eastern, New Delhi, 1992.

Dwyer, Rachel: *The History, Politics and Consumption of Public Culture in India*, Oxford, Delhi, 2001.

Elmendorf, William: *The Structure of Twana Culture,* Washington State University Press, Pullman, 1960.

Eno, Robert: *The Confucian Creation of Heaven: Philosophy and the Defense of Ritual Mastery*, SUNY Press, Albany, 1990.

Farrand, Livingston: *Traditions of the Quinalut Indians,* American Museum of Natural History, New York, 1902.

Gambhirananda, Swami: *Brahma Sutra Shamkar Bhasya,* Adavita Ashrama, Calcutta, 1977.

Gandhi, Mahatma: *An Autobiography: The Story of My Experiments with Truth,* Beacon Press, Boston, 1957.

Halbfass, Wilhelm: *India and Europe: An Essay in Understanding,* State University of New York Press, Albany, 1988.

Hawley, John Stratton: *Songs of the Saints of India,* Oxford University Press, New York, 1988.

Howard Schwartz: *Reimaging the Bible: The Storytelling of the Rabbis,* Oxford University Press, New York, 1998.

John Drew: *India and the Romantic Imagination,* Oxford Univ. Press, London, 1987.

John, Elsner: *Pilgrimage: Past and Present in the World Religions,* Harvard University Press, Cambridge, 1995.

Kantikar, Hemant: *Kalidasa's Abhijnana Shakuntala,* Popular Prakashan, Bombay, 1984.

Kinsley, David R., *Hinduism a Cultural Perspective,* Prentice-Hall, New Jersey, 1993.

Kosambi, D.D.: *Myth and Reality: Studies in the Formation of Indian Culture,* Popular Prakashan, Bombay, 1962.

Lamba, B.: *Fauna of Corbett National Park,* ZSI, Calcutta, 1987.

Louis, Fischer: *Essential Gandhi: An Anthology of His Writings,* Vintage, New York, 1983.

MacDonell, Arthur Anthony: *History of Sanskrit Literature,* South Asia Books, Columbia, 1990.

Mandel, Peter: *Cassette Culture: Popular Music and Technology in North India,* University of Chicago Press, Chicago, 1993.

Michell, George: *The Hindu Temple: An Introduction to Its Meaning and Forms,* University of Chicago Press, Chicago, 1988.

Miller, Barbara Stoler: *The Bhagavad-Gita: Krishna's Counsel in Time of War,* Bantam, New York, 1986.

Mohanty, J.M.: *Gangesa's Theory of Truth*, Visva-Bharati, Santiniketan, 1966.

Nathan, Leonard: *The Transport of Love: The Meghaduta of Kalidasa,* University of California Press, Berkeley, 1976.

Piatigorsky, Alexander: *The Buddhist Philosophy of Thought,* Rowman & Allenheld, London, 1984.

Prajnanananda, Swami: *Schools of Indian Philosophical Thought,* Firma K. L. Mukhopadhyay, Calcutta, 1973.

Ranajit Guha: *A Construction of Humanism in Colonial India,* CASA, Amsterdam, 1993.

Reuchenbach, Hans: *The Philosophy of Space and Time*, Dover Publications, New York, 1958.

Richard Davis: *Lives of Indian Images,* Princeton Univ. Press. Princeton, 1997.

Ross, Carter: *The Dhammapada,* Oxford University Press, New York, 1987.

Sharma, Pushpendra K.: *Hindu Religion and Ethics,* Asian Publication Services, New Delhi, 1997.

Sivaramamurti, C.: *Sri Lakshmi in Indian Art and Thought*, Kanak, New Delhi, 1982.

Smith, Bardwell L.: *Essays on Gupta Culture*, Motilal Banarsidass, Delhi, 1983.

Tobias, Michael: *A Day in the Life of India,* Collins Publishers San Francisco, San Francisco, 1996.

Trimingham, J.: *Sufi Orders in Islam*, Oxford University Press, New York, 1998.

Wells, Oliver: *Salish Weaving Primitive and Modern,* Oliver Wells, Sardis, 1970.

Zimmer, Heinrich. *The Art of Indian Asia*, Pantheon, New York, 1955.

Zion, Bokser: *Abraham Isaac Kook: The Lights of Penitence*, Paulist Press, New York, 1978.

Index

E

F

G

H

I

J

R

S

T

U

V

W

Y

❑❑❑